I0110323

CONCRETE COLONIALISM

CONCRETE COLONIALISM

*Architecture, Urbanism, and the
US Imperial Project in the Philippines*

DIANA JEAN S. MARTINEZ

Duke University Press *Durham and London* 2025

© 2025 DUKE UNIVERSITY PRESS. All rights reserved
Project Editor: Livia Tenzer
Designed by A. Mattson Gallagher
Typeset in Garamond Premier Pro and Knockout
by Westchester Publishing Services

Library of Congress Cataloging-in-Publication Data
Names: Martinez, Diana Jean S., [date] author.
Title: Concrete colonialism : architecture, urbanism, and the
US imperial project in the Philippines / Diana Jean S. Martinez.
Other titles: Architecture, urbanism, and the US imperial project in
the Philippines
Description: Durham : Duke University Press, 2025. | Includes
bibliographical references and index.
Identifiers: LCCN 2024055523 (print)
LCCN 2024055524 (ebook)
ISBN 9781478032380 (paperback)
ISBN 9781478029014 (hardcover)
ISBN 9781478061236 (ebook)
Subjects: LCSH: Imperialism and architecture—Philippines. |
Concrete construction—Philippines. | Architecture and
globalization—Philippines. | Philippines—Colonization. |
Philippines—Relations—United States. | United States—Relations—
Philippines. | Philippines—History—1898–1946.
Classification: LCC NA2543.I47 M37 2025 (print) | LCC NA2543.I47
(ebook) | DDC 721/.04450959909041—dc23/eng/20250529
LC record available at https://lccn.loc.gov/2024055523
LC ebook record available at https://lccn.loc.gov/2024055524

Cover art: From the cover of *Japanese Defense of Cities as Exemplified
by the Battle for Manila: A Report by XIV Corps* (Headquarters Sixth
Army: A.C. of S., G-2, 1945). Image: Combined Arms Research Library,
N10662.

For Mom and Dad

Contents

Preface and Acknowledgments

I write this from Anilao, Mabini, Batangas, where my extended family has gathered for a reunion. One of my clearest childhood memories was of this place, during one such reunion. I was staying at my grandparent's house. The rest of my family was still asleep. Jetlagged, I snuck out of the bedroom and onto the terrace facing the beach. My feet prickled by the terrace's pebbledash, I leaned against the rail of precast balusters, and stood mesmerized by long flashing arcs of silver-sided flying fish leaping above the moonlit surface of Balayan Bay. Hours later the smell of diesel and the sputtering of outboard motors announced the arrival of the early morning catch, as sellers prepared the palengke, just a few meters from the house, by throwing buckets of soapy water over the concrete floor.

My mother was born close to this very spot, in a one room nipa house, where they kept chickens below the main level. One of her earliest memories of her home was of poking through the pitched slatted floor so an egg caught on the bamboo's nodal ridges would continue its roll toward a collection trough—a split shaft of bamboo. Aided by remittances sent by their eldest children, my grandma and grandpa built the town's first concrete house, on a small lane that ran parallel to the beach. Three stories tall, it had the town's first toilet, "windows" of patterned breezeblock, and electric outlets. It was furnished—almost entirely—with ornately carved furniture hewn from a single narra tree felled by a typhoon on a family farm on the island of Mindoro. At family dinners, under buzzing fluorescent tubes, the Batangueño accents of one generation and the midwestern accents of another sharply pinged off the concrete walls of the sala. Though it is rarely noticed, the central character of this book lingers, perhaps only half-consciously, in the memory of every living Filipino, though it was only introduced to the archipelago a few years after my grandparents were born, in 1909.

Throughout the writing of this book my own memories and those of my family members have mixed freely with the images, passages, and articles I have come across over the course of my research. Descriptions of cities and landscapes that I have attempted to reconstruct through reports, photos, film footage, and other archival materials are seasoned by images of grandma and grandpa Sandoval teaching in concrete schoolhouses, and with my Auntie Tinay's description of the kamote patches that sustained my dad's family during the Japanese occupation. Details of my own life are also tightly intertwined with the pages that follow. Through this work I have come to a better understanding of my family and its place in this world. My family, however, do not only provide personal touchstones; this work is complete because of their love and support. There isn't enough room to name all the aunts, uncles, and cousins that I would like to thank. Though each has been important, I am especially grateful to P. J. Dilbert, Pelang, Techie, Shy, and King for opening their home on trips back to the Philippines.

I have long insisted that this book is not written about the Philippines, but is in more significant ways a history of the United States and its marginalized history of colonialism. The importance and centrality of this story to US history, which surfaces in rarely accessed archives, was also revealed to me in deeply personal ways. It is just one of many twists of fate that my partner's great-great-grandfather served in the US Signal Corps in the Philippines. There he dutifully carried out orders to force locals to labor (unpaid) on a telegraph network. Though he saw little more in Filipinos than lazy natives, my children are now his descendants. His great-grandson, John (my father-in-law), and my mother-in-law, Judy, have been important sources of warmth and support throughout the writing of this book. They have cared for me and for their grandchildren with creativity and unflagging energy. History takes strange turns, and it is as much for them that I wrote this book as it was for the family I was born into. For their love, openness, and companionship I have not only them, but their entire family to thank—one that extends to all the Kiwi whānau that kept us safe and sane through the pandemic, especially Debbie, Peter, Rose, Chris M., Jules, Chris H., Sam, Nic, Nick, and Josephine.

I am fortunate and grateful to have a circle of friends and colleagues who have influenced and enriched this work in ways that are difficult to account for. Thank you especially to Hollyamber Kennedy, James Graham, Manuel Schwartzberg-Carrió, Ginger Nolan, Ayala Levin, Addison Godel, Peter Minosh, Remei Capdevila, Aaron White, Dong-Ping Wong, Adam Davidson, Erika Lanselle, Lilly Nguyen, and Katie Hornstein. At Tufts this circle of friends has expanded to include Sarah Fong, Kareem Kubchandani, Lily Mengesha, Mary McNeil, Daanika Gordon, Kamran Rastegar, Kris Manjapra, Adriana Zavala, Christina Maranci, Eric Rosenberg, Diego Javier Luis, Miriam Said, Alice Sullivan, Jacob Stewart-Halevy, Andrew McClellan, Peter Probst, Beatrice Forbes Manz, Matthew Okazaki, AB Huber, James Heard, Amy West, Anne Burgess, and Chris Cavalier.

This project has benefitted from the generous and insightful comments from Jorge Otero-Pailos, Christopher Capozzola, Paul Kramer, Timothy Mitchell, Danny Abramson, Ed Eigen, Felicity Scott, Joanna Merwood-Salisbury, and two especially careful anonymous readers. Thank you especially to Vince Rafael whose insights have shaped and sharpened this book in significant and structural ways. Elizabeth Brogden's editorial work has been a lesson in careful elegance, while Livia Tenzer at Duke UP expertly guided this book through its final stages. I am also grateful for the material support this book has received from the Center for the Humanities at Tufts, the Neubauer family, and Leonard and Jane Bernstein.

I would have never chosen this path if not for those along the way who believed I had something to contribute, including Joan Ockman, Felicity Scott, Mabel Wilson, Esra Akcan, Greig Crysler, Zoë Prillinger, and Luke Ogrydziak. I reserve a special thank you for Reinhold Martin, whose creativity and critical insights have served as a guide, and whose kindness and support I have depended on for many years.

Nothing would have been possible if my father had not modeled an intense curiosity about the world. All has been made possible by my mom's unlimited generosity and humor. And everything has been made more bearable and amusing because of my brother, who laughs, to the great puzzlement of others, at the same random things that I do. Thank you.

My greatest debt is to my partner, Owen Cornwall, who patiently listened to every half-formed idea, helping me fill each out, over breakfast, over chores, in the car, walking the kids to school, even when exhausted and busy figuring out his own ideas. You have supported this work in more ways than I can count or possibly thank you for. Thank you especially for the life we have built with Zoë and Charlie, the deepest wells of love and joy.

INTRODUCTION

The West is known by its deeds, the East by its dreams. The Anglo-Saxon lives in the concrete, the Oriental in the shadows. The American, having found a "proposition" in a field makes haste and sells all that he has and buys that field that he may dig therein and get "results." The Oriental inhales the drowsy fumes of some far off good that was, or is, or is to come— it little matters which—and is content. —GEORGE AMOS MILLER, *Interesting Manila*

In his 1906 travel guide, *Interesting Manila*, George Amos Miller attempted to familiarize his American audience with the peoples of its brand-new colonial territory by comparing the industrious American, racially defined as the "Anglo-Saxon," to the passive "Oriental," a figure whom Amos describes as enveloped in a vapor of indifference. Miller was of course not speaking of "concrete" in the material sense, but rather using the term to describe an American that invested in a *real* economy—one characterized by personal investment and quantifiable returns.[1] But by 1913, when George Hamlin Fitch wrote the travel guide, *The Critic in the Orient*, Manila would be a city literally transformed by the material. Fitch opens his chapter on the Philippines by describing Manila's approaching horizon as a huge mass of concrete, writing that it was "now the favorite building material of the new Manila. Not only are the piles and docks made of this material," he remarked, "but all the new warehouses and business buildings as well as most of the American and foreign residences are of concrete." Fitch concluded that the material—"clean, cool, and enduring"—met "every requirement of this tropical environment."[2]

In the seven-year interval separating the publication of these two travel guides, the US colonial administration had built the government-owned Manila Hotel, the General Hospital, the first buildings of the University of the Philippines, Manila City Hall, concrete-lined reservoirs, concrete lighthouses, hundreds of cisterns both small and large, and countless other buildings and public works projects, all out of reinforced concrete. Prior to 1898, there was not a shipload of Portland cement per year that arrived to the islands. By 1913, millions of barrels had been shipped to the Philippines. What came into the Philippines as a shapeless quantity of powder and nested stacks of reinforcement, was mixed with local sand, aggregate, and water and poured into a vast number of forms and shapes, ranging from the intricate volutes, dentils, and metopes of the new government buildings to the 8'-diameter tubular sections of what US officials touted a "sewer and storm-water drainage system superior to those of any other city in the Orient!"[3] Large volumes were poured into Manila Bay's hulking modern fortifications, and thin layers covered vast swaths of earth, from the far-reaching networks of roads and bridges, to the concrete that partially surfaced the ground of the new sanitary *barrios*—the modernized foundation of the native *bahay kubo*.[4]

Originally a logician's term meaning "actual and solid"—and used in opposition to the word *abstract*—*concrete* only came to refer to the manmade material in the mid-nineteenth century.[5] The popularization of its usage mapped onto major advances in reinforced concrete construction. But how can any one material be more "actual" than any other? Modern reinforced concrete's superconcreteness lay not in its opposition to abstraction, but in its ability to narrow the gap between an abstract conception and its realization. Human endeavors, Tim Ingold argues, are "forever poised between . . . the pull of hopes and dreams and the drag of material constraint."[6] Reinforced concrete construction, in addition to a number of technological innovations introduced around the same time, significantly eased the friction between acts of design and those of construction. Indeed, modern modes of construction tend to render labor more abstract (having the converse effect of rendering the architectural *idea* or design as more concrete than the labor that built it). Compare, for example, a hand-laid brick wall to the surface of a cast concrete wall. The dimensions of a typical brick suggest a relationship to the hand of the laborer, and by extension to a relationship to labor time. Variations in brick bonds, meanwhile, are signatures of skilled craftsmanship. By contrast, the scalelessness of concrete, along with its lack of inherent texture, obscure the presence of labor.[7] This tighter relationship between the idea and its concrete realization plays an important (if not central) role in the emergence of an American "concrete culture" that is particular to a society able to so quickly realize its "big plans."[8]

Answering both natural and manmade disasters with unparalleled strength and apparent durability, reinforced concrete enabled a sensible progress unobstructed by the prohibitions of cost and a wide variety of risks—whether meteorological, seismic, biological, political, or even moral. These benefits seemed even more pronounced in the tropical colony, for—whereas its strength and fireproofing ability pushed the cities of temperate metropoles to heights once considered too perilous—the material promised an imperviousness to an even greater variety of hazards seen as endemic to tropical climates. This was especially the case in the Philippines, where concrete's resistance to fire, earthquake, rot, microbe, termite, and typhoon shored up many of the doubts surrounding the US's first major colonial endeavor in East Asia. This was of central importance, as the US's colonization of the Philippines was often argued—either for or against—on quantifiable as opposed to ideological grounds, reflecting the US's turn away from a coherent narrative of its founding ideals of life, liberty, property, and equal protection under the laws, and toward an emphasis on quantifiable and verifiable goals—a governance informed by the application of rationalized and scientific methods to the operations of the state.[9] For example, though the Organic Act of 1902, which served as the colony's de facto constitution from 1902 to 1916, included a bill of rights, it also included as a condition of independence the requirement to conduct a census (a collection of population metrics used to generate a managerial colonial policy). Of particular relevance to this book, the census took into account not only race, marital status, and parents' birthplaces, but also included categories like "material of house," which was used as a hard measure of a native's level of "civilization," at the same time that it defined a measurable field of intervention.

Reinforced concrete construction was still a new technology at the time of the outbreak of the Spanish-American War. It was, however, at precisely this time that US producers and promoters of Portland cement began to associate the material with the construction of an era of American greatness—a "Concrete Age," as announced by the title of an early twentieth-century trade publication. Classifying "ages" according to material (e.g., the Stone, Bronze, and Iron Ages) was a practice formalized and popularized in the mid nineteenth century.[10] In view of a past now so systematically defined in terms of its materiality (and the technological advantages that those materials afforded), Americans began to see themselves in the grandiose terms of an epochal and civilizational history—not only using, but identifying with, concrete's durability and strength, and equating it with their own promising and vigorous future. Thus, it was not only that, as Michael Adas has argued, "advocates of U.S. expansion have . . . consistently assumed that the adoption of American technologies (and material culture more broadly) also entailed the incorporation of American values, ways of thinking, and modes of organizing everything from factory workers to political systems,"[11] but rather that material culture and "American values, ways of thinking" were coextensive, converging around the various agencies and consequences of reinforced concrete construction.

This is not to say that the introduction of reinforced concrete was an unimpeded process from conception to execution. This book contains several accounts of failure, the causes of which include inexperience with the still experimental material, faulty design, poor workmanship, labor conflict, native resistance, incorrect admixture ratios,[12] natural disaster, and ballistic forces in times of war. Concrete, as it turns out, is also not as durable as it was initially believed to be: Lucia Allais and Forrest Meggers point out that the failure of all modern reinforced concrete through carbonation was calculated in 1968 to take about 100 years, putting structures built at the turn of the century on the brink of structural failure.[13] That is to say, this book does not even account for the most destructive consequences of concrete colonialism, some of which are yet to be seen.

Today, concrete is the most commonly used building material in the world. Why, then, focus on the US colonial project in the Philippines? Why not British India, where—a few years before the first shipment of cement arrived in the Philippines—Major E. R. B. Stokes-Robert built a reinforced concrete bridge over a small river in 1901, or where plain (unreinforced) concrete blocks had been used in harbor works since the 1870s?[14] Why not Egypt, where the Hennebique central office built impressive railway bridges starting as early as 1903, or Algeria, where Hennebique opened an agency in 1893?[15] Or French Indochina, which—since the early twentieth century—produced far more Portland cement than the Philippines ever did? Or Brazil, which along with a newly independent India embraced concrete modernism as part of "a powerful tool in the process (and project) of decolonization"?[16] Why not the former Soviet Union, which immediately conjures images of both heroic concrete infrastructures and dismal *Khrushchyovkas*? Or China, which has used as much cement in two years as the United States did in the course of the entire twentieth century?[17] Why not Angola, Nigeria, or the Sudan, all of which are major targets of China's ambitious African development strategies? And why not the United States itself?

Though these sites are not the focus of my book, their stories are intertwined with this one. Concrete colonialism is a story that unfolds, though in different ways, across the globe, as pieces of a puzzle with both historical and emerging complementarities. Concrete colonialism in the Philippines, however, offers a unique vantage point from which to view how this concrete world came into being. Most crucially, nowhere else (in terms of its early history at the beginning of the twentieth century) was reinforced concrete used as pervasively as it was in the Philippines, where its use was adopted as colonial policy. Whereas by at least 1906 reinforced concrete construction was the nearly exclusive mode of construction for government-built architectural and infrastructural projects in the Philippines, reinforced concrete buildings were, outside of the Philippines, relatively rare in colonial territories, especially the regions today referred to as East, Southeast, and South Asia, until the 1920s. Exceptions included experimental pedestrian bridges in Japan (1903–1904), several multistory commercial structures in Guangzhou (ca. 1905), the Kunstkring in the garden city of Menteng in Indonesia (1914), and the aforementioned projects in India. In British and French colonies colonial architecture—including the grand opera houses of Indochina and Lutyens' Delhi—were built using traditional stone and brick masonry. One of the first large-scale specifications of reinforced concrete construction in a colonial territory outside of the Philippines was, in fact, a project deeply influenced by Daniel Burnham's work in the Philippines—the hill station of Dalat, whose master plan was drawn up by Ernest Hébrard in 1923. Though a zoning plan for Dalat by Paul Champoundry, which also specified the use of reinforced concrete, was completed in 1906 (i.e., after the publication of Burnham's Manila and Baguio plans), major construction using the material did not occur until after the publication of Hébrard's plan.[18] This book then considers the significance of the early and nearly exclusive use of reinforced concrete technology in the US colony, and reveals, as I aim to demonstrate, important aspects of how the United States developed as a global hegemonic power—at the very moment of the US's meteoric rise.

What was invoked in official documents and public speeches as a durable and scalable means of developing the United States' first far eastern colony was also, at the end of the nineteenth century, understood as a means of reinvigorating and stabilizing the retarded growth of the US economy through the continuous reinvestment of surplus capital in an expanding set of foreign territories spread across the globe.[19] In the colony, these investments took the form of public works projects—roads, sewer systems, water works, irrigation systems, and government buildings, which were themselves designed to attract more international capital. This process, which generally aligns with what we might today call economic development, is not usually associated with colonial sovereignty, but with *indirect* neocolonial arrangements of power. What the story of concrete in the Philippines allows me to do, then, is to frame what is usually presented as the end of empire as, rather, the beginning of an imperial reconstruction.[20] Relatedly, this allows me to present a counternarrative to those that valorize the technology's adoption as a "tool in the process of decolonization." By contrast, I argue that concrete construction in the Philippines spans periods of colonial and national building, which are here presented as phases of a continuous imperial expansion choreographed by former imperial powers—a story obscured by liberatory narratives of the postcolonial nation-state.

What Is Concrete Colonialism?

What is concrete colonialism? And what distinguishes it from other types (in a rapidly expanding academic typology) of colonialisms? My contention is that concrete colonialism is distinct from but related to many other forms of colonialism including but not limited to extractive, settler, penal, internal, plantation, legal, trade, and missionary colonialisms.[21] To understand its particularities requires an address of two basic questions, namely, what is concrete? and what is colonialism? Separately these terms might seem overdetermined, but a close examination of each reveals a specific and unfolding relationship that produces historically and materially specific effects. A basic definition of colonialism is of an arrangement in which one population exerts control over another, usually for the purposes of extracting resources and hoarding wealth (a definition that does not necessarily entail colonial sovereignty). Colonialism, however, was never assembled in quite the same way. As a term, *colonialism* is too often used as shorthand when referring to complex relationships between humans, land, resources, materials, and their respective agencies. As such it is common to make claims that colonialism itself *acts* or explains certain historical conditions. My contention is that the term *colonialism* does not itself explain anything. Rather, it is a constantly evolving set of conditions that itself has to be explained. This same rule applies to other master terms like *capitalism*.

Karl Marx himself did not describe the mill as the outcome of "capitalism" but, rather, as productive of a specific type of capitalism. In a similar way, *concrete colonialism* describes concrete as productive of a specific type of colonialism—in this case an apparently durable form that outlasts a legally defined colonial sovereignty.[22]

The architecture historian Sigfried Giedion provides a very good answer to the question "What is concrete?," describing it as an "aggregate body" made "from slender iron rods, cement, sand, and gravel," which combines "the properties of these almost worthless materials ... [to] increase their separate capacities many times over."[23] Generally speaking, the five ("almost worthless") component materials can be divided into two categories: those that are locally sourced and processed and those that are industrially produced. The former category includes sand, aggregate, and water, while the latter consists of steel reinforcement and Portland cement (which are themselves made from a diverse set of raw materials). Forms of labor are embedded within each component—aggregate has to mined and crushed, sand has to be sourced and sifted, and water has to be made relatively clean. Reinforcing steel and Portland cement, meanwhile, combined the work of machines with the manual labor of miners, truck drivers, kiln operators, metal benders, engineers, designers, and managers.

Reinforced concrete is itself not a commodity, but is rather made up of a number of different commodities. Unlike "soft" or "non-durable" goods (e.g., textiles, tea, coffee, salt, coal, and oil), Portland cement and reinforcing steel were not metabolized, worn, or consumed as such. When unmolded to reveal its final form, reinforced concrete acts in near contradistinction to its exportable, tradable components. After passing through a brief liquid state, the admixture forms into a solid, strong, heavy (and at times seemingly indestructible) mass. During the settlement of the American frontier, timber construction was susceptible to both destruction by fire and the rising price of lumber (as the lumber industry realized the finitude of US forests). Reinforced concrete provided permanence at a fraction of the cost of any other durable material. In the tropics, concrete replaced locally available materials like bamboo and nipa, organic matter yielded from a tropical environment that by virtue of its interminable cycles of renewal and decay prevented primitive accumulation. Concrete, then, not only significantly and substantially shaped the nature of the US colonial project; it also allowed the United States to achieve an ambitious colonial goal—to reshape and reform what it viewed as tropical conditions that were inherently hostile to capitalism. These tangible, visible reforms of the environment (inclusive of the people who inhabited it) became the ideological basis of an American *civilizing mission*—allowing US colonizers to overcome the internal contradictions of a colonizing power that held "liberty" and "self-determination" as foundational values. Portland cement, then, was not just a durable good; it was the commodification and expansion of durability itself.

The story of concrete, however, begins long before the site of emplacement, and ends long after it. Concrete aggregates a number of raw materials, forms of labor, and industrial processes. Its site of production, then, is divided between limestone and iron ore quarries, rebar and Portland cement factories, the railways and oceans that it moves across, its site of emplacement, and the site of its eventual disposal. Thus, though reinforced concrete's structural performance and its overall durability revolutionized building construction in the metropole, it was the transportability of its components that allowed that same revolution to happen almost simultaneously in Europe's and the United States' tropical colonies. It is the material's multi-sitedness—its sites of extraction, processing, and production, and the global circulation of its component parts—that renders it of particular importance to processes of colonization. In this book I not only analyze concrete, but I also use it as a lens that allows one to view—within a single epistemic frame—a multiplicity of classed and racialized subjects—including the American steel benders, Vietnamese Portland cement laborers, dispossessed Indigenous Americans, and the native Filipino laborer—as subject to the same set of evolving and interconnected imperial practices.[24]

The Imperial Debate

In the immediate aftermath of the Spanish-American War representatives of both the United States and Spain met in Paris to hammer out the conditions of a peace agreement. The resulting Treaty of Paris included securing national sovereignty for Cuba and transferring possession of the Philippine Islands, Puerto Rico, and Guam to the United States. Though the treaty was signed within days in the Spanish Cortes, the US Senate took weeks to ratify the settlement. The main sticking point was that the acquisition of the Philippines (at a cost of $20 million) would mean—beyond the shadow of a doubt—that the United States was an imperial power. This "condition" of victory thus brought the nation face to face with a particularly vexing internal contradiction. As with any treaty verification, its passage required a two-thirds majority vote in the Senate. Senators deliberated: Was colonization not anathema to the foundational principle of American democracy, that of self-determination? Or had the United States grown so great that empire was an inevitable responsibility? Senator George Hoar from Massachusetts argued, "(t)his Treaty will make us a vulgar, commonplace empire, controlling subject races and vassal states, in which one class must forever rule and other classes must forever obey." Hoar's fellow Republican senator from Massachusetts, Henry Cabot Lodge, countered by warning that, if the Treaty of Paris was rejected, the people of the United States would be deemed "incapable of taking rank as one of the greatest world powers." Here, the widely celebrated ideological (abolitionist) and material (industrialist) motivations for the Civil War came into direct confrontation. Cabot Lodge was hardly a disinterested party. The descendent of two prominent Boston Brahmin families (with fortunes built on international commerce), the Philippines represented—especially for him—an open door to a commercial theater in which the United States had long struggled to gain a foothold. On February 6, 1899, the Treaty of Paris was ratified in the Senate by a margin of just one vote.

Shortly thereafter, the United States found itself in a familiar place—in a violent war of aggression against an indigenous population. This time, though, US troops were sent some seven thousand miles away from what had been assumed to be the country's western terminus. A day before the ratification vote, leaders of the First Philippine Republic declared war against the United States, which they viewed as a continuation of their struggle for independence, and as a response to what they viewed as a betrayal. Filipinos had fought alongside the United States in the Battle of Manila Bay, under the impression that the revolutionary republic was waging a battle of liberation and not of conquest. The pro- versus anti-imperial debate that began on the Senate floor intensified as news of both mounting casualties and atrocities committed against the native population reached domestic shores. The capture in 1901 of Emilio Aguinaldo, the leader of the First Philippine Republic, did not end the war, as US military leaders had believed it would. Though the Philippine "insurgency" (as the United States referred to it) was declared over in 1902, hostilities between the United States and various of the archipelago's militant groups (some closely affiliated, and others more loosely, with the First Philippine Republic), continued well beyond that date, in a conflict that suffered a higher casualty rate than the US Civil War.[25]

Though resistance to US occupation was never extinguished, by 1906—the year that Miller published his *Guide to the Philippines*—even the most fervent anti-imperialists began to accept annexation as a fait accompli, and were drawn into a debate over what to do with the archipelago and its peoples.[26] For example, William Jennings Bryan—perhaps one of the most active and vocal members of the American Anti-Imperialists League—appealed for the establishment of a "stable form of government" in the islands, followed by a policy that would "protect the Philippines from outside interference while they work out their destiny." This was a policy that, as pro-imperial spokesmen pointed out, mirrored the substance of their own program.[27] In fact, most of the "anti-imperialists" favored the overseas expansion of the "American economic system"—which, in actual terms, meant the expansion of its markets, its systems of labor, and the development of material resources. These were imperatives that required a massive constructive undertaking that included the construction of forts (to protect the archipelago from "outside interference"), ports (to handle increased commercial traffic), civic structures (to house a "stable government"), schools (to educate a labor force), and transportation infrastructure (to move material resources from source to port).

Stripped of its ideological armatures, the dispute between "anti-imperialists" and "imperialists" revealed its underlying immateriality. What *Concrete Colonialism* examines, then, is the very material that the "imperial debate" obscures.

The belief that the expansion of a US economic system was not a form of colonization is how someone like Andrew Carnegie (whose main objection to colonialism was a racist fear of Filipino invasion) could adamantly claim to be anti-imperialist, even as his corporation profited from and played a central role in the construction of what is now recognized as a global US empire. Carnegie assumed that "colonization" was a new endeavor for the United States when, in truth, the United States had been a colonizing power from its inception.[28] Frederick Jackson Turner articulated this at the World's Columbian Exposition of 1893, held in Chicago, in his famous speech, "The Significance of the Frontier in American History," which opens with the declaration that "up to our own day American history has been in large degree the history of the *colonization* of the Great West."[29] In the aftermath of the Spanish-American War, Turner further developed his thesis writing that the US's colonial policy was always "hidden under the phraseology of 'interstate migration' and 'territorial organization.'"[30] In other words—though not expressed as a conscious pursuit within the United States Constitution—colonization was a central feature of the American imperial constitution. Obstructing the conception of the United States as a colonizing power, however, was the fact that what were long held as the US's founding events—the signing of the Declaration of Independence, the framing of the Constitution, and the War of 1812—were motivated by, or at least framed as, a casting off of the yoke of empire. However, as Turner argues, American colonial policy can be found in the US's continuous history of expansion. This is a history that recognizes "interstate migration" as a subterfuge for settler colonialism, and that acknowledges that "territorial organization" was in fact a technique of colonial land acquisition. These were techniques that allowed white settlers to not only live on the land, but to change it, to make use of it for their own purposes, driven by what was presented as a moral imperative to render land more economically productive than any yet settled in human history. I both pick up where Turner left off—by focusing on the rapidly evolving forms and techniques of colonial dominance at the precise moment the United States pushes past its assumed continental edges—and part ways with Turner at the point that his methodology is used to construct a positivist account of US empire. That is to say, our paths diverge at the juncture where his "frontier thesis" was presented as the font of American "meaning."

Dozens of historians have wrestled with the persistent amnesia surrounding the US's colonization of the Philippines. Despite a voluminous and growing literature addressing this history, new versions are repeatedly received as a surprise. This is largely because it continues to appear as an aberration to the dominant narratives of US history. Recent heroic attempts to make sense of the colonization of the Philippines *within* US history have invoked the "hidden" history of the Philippines as the most outstanding "proof" of "formal" US empire, defined as those territories that have fallen under the legal jurisdiction of the United States. In this version of the story, US colonialism "ends" (at least partially) on account of "empire-killing technologies," which allowed the United States to "wean" itself from its colonies by replacing raw materials unavailable on the US mainland on which it depended—including rubber, nitrates, silk, and sisal—with chemically synthetic versions. According to this history, large chunks of the US empire dissolve into a map of atomized points—a globally distributed archipelago of military bases—that the author presents as the "last" of US empire's overseas territories.[31] While US military empire is certainly one persistent aspect of concrete colonialism, this book also attempts to address a number of durable colonial forms by turning toward concrete colonialism's sensible and durable presence.[32] It is through a description of this evidence that this book makes its most ambitious and general appeal, by asserting that both empire and colonialism persist—in concrete forms—despite claims of its conclusion.

The Unity of Racial Capitalism, Modernism, and Empire

Concrete Colonialism contributes to a literature that challenges the historical separation between colonialism and "postcolonial" forms of exploitation by adding new material dimension to the argument that as Naoko Shibusawa put it, "empire, racial capitalism, and modernity are intertwined, rather than separate categories."[33] Extending key aspects of Cedric Robinson's concept of racial capitalism, Shibusawa emphasizes that capitalism is a "rupture in the long world history of empire." Reinforced concrete, I argue, plays a particular and specific role in this rupture, one that registers particularly acute and legible effects in the US colony.

A central distinction between precapitalist empire and *modern* empire is, Shibusawa contends, a "reversal of the relationship between political and economic actors. While economic actors served at the pleasure of the political leadership in the pre-capitalist era, the political system serves capitalists in the capitalist era."[34] Indeed, in the Philippines, the ranks of the colonial administration were packed with captains of industry and the leading men of business, like William Cameron Forbes (a central figure in this book). During Forbes's inaugural address as the third governor-general of the Philippines in 1909, he made clear his intention to avoid "the *unprofitable* consideration and discussion of the future political status of the Islands,"[35] because, he stated plainly, "What is needed here is capital."[36] The speech that followed focused on a detailed plan to execute an ambitious archipelago-wide program of capital-intensive infrastructural projects. These projects—all of which, Forbes insisted, should be built out of reinforced concrete—took advantage of the "assistance of outside capital" but were also planned in order to "better attract accumulations of wealth already made in other countries."[37] On this benefit of colonialism to capitalism Forbes was candid, as he was about the tropics' ability to yield products unattainable in temperate zones (coffee, chocolate, sugar). He failed to explain, however, the primary advantage of colonialism to capitalism: the expropriation of labor at a cost less than the value that the workers produced, and, more crucially, at a cost that was generally less than could be secured in the United States. Directing native attention away from this global inequality, Forbes emphasized the projected benefits of industrial development, which would bring, he argued, prosperity to the islands in the form of higher wages, better houses, and generally improved living conditions. A modern system of wage labor—sometimes presented as part of a campaign to globally vanquish the dehumanizing practice of chattel slavery (Forbes was descended from a proud line of Brahmin abolitionists and made it his special duty to see to the elimination of enslavement practices amongst the native populations)[38]—was, as I aim to demonstrate, just one of the ways that racial capitalism was modernized by US colonizers in the Philippines.

To clarify, though by the eighteenth century chattel slavery already served regional and global capitalisms, by that time increasingly large and increasingly organized slave rebellions and the threat of Black revolution had rendered slavery an untenable system. Formal emancipation, however, did not abolish racial capitalism; rather, as Cedric Robinson argued, "metropolitan capital changed its tune," reforming and reconstructing the system by replacing slavery, or the "unwaged proletariat" with various forms of labor, or "waged slavery," namely, "coolie labor, peonage, sharecropping, tenant-farming, forced-labor, penal labor, and modern peasantry."[39] Robinson presents these forms of labor as part of a capitalism that he describes as "an anarchic globalism of modern capitalist production and exchange," and against what Marx "imagined as . . . a geometric whole whose elementary and often hidden characteristics (price, value, accumulation, and profit) could be discovered with arithmetic means and certainty." It is Marx's commitment to theoretical elegance that, Robinson argues, leads him to consign categories of difference (gender, race, culture) to the dustbin, as such "unimportant . . . proportion(s) of wage labor" that they were tossed, along with "slave labor and peasants, into the imagined abyss signified by precapitalist, noncapitalist, and primitive accumulation."[40] *Concrete Colonialism* takes up Robinson's corrective by not only demonstrating how race served as an important element in the development of and justification for the colony's extensive penal and corvée labor program, where convicts and other colonial subjects were forced to work on an extensive program of public works projects, but also the development of a far more extensive modern exploitative system of wage labor that in both direct and indirect ways is shaped by concrete. Concrete, for example, was a medium through which colonists hoped for (and actually achieved) the multiplication of value extracted from racialized labor by eliminating traditional modes of building such that the routine labor required by those structures could be repurposed toward the construction of infrastructural projects; by decreasing the time it took to move products from sites of production to sites of export through the construction of concrete infrastructures; and through the development of native bodies themselves—the goal that subtended the bogus science of "race development" addressed in most detail in the chapter "The 'Master Material' and the 'Master Race.'" Whether the benefits of concrete construction were real, reified, imagined, or exaggerated, the use of concrete drew racialized subjects ever more tightly into the material circuitry of US empire.

Notes on Method and Archive

This book, in the main, considers two major archival "sources"—various forms of "technical literature," on the one hand, and a "collection" of concrete artifacts, on the other. The "technical literature" includes colonial and government reports, self-interested industry periodicals (such as *Building Age, The Concrete Age, Engineering World*, etc.), and sometimes ambitious (though likewise self-interested) histories like *The Romance of Cement* and *History of the Portland Cement Industry in the United States*.[41] These volumes often included lofty claims of concrete or Portland cement's imperial agency, as is the case with the following excerpt from *The Romance of Cement*, published by the Edison Portland Cement Co. in 1926:

> To England we yield the palm for discovering the secret of cement making; and to Ancient Rome, for structural grandeur. But credit for the latest and most engrossing chapter in the Romance of Cement belongs by good right to America. Prophesy the future of industry and you will unfold the future of cement, for day by day cement is becoming more important—actually indispensable—in the progress of this nation. It is the means to ends of which only the great modern engineer, architect, and builder may dare dream. But it is more—it is the end in itself, for in its rugged durability, it is as permanent as anything we know. Every day will reveal new uses for Portland cement; every generation will leave its mark—in cement; every new generation will scan the history and add its own chapter—that is the Eternal Romance of Cement.[42]

More consequential than these imperious claims, however, was the fact that this technical literature was filled with articles on new methods of construction, advertisements for new products, standard coefficients, mix ratios, safety factors, and labor requirements. In short, this literature provided a sort of how-to manual for building empire. The use, usefulness, and effects of new products, new methods, and new materials is seen throughout the reports of the Army Corps of Engineers and the War Department, as well as—and most importantly for this book—the *Quarterly Bulletin, Bureau of Public Works* (later the *Bulletin*), which carefully documented virtually every project executed by the Philippines' Bureau of Public Works (BPW) between 1913 and 1931.[43] It is in this literature that we can perhaps most clearly observe the presentation of the "how" as the "why" of empire. My argument, then, that the material's very properties shaped the policies and practices of US colonialism, is in some ways a straightforward reflection of the assertions made on the behalf of concrete itself—a material that promised (if it did not deliver) what had up until that point seemed a contradiction: a permanent future, expediently built. Simply put: *Empire made easy.*

Much of this "archive" cannot be found in the Philippines, a problem recognized in 1961 by one E. Victor Niemeyer, of the defunct United States Information Agency, who observed that "the bulk of the source materials for a major portion of Philippine history (i.e., the US colonial period) is outside the country in widely scattered archives and libraries." It is in, for example, the National Archives, the University of Michigan, Houghton Library at Harvard, the St. Louis Public Library, and the Newberry Library in Chicago—where much of the archival material for this book was sourced.[44] And it is for precisely this reason that Ateneo de Manila University established the American Historical Collection of Filipiniana. Beyond a collection of unique material artifacts, the documents contained in that collection are mostly duplicates of what one may find in the United States (and the serials and documents included therein are often less complete than their US counterparts). The displacement of this archive is why concrete serves as a particularly valuable resource and framework. The collection of architectural objects that I analyze in this book are fragments of a history that remain in plain sight—as half-ruined relics, as outdated infrastructure, or as preserved or renovated monuments that (while found in a place called the Philippines) are, I argue, better understood as part of a larger imperial network. I have used the archive of "widely scattered" documents, on the one hand, to render the concrete colony more vivid for the reader, and, on the other, to restore a history to these fragments, many of which remain present throughout the archipelago available for rereading, reassessment, and reinterpretation.

The Filipino voices that are highlighted in this book are mostly those of the native elite (familiar names like Manuel Quezon, Isabelo de los Reyes, Sergio Osmeña, et al.). Native criticism of the projects addressed in this book, which can be found in *El Renascimiento* and *La Vanguardia* (both deeply critical of the US colonial regime and reflecting, on the whole, the point of view of metropolitan colonial subjects), is not typically focused on the architectural objects themselves, but rather on exploitative practices like corvée labor, and more generally on poor pay and labor conditions. In general, objections to concrete projects themselves (especially very large ones like dams and irrigation projects) were and are more common among rural and agrarian populations (who more directly suffer their negative effects, and whose objections were left mostly unrecorded) than they were among the growing urban proletariat.[45] Though the most organized of these objections were recorded, far more were simply suppressed, poorly documented, or not recorded at all. That there is little recorded evidence of native objection to infrastructural projects themselves has to do with the fact that Filipinos living in cities and towns desired (for the same reasons that anyone else would desire) the sanitary improvements, education, and infrastructural services promised (and sometimes delivered) by the colonial regime. Indeed, many of the concrete projects were designed as a means of building trust and consensus among the urban and mostly lowland colonial population. Just as native criticisms of concrete colonialism (or the lack of them) cannot simply be taken at face value, neither can any other archival source be treated as straightforwardly reliable. Like many before me, I must contend with my dependence on a set of deeply compromised sources—a colonial archive that should never be treated as plainly legible. I thus treat my archive not as a site of "discovery" but as one that requires interpretive labor in the interest of attempting, as Walter Benjamin famously implored, to "brush history against the grain."[46]

Territorial Remediations

This book presents territory not only as land enclosed by a geopolitical border, but as a medium—one that can be shaped, fortified, strengthened, or otherwise modified. As such, though territory can never be reconquered (by the same power) in the strictly geometric or cartographic sense, a region's resources and qualities (inclusive of its people) can be reorganized in order to render that territory more productive, or more suitable to present needs—a phenomenon that William Cronon described as "changes *in* the land."[47] Whereas the close of the frontier may have motivated a psychic need for an imperial dive into the Pacific, it was the continuous development and redevelopment of the resources and *qualities* of the American interior that produced the range of constantly evolving colonial techniques and policies that are the primary interest of this book. Thus, though the frontier was a closed historical chapter—a chapter in fact "destined" for closure—a history of territory as a medium allows us to not only place the Philippines within a cartographically mappable history of territorial expansion, but also to propose a *colonialism of permanent expansion*. The frontier is thus re-presented here, not as a horizon that "closed" at the end of the nineteenth century, but as a constant and continuous material reconfigurability.[48]

Within this framework, the annexation of the Philippines appears not (as it was sometimes regarded by anti-imperialists at the time) as a scandalous and singular event—an aberrant, albeit limited, flirtation with "formal empire."

Rather, this history is one that traces a set of colonial practices with origins in the reorganization of what was assumed to be already "settled" land. Accordingly, this book is an attempt to trace heterogeneous, ad hoc, and constantly shifting colonial methods that nevertheless share a common material basis. The object of *Concrete Colonialism* is thus not the United States or the Philippines as such, but rather the continuously organized and reorganized material relationships between and within them. Indeed, as this book argues, the colonial experiments conducted in the Philippines played a central role in structuring the US's relationship to the rest of the world—a complex and constantly renegotiated relationship between the US's expanding interior and its increasingly fictional exterior. My intention is to highlight the pivotal role that the colonization of the Philippines played in the formation of this twisted, shifting, and global American topos.[49]

This history, then, is not conceived of as a contribution to "global history," defined as a practice driven by the representative inclusion of every corner of the globe. Rather, it critically situates the Philippines within the transformative processes of globalization through which the United States establishes its global hegemony. This process, I contend, begins with the development of the land. This was a process accelerated in the Philippines by two key factors: the first being the colony's absence of protracting democratic processes (seen by many reformers during the Progressive Era as inhibiting the pace of progress), and the second being the use of reinforced concrete. For, whereas heroic feats of US engineering like the Erie Canal predate the widespread use of modern Portland cement and steel reinforcement, the Panama Canal—a project many magnitudes larger and more legibly global in its scope—would not have been possible without modern reinforced concrete technology. It was around the time of the Panama Canal's construction (beginning in 1904) that we see an explosion of reinforced concrete projects in the Philippines, especially after the establishment, in 1905, of the Philippines' Bureau of Public Works. Though the canals, culverts, dams, standpipes, highways, schools, piers, customs houses, markets, and monuments executed under that Bureau's auspices lacked the singular spectacularity of the Panama Canal, collectively these projects remade the Philippines. By accelerating intra-island transport, interisland connections, and international traffic, they helped to orient the archipelago's resources toward an international market. Though this massive construction project, conceived of at the scale of the entire colony, closely resembles neocolonial strategies of economic development, they were deployed in the Philippines as colonial techniques. This is, in part, why the US colonization of the Philippines is both easy to marginalize and difficult to historically contextualize. This history, seemingly out of sync, bridges the gap between the nineteenth-century expansion of the French and British Empires and the neocolonial practices of "development" associated with the post–World War II era, aiming to expose these historically separated narratives as continuous.

Concrete, Architecture History,
and an Expansive Disciplinarity

Though this is an interdisciplinary study, and aims to speak to a broad audience, I am trained as an architect and as an architecture historian, and I teach architecture history. It is not only because of this, however, that I write from the perspective that I do. I believe that architecture history offers a unique lens through which to view and analyze the US colonial project in the Philippines. This view, however, is sometimes obscured by the deeply coded knowledge that circulates within limited circles of expertise. The sources that I analyze often require a familiarity with building materials, architectural traditions, and with the standards and conventions of architectural representation. These documents often belong to a class of knowledge never intended to be accessible to the lay reader, and yet they contain within them knowledge of historical consequence. Translating and contextualizing these plans, artifacts, and other sources reveals heretofore understudied aspects of US empire and something about how power within it worked.

In addition to this, the US colonial project is one that not only involved architects and engineers, but one in which those figures took on powerful positions within the colonial government. Indeed, that knowledge of the US colonial project in the Philippines is relatively widespread within the field of American *architecture* history is by virtue of the fact that one of its main protagonists, Daniel Burnham, prepared a pair of grandiose master plans for the archipelago—one for the capital city of Manila and another for Baguio, a brand-new summer capital in the mountain province of Benguet. The effect of this particular inroad into the annals of architectural history, however, is that the story of US colonialism has been embedded as a single chapter (or, more often, as a surprising footnote) in monographs dedicated to one man's heroized career. Burnham's prominence in the secondary literature belies both the limited nature of his direct involvement in the project and the large cast of characters that played more significant roles in shaping the US's colonial project in the Philippines. Thus, though Burnham—the widely acknowledged father of American urban planning—serves as an important figure and historical touchstone in and for this book, neither his biography nor his famous plans serve as its central object. Rather, I treat Burnham as a subject formed within this particular historical milieu.

I do not, however, as this assertion might suggest, treat Burnham as a mere symptom of history. This story is not one that can be understood by diligently tracing the contours of blandly predictable predeterminations, technological or otherwise. Though Burnham is not the focus of this study (it is indeed here in the introduction that he receives the most sustained attention) he was and will be portrayed as an important historical agent—one who possessed particular sensitivity to the materials, techniques, and conditions of his time. Toward those ends, what is most important to know about Burnham—an opinion broadly shared by his most vehement critics, his most steadfast boosters, and by his most thorough biographers—is that Burnham was not an architect as conventionally understood. Only a few drawings in his actual hand survive, and those that do survive show no evidence of remarkable artistic talent. To the extent that his work is ever appreciated on an aesthetic register, those aspects are fully attributed to the preternatural artistic talents of his prematurely deceased partner, John Wellborn Root, or to the various Beaux Arts–trained protégés that succeeded him. For his part, Burnham was—especially in his own time—regarded first and foremost as an effective administrator and businessman. Frank Lloyd Wright eulogized him as an "enthusiastic promoter of great constructive enterprises . . . a great man," but by no measure "a creative architect."[50] Indeed, his impact on the profession of architecture is best characterized by his full embrace of "bigness, organization, delegation, and intense commercialism"—a sworn devotion to "big business" that his self-proclaimed rival, Louis Sullivan, regarded as toxic to an architectural *vocation* that supposedly operated on an unassailable and autonomous plane of "culture."[51] Indeed, Burnham's office is widely acknowledged as the US's first corporate architecture firm. Even in this capacity, however, Burnham's historical role is both mischaracterized and underestimated. His contributions relative to the architecture (i.e., the organization) of the American corporation itself is more important to understand than the significant role he may have played in the production of American corporate architecture (i.e., corporate buildings themselves), though I treat these two architectures not only as closely related, but in fact as *structurally* and *materially fused*.[52]

It is, of course, no stretch to think of Burnham and concrete together. Much of the work that is credited to him was built in part or in whole of reinforced concrete. Despite this, if Burnham is associated with any material, it is usually with the airbrushed plaster staff that fleshed out the steel skeletons of the World's Columbian Exposition, a historic feat with which his name will be forever bound. Burnham's association with this ephemeral material was usually invoked to identify the architect with an artless and crassly modern reproducibility, and to substantiate criticisms that characterized his work as flimsy simulations of "real" architecture—"a mode of architecture" that Lewis Mumford sneered "was little but veneer."[53] Most of Burnham's work, however—superficial or not—was (relatively) permanent, built as it was in whole or in large part out of reinforced concrete. While concrete acted similarly to plaster in many ways—in its plasticity, the portability of its components, its ease of use, and its managerial requirements—it was its opposite in one critical respect: Whereas plaster staff is unable to withstand tests of weather exceeding a number of months, reinforced concrete rivals the strength and permanence of stone. Therefore, it mattered little that Louis Sullivan considered Burnham little more than an "expert salesman ... of the materials of decay."[54] The architecture that he built after the exposition endured. That is to say, the most significant difference separating Burnham's Dream City from the "real" cities of Manila, Chicago, and Washington, DC, was—at least initially—merely a material one. And so it is to concrete that this book turns. Concrete, in short, allows me to address a far more ambitious, empire-wide project than the ones laid out in Burnham's famous "big plans"; it allows me to address the elasticity of the colonial project and to chart concrete's relationships and interactions with a highly mobile set of contingencies, including rapidly evolving technologies, the spread of disease, a global labor movement, and the rise of internationalism.

Academics trained in a variety of disciplines have written about the history and social, cultural, and political effects of reinforced concrete at the grandest of scales. The environmental historian Vaclav Smil, for example, argues that cement and steel (the industrially produced components of concrete) are two of the four "material pillars of modern civilization,"[55] while anthropologists like Eli Elinoff have claimed it as the first element of the Anthropocene.[56] Taking a finer-grained approach, the historian Amy Slaton examines concrete's global effects at the crossroads of science, technology, and industrial labor. What these historians present as a world-changing, indeed epochal, technology, has so far appeared only as a minor character in books on the US colonization of the Philippines, including Warwick Anderson's *Colonial Pathologies*, Paul A. Kramer's *The Blood of Government*, David Brody's *Visualizing American Empire*, Rebecca Tinio McKenna's *American Imperial Pastoral*, and Peter W. Stanley's *A Nation in the Making* (pathbreaking works that have deeply influenced my own). The near absence of a consideration of concrete in these books is surprising considering that, after 1905, virtually all permanent buildings executed by the US colonial government were built out of it.

Another book that has significantly influenced this one is Benedict Anderson's *Imagined Communities* (a book that towers both within and in some ways over Philippine and Fil-Am Studies). Most directly, this book contends with the figure of the nation as an outcome of print capitalism. I do not oppose that argument here, but instead offer some ways to think through how daily contact with this modern material works in ways different from and alongside the world that print capitalism made. More significantly *Imagined Communities* has served as a model for constructing a narrative that traverses an interconnected history of modernity though an examination of particular places and the effects of media on and within it. Different media, however, render different effects. Examining the US colonial project in the Philippines through the use of what was both believed to be—and actually was—an environmentally transformative material allows me to link what Immanuel Wallerstein calls the "world system" to a sensible and grounded reality by permitting me to tell specific stories that reveal something about the nature of US empire as such.

Though I situate this study of the Philippines within a history of the "world system," it is very likely that this book will be relegated to a disciplinarily ossified geographical "area." As Vicente Rafael and Rey Chow have argued, by privileging the nation-state as the elementary unit of analysis, "areas" are conceived "as if they were the natural—or at least, historically necessary—formations for the containment of differences within and between cultures."[57] The study of "areas," Rafael extends, is not only the legacy of Orientalist discourse, but more significantly has been integrated into institutional cultures (like those of universities)—that silo work produced within these areas into the delimited categories of a liberal pluralism, in turn precluding the possibility of scholarly relevance beyond the nation or area addressed.[58] Indeed, a historical grasp of a globalized system of architectural production remains elusive because most histories that address an architectural periphery are presented and represented as totems of national or regional difference.[59] The history of reinforced concrete architecture pushes against this tendency, as in many cases this architecture is better understood in terms of its similarity with structures built across the globe rather than in terms of its differences from them. Taking seriously this serialization and global ubiquity challenges both the persistent re-inscription of isolatable national and regional frames, enabling me to describe the global entanglements that are the very nature of materiality.[60]

Though many other thinkers engaged with material have informed this book in one way or another, none brought me to materiality as a "method." Over the course of my academic training I have accepted Bruno Latour's insight that materials matter or "act" in complex networks of people and things, and subscribe to Marx's argument that all aspects and institutions of human society are the outgrowth of material conditions. Though this is the ontological ground on which this book rests, I arrived at this subject matter (or matter as a subject) through my home discipline of architecture history in which a focus on build-ing material is a long-established convention. This "approach," which can be traced at least as far back as John Ruskin's *The Stones of Venice* (1850), Gottfried Semper's *Der Stil* (1861–63), and Banister Fletcher's *The Influence of Material on Architecture* (1897), emerged in the wake of the Industrial Revolution—when industrially produced materials began to radically transform the building trades. This body of literature expanded when architecture historians—many of whom either heroized or worked closely with a European Avant-Garde—positively advocated for the use of industrial materials. These histories included Sigfried Giedion's *Bauen in Frankreich, Bauen in Eisen, Bauen in Eisenbeton* (1928), Peter Collins's *Concrete* (1959), and Reyner Banham's *A Concrete Atlan-tis* (1986), to name only a few of the most significant examples.

None of the books mentioned above would have much to say about the architecture or infrastructure I write about in this book. Though Banham and Giedion look at infrastructure, warehouses, and grain silos, that is, structures not usually considered architecture, I do not treat this "non-architecture" as they do, as unwittingly produced source material for true modernist form. Those structures I address that *are* considered architecture, meanwhile, would typi-cally be seen as examples of a substandard and/or retrograde academicism. In some respects, this book has more in common with histories written by those considered foundational figures in American architectural history, includ-ing Lewis Mumford, Montgomery Schuyler, Carl Condit, and Henry-Russel Hitchcock, who—when compared with their European counterparts—were forced to reckon with the unity of industrial and architectural production and were (save for Hitchcock) less bothered by the American tendency toward historicism. However, as is the case with the aforementioned European histo-rians, architecture generally constitutes the *end* of their investigations. This was certainly the case with Schuyler and Mumford, who not only identified the Beaux Arts style as a mindless reflection and a soulless reaction to the "imperial" forces of industrialization, but also aimed to resolve historical con-flict by championing the "organic" architecture of Louis Sullivan and Frank Lloyd Wright, which they argued was—by virtue of its sponsorship of craft traditions—inherently more "democratic." This history makes no such en-dorsements. Rather, I recognize that because both Sullivan and Wright made abundant use of industrial materials, in addition to the fact that they themselves worked with and for multinational corporations, they too are a part of the same imperial history.

This is not to say that architecture historians have not themselves consciously attempted to turn away from their own hagiographic tendencies. Particularly relevant to this work were attempts to expand architectural history scholarship to include the "history of building practice" more broadly, which the British historian of (mostly) British architecture John Summerson described (upon the founding of the Construction History Group and its journal *Construction History*), as "involv(ing) the total process of getting a building up on site, including everything from the recruitment of labour, selection of materials, transport of materials and equipment on the site, down to the supply of drawing materials for the office, the method of payment to builder and architect and so on and so on."[61] Summerson explained this foray into "building practice" by referring to an editorial in the first volume of the *Builder*, published in 1842, where the editor, Joseph Hansom, considering the *Builder's* potential readership "lists all the people who, he believes, ought to be interested and who form what he calls the 'building class'" ultimately listing "no fewer than 102 types of readers,"[62] each of which is involved with building, brokering, designing, expediting, and trading things somehow related to the building industry. In short, what Hansom illustrates is what Latour called a "network." Perhaps even more significantly, Summerson notes that what impressed him most about Hansom's list "was the tremendous ramification of the 'building world' and its unique relationship to society." I mention this to, on the one hand, declare my sympathy with architectural scholarship that defines as its object the description of the built world's "relationship to society" and on the other to state that what may at times seem a methodological "detour" from the conventions of architecture history has on various occasions and for a variety of reasons entered the mainstreams of architectural discourse. Methodologically speaking then, this book makes no claims to originality or radicality. The central contribution of this book with respect to architectural history is my insertion of the Philippines as an important node within the history of global architectural practice, and by extension to provide a historical context for the global professional practice that all architects engage with today.

Recent contributions to architectural histories of concrete contextualize, as this work does, architecture within both particular and global historical frameworks, aiming to demonstrate architecture's interactions between social, economic, political, institutional, and cultural formations. This includes Adrian Forty's *Concrete and Culture* (2012), a wide-ranging global history of concrete and its cultural effects; Michael Kubo, Chris Grimley, and Mark Pasnik's *Heroic: Concrete Architecture and the New Boston* (2015), an analysis of Brutalist architecture in Boston, set in the historical and political context of President Lyndon Johnson's New Society; and Martino Stierli and Vladimir Kulić's *Toward a Concrete Utopia: Architecture in Yugoslavia* (2018), an exhibition catalogue containing scholarly essays that highlight the pivotal role that concrete played in partially realizing an architectural techno-modernism that embodied Yugoslavia's "third way" approach to development.

Though this book has benefitted in significant ways from this scholarship, it sets itself apart from those architecture histories not only because I address a part of the world that is almost never addressed in mainstream architectural histories, but also because none of the architecture I write about is likely to be admitted into an architectural history "canon." This is the precise reason I am interested in the material castoffs of a supposedly more august architecture history. I take as my task (after Walter Benjamin) the recovery of these "historical leftovers" as evidence of repressed histories, and as histories of the repressed. It is, in other words, because these objects are forgotten, left out, and left to ruin that I seek to reunite them with history as a whole.

Organization of Chapters

Concrete Colonialism unfolds over ten short, thematic chapters that are arranged in a loose, sometimes discontinuous, and often-times overlapping chronology that pulls the reader forward in time. Together, these chapters neither present a coherent story nor attempt to offer a comprehensive account. Rather, I have structured this book as a collection of episodic reflections that demonstrate the proliferation of possibilities enabled by concrete—a set of stories and agendas that, though diverse, are nevertheless bound together by a single (hybrid) material. None of these chapters follow a straight line. For example, though I may address a particular agency because it was invoked to fulfill a particular imperative, I follow not only when those objectives are achieved, but also address failures, detours, contingencies, unforeseen effects and short- and long-term consequences that are also a part of each story.

The first chapter, "'The Master Material' and the 'Master Race,'" situates the reader within the broader historical context of the rapid expansion of reinforced concrete construction across the globe, particularly focusing on a topic that recurs throughout the book: namely, that of race and racial capitalism. In this chapter I examine how a material that is perceived and in fact possesses the ability to radically transform the environment is viewed as a tool with which to develop race (understood to be shaped by environmental pressures). Each subsequent chapter is dedicated to a quality and/or agency of concrete, namely stability, salubrity, reproducibility, scalability, liquidity, artifice, plasticity, and strength. This heuristic allows me to account for the heterogeneous agencies of concrete, and to relatedly highlight how a specific quality is invoked with respect to the American colonial regime's shifting imperatives.

The history of *Concrete Colonialism* opens not in Manila, but in Chicago, where Daniel Burnham and John Root first experiment with the "floating raft foundation"—the central character of the second chapter, "Stability." This technology, among others, allowed the young firm not only to build the world's first skyscrapers in a remediated muddy morass, but also enabled the settlement of Chicago's particularly difficult geological conditions—thus opening up the possibility of settling almost any land, anywhere.[63] This history of the changing land is introduced to dislodge the image of the westward moving line of the frontier, in order to turn toward a colonial practice rooted in the environmental transformation of the American interior. The chapter reassesses Burnham's World's Columbian Exposition in environmental terms, shifting focus away from its plan and toward the changing quality of the ground, the unassuming site of what Root calls a "material revolution." The chapter closes with the arrival, in 1903, of the floating raft in Manila (two years before Burnham's own arrival to the archipelago) where it was used to buoy the government-owned Insular Ice and Cold Storage Plant within Manila's unstable deltaic silt. The construction of this building is prioritized on account of a widely held belief that American ice and food stores were necessary to stabilize the Anglo-American body against the deleterious effects of the tropics. I conclude this chapter by considering "stabilization" in a broader sense, by arguing that the aim of colonial rule as laid out especially by William Cameron Forbes was to answer to, in his words, the "demands of capital" by providing and maintaining a stable government and environment.

Focusing on the years during and immediately after the Philippine-American War, chapter 3, "Salubrity," examines the use of concrete in colonial sanitation projects. I compare two different approaches to sanitation: The first is Manila's modern and "comprehensive" sewer system; the second is an essentially "self-help" housing scheme for Manila's native urban poor called the "sanitary barrio." This chapter both situates this housing scheme within a longer history of what Friedrich Engels called the "housing question" and demonstrates how a supposedly universal scientific knowledge was differentially applied based on race and class, thereby taking to task the common argument that one of the failures of modernism was an unwillingness to accommodate native culture.

The story of the sanitary barrio demonstrates how a valorization of vernacular forms, native construction, and "cultural preferences" were co-opted toward colonial purposes—in this case being used to justify lower standards of sanitation for a colonial subject population.

"Reproducibility," chapter 4, opens with Daniel Burnham's arrival to the Philippines in 1905 and with the construction of the first architectural projects associated with his Philippine plans. These projects, namely the Manila Hotel and the Army and Navy Club, were built with the express purpose of attracting foreign capital to the Philippines. They were central to what William Cameron Forbes (governor-general under Theodore Roosevelt) described as a "material approach" to colonial governance, which amounted to the programmatic pursuit of an expanded economic reproduction. Relatedly, this chapter also addresses one of the most controversial agencies of concrete construction—its facilitation of the architectural replica. In bringing Forbes's "material approach" and architectural reproducibility together, I aim to describe a relationship between economic reproduction and technological reproducibility as such. In this chapter, I introduce William E. Parsons, who was hand-picked by Daniel Burnham to serve as the executor of his Philippine plans. Parsons introduces standardized plans for schools, prisons, and open-air markets, though he avoids replication for monumental civic programs. Despite this, economic constraints eventually give way to the fully replicated monument in the form of dozens of identical provincial capitol buildings, copies that sow doubt over the supposedly ideological motivations of the US colonial project.

Chapter 5, "Scalability," shifts focus away from the urban context to an archipelago-wide project to develop the colonial interior. Through a brief address of big projects and big things this impressionistic chapter attempts to capture a project conceived and executed at the scale of the archipelago itself. Here I focus on the construction and maintenance of roads, dams, and irrigation systems, which are built using a combination of imported industrial machinery and large masses of often unpaid (prison and corvée) labor. In conjunction with the port works these projects enabled the movement of mineral, forest, and agricultural resources out of the Philippines. This chapter spans both a wider geographical area and a longer period of time than the others, covering vast, open-ended initiatives that consolidate the colony's social, cultural, and economic integration into an interconnected world system.

The short chapter 6, "Liquidity," focuses on the regional production of Portland cement, and on the role its production plays in the material development of the region as such. Here, I explain why Portland cement was not successfully produced in the Philippines until 1922, which is surprising considering that virtually all public buildings have been constructed out of reinforced concrete since 1905. Though Portland cement was not produced in significant amounts in the Philippines until after 1922, it is between 1905 and 1922 that the Philippines becomes a leader in concrete research, sharing its findings with regional producers in the interest of improving the quality of the regional product. In this capacity, the United States played an important and early role in the materialization of regional economic ties, providing an important precedent for intervention into and administration of economically defined "areas" more commonly associated with the development politics of the postwar era. This chapter functions as an interlude to mark a historical shift in the US's approach to the Philippines from a more explicitly colonial project to a nation-building project—a shift initiated by changes introduced by the first Democratic administration to take power since the beginning of the US colonial period. Though the architecture—especially in the following two chapters—is presented as ideologically distinct from those buildings built by the regime of Republican president William Howard Taft, it is materially continuous with those buildings and with the larger project.

Chapter 7, "Artifice," examines how an architectural cult of materiality interacted with the politics of nation building in the Philippines where new stakes for material expression emerge in the wake of Woodrow Wilson's election, the growing importance of liberal internationalism, and, relatedly, the 1916 passage of the Jones Law—the first formal promise made by the United States to grant the Philippines political independence in the form of national sovereignty. Architecture produced during this transitional period reflected a new remit to represent the United States as a moral example—not only for its soon-to-be former colonial subjects, but also for a community of nations increasingly wary of imperial expansion. Under these conditions, concrete's prosaic appearance became a liability. Ralph Harrington Doane, the last American consulting architect to serve the Insular Government, referred to concrete as an industrially produced "bastard material," unsuitable for a monument. Unable to source stone slabs, Doane develops a concrete using a local marble aggregate, aiming to remediate concrete's characterless industrial appearance. Doane presents this reformed material as a rich prefiguration of national sovereignty. The actually superficial narrative of national recognition presented in this chapter should, however, not be mistaken as part of a liberating project of "decolonization" or decolonial thinking (terms that were not used at the time).[64] Instead, what I present is a description of how formal and political decolonization (mostly associated with the post–World War II decolonizations of Asia and Africa) was a process shaped by former imperial powers in pursuit of their own interests.

"Plasticity" addresses, as "Artifice" does, concrete's ability to take on the appearance of something other than itself. However, whereas chapter 7 examines concrete's ability to take on the appearance of another material, chapter 8 turns toward how this material is called on to transcend materiality as such. It does so, here, in order to take on an ideological form. Focusing on a process and period of "Filipinization" (a Wilson-era transitional colonial policy that embraced Philippine national culture and native elite political control), I examine how architects during this period turned to sculpture as a medium through which they explored and developed a "native" canon, here used in the art-historical sense of a system of ideal proportions. Specifically, I look at how a Filipino native elite took on a project of self-racialization outlined for them by former imperial powers as a strictly delimited arena of political agency. The thematization of the native body—which, I argue, lies at the historical origins of the ethno-state—is illustrated mainly through the life and career of the architect Juan Arellano, alongside the origins of one of his most important commissions: the Philippine Legislative Building. This was a project designed and built just after the United States made its first formal promise to grant the Philippines its national sovereignty, and the building's heavily loaded decorative program was intended to provide an exemplary image of how postcolonial nations would fit into an imagined new world order—one in which cultural and ethnic identity served as the symbolic currency of Wilsonian internationalist politics.

The American colonial period in the Philippines both begins and ends with war. "Strength" examines US military installations in the Philippines and covers projects built both at the beginning of the US colonial period and at the time of its only apparent conclusion—during the lead-up to World War II, when the archipelago became a conspicuous target for an expanding Japanese empire. Over the course of this chapter, I present the military buildup of the Philippines as the beginning of a transformation of American territory from one largely thought of as a contiguous land mass to a globally distributed, militarized archipelago. This chapter ends with the near total destruction of most of the concrete architecture and infrastructure addressed throughout the book. The colonial city that once stood as concrete proof of colonialism's benefits was revealed in the aftermath of war to be a dangerous geopolitical gamble from the outset.

Picking up in the immediate aftermath of Manila's destruction in World War II, I conclude in chapter 10 with a short chapter dedicated to "Reconstruction," placing Manila's rehabilitation in the context of other US histories of reconstruction. This was an effort that preceded the Marshall Plan, a development project otherwise considered unprecedented, but which finds its immediate precursor in the Philippine Rehabilitation Act—a pledge to rebuild all that had been destroyed in World War II only if it accepted various compromises to Philippine sovereignty, including trade terms greatly beneficial to the United States and the right to build and maintain military bases on the archipelago. Here, I present not the conclusion of concrete colonialism, but rather the possibility of its perpetuity.

I

THE "MASTER MATERIAL"
AND THE "MASTER RACE"

J. C. Witt, a young scientist and chemical engineer, opened his article, "Why Concrete Is the Master Building Material in the Philippines," published in 1921, with praise for a different material altogether: bamboo. It was, in his words, "in many respects an ideal material," being cheap, readily available, easy to work with, straightforward to repair, resilient in an earthquake, and above all comfortable in the tropical heat. According to Witt, however, "such construction" was "not suited to building other than the simplest type of dwelling." Other local materials were equally inappropriate for purposes that Witt left vaguely defined, including wood (susceptible to the "constant and untiring" work of tropical bugs), local brick ("underburned . . . [and] of little strength"), and the volcanic local stone, called "tuff," which was "too soft for use in any but a very thick wall."[1] Indeed, the volcanic stone masonry of Manila's impressive fortified city, Intramuros, were over twenty feet thick in parts. Thus, beyond the walled city, and the imposing churches built in the center of each town, the Spanish had built relatively few permanent structures in the archipelago during its more than three hundred years of colonial rule. By contrast, in its five decades of colonial rule, the United States resurfaced huge swaths of the archipelago, reshaping its landscapes and transforming its towns by emplacing millions of tons of reinforced concrete. Concrete was, however, the master material in the Philippines, not only because of its pervasive use, but also because it alone would transform both the land *and* (US colonizers believed) the people that lived on it.

The Imperial Material

Although the 1905 plans for Manila and Baguio by architect and city planner Daniel Burnham were the most prominent outcome of his work in the Philippines, his most consequential was, perhaps, his often-overlooked recommendation for an architecture of "flat walls, simply built of concrete."[2] It introduced not only a novel material but a new kind of colonization—one in which campaigns of native dispossession were followed almost immediately by the construction of durable forms of settlement. The combustible timber boom towns of the American frontier were remade as solid, interconnected hardscapes, a construction enabled by innovations in cement manufacture and the increasing popularity of reinforced concrete construction systems including the Hennebique "stirrup" system (1879), the Ransome twisted bar system (1884), the Kahn trussed bar system (1902), C. A. P. Turner's flat-slab mushroom system (1908), the Patent Indented Steel Bar Co. system (1911), and dozens more.

The specification of reinforced concrete rose precipitously in the aftermath of San Francisco's Great Earthquake and resulting fire of 1906, which left only two buildings unscathed: Julia Morgan's clocktower on the Mills College campus in Oakland (built using the Ransome system) and a Bekins warehouse in San Francisco (built using the Kahn trussed bar).[3] The resilience of Kahn's system, in particular, was confirmed in 1907 after earthquakes in Kingston, Jamaica, destroyed everything but the government rum warehouse and the Singer Sewing Co. building; in 1908 when "a lunatic asylum and four or five houses all built of reinforced concrete"[4] in Messina, Italy, survived a seismic event of XI (extreme) on the Mercalli scale intact; and when the nearly-complete government-owned Manila Hotel "stood up perfectly"[5] against the 964 recorded shocks that struck the Philippine capital in January of 1911. Julius Kahn used the material's earthquake resistance to secure the position of his company Trussed Concrete Steel (or TrusCon) within an international market (commissioning the publication of the book *Earthquake Proof Construction*, by Lewis Alden Estes, from which all the above examples were taken). By the mid-1930s, the Kahn system could be found in over 134 cities across the United States, as well as in Europe, Mexico, Brazil, Africa, China, Japan, and the Caribbean. Across the globe's seismically prone areas in particular, reinforced concrete took almost immediate hold of the building industry.

What the global success of TrusCon points to is that concrete's status as the "master material" in the Philippines had as much to do with the dynamic and developing features of a global market as it did with conditions unique to the archipelago itself. The US's unique political arrangement in the Philippines, as the only US territory to hold formal colonial status, did, however, render various advantages to the growth of the market for concrete products in the Philippines. For example, the Philippines was seen as a new market through which the US government aimed to stabilize the price of overproduced commodities by ramping up exports.[6] If the colony's private sector did not generate enough demand, the colonial government (under the control of the federal government) could stimulate its own demand by initiating massive construction projects. In those cases, US producers shipped cement and reinforcement as ballast on military vessels as tariff-free freight.[7] Even when US demand for domestic cement was high (as it was throughout the early twentieth century), imported (non-US) concrete continued to benefit the colonial government, as each "foreign" barrel was subject to a seven-cent tariff—a significant source of revenue for the Insular Government. The colony, in other words, provided a variety of stabilizing advantages to the otherwise volatile process of global industrial development. These arrangements disincentivized the development of the Philippines' Portland cement industry (among others)—driving the colony's and the metropole's economies in opposite directions even as the very materiality of the cities began to converge.

Making Race Masters: US Imperialism and "Race Development"

Today, "development" is considered shorthand for *economic* development—a set of practices that are generally associated with the neocolonial imperatives of the postwar period—but the economy was not always imagined as development's primary, much less exclusive, object. Development theory, as anthropologist George W. Stocking Jr. argued, grew out of Darwinian evolutionary theory as laid out in *On the Origin of Species* (1859) and in the academic scholarship that followed in its wake in the 1860s and 1870s.[8] In those decades, older civilizational rationales for the colonial exploitation of "savage" nations and peoples were reinterpreted through the lens of evolutionary theory. "Savage" and "superior" nations and peoples were reinscribed into both academia and society at large as "races" occupying a spectrum from "primitive" to "advanced." By the turn of the twentieth century, this hierarchical order had been institutionalized within the flourishing disciplines of ethnology, anthropology, and sociology, and popularized at World's Fairs, traveling sideshows, and "scientific" magazines. In the interest of reconciling the work being done in these new disciplines with what they called a new "point of view towards primitive races" in 1910, two professors at Clark University founded the *Journal of Race Development* (*JRD*), providing what was perhaps the most candid account of the racial origins of development practice.[9]

What was known for a brief moment at the turn of the century as "race development" included (but was not, as its name might suggest, limited to) the "science" of eugenics. At times, proponents of "race development" viewed education, and other social and environmental interventions, as an "altruistic" means of improving "weaker races."[10] As such, race development encompassed multiple itineraries situated within a variety of disciplines, which included sociology, anthropology, sanitary science, urban planning, political science, international relations, and economics. Though the reasons for why the object of development shifted from "race" to national economies are complex, *that* these practices emerged out of an imperative to improve the world's under- and "undeveloped" races is plainly illustrated by the journal's renaming in 1919, when it was given the title *Foreign Affairs*, after merging with the *Journal of International Relations*. What is now simply referred to as "development" thus took shape not in the postwar era, but half a century earlier in the Philippines, Puerto Rico, Haiti, and other US-occupied territories as a set of practices and techniques that defined the US's "unique approach" to colonization—one that attempted to evade the apparent contradictions inherent to US empire by appending the logic of evolution to the ascendance of a distinctly American civilization. This developmental approach drew from practices cultivated in the conquest of the US interior, and included the rapid construction of sanitary, transportation, industrial, commercial, and institutional infrastructures.[11]

Though the founders of the *JRD*—history professor George Hubbard Blakeslee and psychology professor Granville Stanley Hall, both of Clark University—launched it as an academic journal, their explicit interest lay in the world of "practice." They were particularly invested in the opportunities for study offered by the US's new colonial approach in the Philippines—one which was, they argued, distinct from both the exploitative colonialism of Continental powers and the paternalistic colonial approach of the English (both of which were understood to be permanent arrangements). By contrast, the American approach was based on the idea of improving "weaker" races—a finite colonial arrangement that both mobilized existing anthropological knowledge while also serving as a new field of "useful" study.[12]

The work of "race development" took shape as an attempt to both systematize and instrumentalize what historians considered to be up until that point an "organic" process of national development, most often viewed by those same historians as a story of cultural and economic ascendance. One embarrassing exception, Blakeslee pointed out, to the US's rise to global prominence was the fact that the "negro problem" was "still not solved" thirty years after the end of Reconstruction.[13] However, despite the incomplete address of this "problem," it established a foundation of empirical knowledge that gave the United States a distinct advantage in defining modern colonial practice. As Hall points out in the journal's very first article, "The Point of View Towards Primitive Races," the "Philippine problem" could simply be annexed to a field of theory and practice built on existing knowledge gained in dealing with the US's other Indian, Negro, and immigrant "problems."

In 1912, Howard W. Odum, JRD contributor and the eventual founder of the journal Social Forces, made a first (and last) attempt to define race development in scientific terms. In his article, "Standards of Measurement for Race Development," Odum submitted various metrics by which racial progress could be measured.[14] Among other acknowledged influences, Odum's definition built on Franz Boas's groundbreaking, freshly published assertions of racial plasticity, which first appeared in the pages of American Anthropologist in 1912. In that article, "Changes in the Bodily Form of Descendants of Immigrants," Boas challenged the hereditary basis of human racial categorization. Tracking the head size of recently arrived US immigrants from Central and Southern Europe and their descendants, Boas determined that there were measurable discrepancies in skull circumference and body form within the course of a single generation—changes attributable to the "effect of social and geographical environment upon man."[15] It did not take a huge leap of imagination to jump from Boas's observations of racial plasticity to Odum's presentation of race development as a constructive project. After all, New York—the "environment" in which Boas's immigrants lived—was nothing if not human-made; and, if environment had the power to shape race, the race developer could begin to pursue a "positive" direction for the "weaker races." Race developers thus identified a new task: quite simply, to construct environments and shape social conditions considered most conducive to racial development. Boas's ideas were (and continue to be) considered representative of a "progressive" theory of development, as opposed to a more "conservative" idea of racial fixity. In the early years of the journal's publication, the implied task of race development was to assume the mantle of responsibility incumbent on "advanced races" to intercede in the process of evolution itself. This power to steer evolution—as *race masters*—was presented by some contributors to the *JRD* as an evolutionary telos. As frequent contributor Ellsworth Huntington put it, the development of weaker races was "the culminating phase of organic evolution."[16]

While the project of "race development," per se, faded into near obscurity, its objectives remained central to the shaping of both colonial (and, later, Philippine) national policy toward the archipelago's "weaker races." The central contention between those who supported colonial retention and those who advocated for Philippine national sovereignty was not whether certain natives were "primitive" or "undeveloped," but rather *who* would be in charge of those "undeveloped" races. In fact, this was the very topic of Maximo Kalaw's article "Recent Policy Towards the Non-Christian People of the Philippines," published in the first issue of the *JRD* to appear under its new title, the *Journal of International Affairs*. Kalaw's approach barely differed from that of the staunchly retentionist Secretary of the Interior Dean Conant Worcester, the central difference being that Kalaw believed the "most advanced" races within the Philippines should carry on the work of developing the "weaker races," while Worcester believed effective race development was only possible under a colonial regime administrated by white Americans and Europeans.

Worcester's arguments for colonial retention took the form of a massive two volume "history" of the Philippines titled *The Philippines Past and Present* (1914). The frontispiece of the second volume shows a Bontoc Igorot as an "uncivilized" adolescent beside a photo of the same person as a young adult. The caption reads: "The Metamorphosis of a Bontoc Igorot: Two photographs of Pít-a-pit, a Bontoc Igorot boy. The second was taken nine years after the first" (figure 1.1). The images not only aimed to depict "an 'evolving' Filipino polity," but also demonstrated the potency of American colonialism.[17] Here, colonial sovereignty is legitimized not only on account of an assumed racial superiority, but also by its biopower, articulated here as a demonstrated ability to manipulate evolutionary forces.

Human transformations were perhaps the most powerful before-and-after pairings, but they were by no means the most common. Far more photographs were dedicated to public works projects executed throughout the archipelago. For example, Worcester places "An Old-style Schoolhouse with Teachers and Pupils" next to "A Modern Primary School Building," while a photo of "A Typical Old-style Bridge" was placed by one of "A Typical Reënforced Concrete Bridge"

THE METAMORPHOSIS OF A BONTOC IGOROT.
Two photographs of Pit-a-pit, a Bontoc Igorot boy. The second was taken nine years after the first.

FIGURE 1.1. "The Metamorphosis of a Bontoc Igorot." From Dean C. Worcester, *The Philippines Past and Present* (New York: Macmillan, 1914), vol. 2, frontispiece.

(figure 1.2). Though Worcester only explicitly mentions concrete a few times throughout the text, the material quite literally fills the frame of most of his "after" photos. The spectacular changes to the Philippine environment enabled by concrete lent credence to Worcester's claims for a colonially induced racial "metamorphosis." It is no mere coincidence that ideas of "race development" took hold at the precise moment that reinforced concrete rose from relative obscurity to become *the* dominant material of modern construction. Citing its speed, strength, availability, and affordability, producers and promoters began to link concrete construction to the best that a modern and "advanced" civilization had to offer, with colonial officials like Worcester positing a deterministic relationship between the environment and the cerebral, behavioral, and physiognomic features of various human races. Very simply, if the environment could be so radically transformed, then race—thought to be the product of its environment—would follow in turn.

Indeed, it is as developmental tools that James Beardsley, who served as the director of the Bureau of Public Works, viewed his projects. In his words,

A TYPICAL OLD-STYLE BRIDGE.

A TYPICAL REËNFORCED CONCRETE BRIDGE.

FIGURE 1.2. Comparison between "native" architecture and architecture built during the US colonial occupation. From Dean C. Worcester, *The Philippines Past and Present* (New York: Macmillan, 1914), vol. 2, 879.

"I cannot help believing that these practical utilitarian works . . . are powerful instruments useful in . . . the development of our dependencies and their people." Filipinos he argued did not understand "the value of thrift," a trait which they lacked on account of never having provided "for themselves sustenance and shelter during the ice-bound months of a northern winter." In various ways public works projects substituted for this environmental deficiency. Paying taxes for the construction of public works projects were, for example, "a first lesson in public thrift." Wages earned in constructing the projects taught the natives the "dignity of labor," while witnessing the construction that returned taxes to Filipinos in the form of public works would, on account of their utility, durability, and return on investment, help natives develop a trust in government. Public works projects (built, in the Philippines, exclusively out of reinforced concrete), were, in other words, at the center of a far-reaching project of social reform.[18] Concrete was racialized in even more particular ways. In an article that described methods of building with reinforced concrete particular to "tropical conditions in the Orient."[19] J. C. Koch, an engineer working for the Bureau of Public Works, detailed how he revised standard engineering equations, multiplied safety factors and used "low[er] constants" than he would have used in the United States, demonstrating how reinforced concrete implied two racially defined groups—the self-possessed white American engineer and the unskilled Filipino laborer.[20]

This is all to illustrate that the relationship between race and architecture as articulated by race developers was distinct from that proposed by Eugène-Emmanuel Viollet-le-Duc (1814–79) in *The Habitations of Man in All Ages* and Gottfried Semper (1803–79) in *The Four Elements of Architecture*, which present race and style as analogous expressions of environmental determination.[21] For these two architects the end goal of the architectural branch of ethnographic "science" was to valorize regionalist architecture as an organic expression of racialized humans, a value reflected in Viollet-le-Duc's concluding exhortation in *Habitations*: "know thyself." Though Worcester's development mission emerges out of the same ethnographic logic as Viollet-le-Duc's (both believed in the possibility of racial "improvement"), Worcester believed that the culminating stage of evolution was for the most advanced race to seize control of the process of evolution in order to develop all forms of "inferior life."[22] Thus, when Worcester placed a photo of an old building type next to a new building type, it was not to present a new Philippine type as a form of native self-realization. Rather, his point was that these buildings and environmental transformations—tools of a master race—would themselves act on the undeveloped races of the archipelago, the objects of colonial practice.

Forbes's Policy of "Material Advancement"

When William Cameron Forbes first arrived in the Philippines, he observed "a great deal of very foolish construction going on." Most buildings in Manila (built by the US military in the early years of the civil government) were constructed of Oregon pine or other cheap wood commonly used by the military and early civil government. As commissioner of commerce and police, Forbes issued orders that outlawed the use of Oregon pine for permanent construction, specifying that "nothing should be built which was likely to fall during my lifetime," a longevity that could only be ensured through the use of reinforced concrete.[23] This was the centerpiece of Forbes's guiding policy of "material advancement"— an approach to colonial governance that he outlined in succinct detail in a speech delivered before the twenty-sixth annual "Lake Mohonk Conference of the Friends of the Indian and Other Dependent Peoples," in 1908, just a month prior to his inauguration as the fifth civil governor-general of the Philippines.[24] Forbes opened his remarks with praise for his predecessors, such as former governor-general William Howard Taft, who would serve as president of the United States starting in 1909, and other (exclusively American) "giants of Philippine history." These men had, in Forbes's estimation, admirably solved the immediate problems of "public order, government administration, finance, health, justice, education, currency, and separation of Church and State." This preparatory work cleared the way for what Forbes presented as a new stage of colonial governance, characterized by the "constructive work which the government can properly undertake with the object of stimulating industry and promoting development."[25] In essence, Forbes presented the colonial state as a means to achieve capitalism's ends. Forbes concluded by arguing that the state's role should be reduced to three specific areas (each with concrete ends):

1st. To develop the physique of the people, so that it is physically possible for them to do an able-bodied man's labor.

2nd. To open up the means of communication, so as to provide for the most economical handling of the products of the islands.

3rd. To stimulate the production along the more modern lines in order to make the labor which we have efficient.[26]

Collectively, these goals were aimed at reproducing the conditions necessary for industrialization. By presenting Taft's work as a "problem solved," Forbes attempted to supersede the contradictory implications of both an American colonial democracy and McKinley's guiding policy of "Benevolent Assimilation" (one that, in Vincente Rafael's words, "foresaw the possibility, if not the inevitability, of colonialism's end"[27]). By replacing messier political concerns with accumulative (i.e., not terminal) goals, Forbes also staged an argument for colonialism in perpetuity.

Restating his position in a speech delivered in the Moro province of Zamboanga—a particularly troublesome hotbed of insurgent activity, Forbes argued, "The real problem before the Philippine people is not their political status. . . . The real problem is the industrial development, and by industrial, I mean agriculture, manufactures, and commerce." Offering his "advice to . . . people who have been thinking about political changes," Forbes suggested they "get busy and devote their attention to the practical questions confronting us—things where there is something to be done," to work with him to "better [the Filipinos'] conditions" by increasing the production of "rubber, hemp, coconuts, sugar, tobacco, lumber, and other things by which money can be made." These were changes that "no change in the civil status of the government" could accomplish. "The government," Forbes concluded "is good enough now, it is all right."[28]

As an appointed official, Forbes was not beholden to native popular will, answering only to the concrete, "real" or "material" needs of the colony as an organization. Though he operated in the absence of a voting polity (that is to say, under colonial conditions), on account of the contradictions of a colonial democracy Forbes still had to prove his effectiveness as a leader to a fully enfranchised stateside citizenry. He did not do this by attempting to communicate the will of colonial subjects, but by presenting the object of his governance as economic. For example, when the retention of the Philippines became a hotly debated question in the halls of the US Congress, Forbes defended himself against William A. Jones's charges of misgovernance by offering a series of figures on average wage rates (from ten cents a day under the Spanish to twenty cents a day by 1908), annual export revenues (from $19,821,347 in 1900 to $53,683,326 by 1913), total mileage of road paved (4,531), artesian wells drilled (828), lighthouses erected (89), bridges and culverts built (2,380), cigars rolled, money orders sold, and so on, all of which he presented collectively as a "progress barometer."[29] Reinforced concrete played a crucial role in the realization of nearly all of these metrics. Colonialism, therefore, was not only an economic or sociological lens through which Forbes and others quantified and assessed the colony and the postcolony; the economy was *made* calculable through the use of concrete.[30]

As a material capable of manifesting calculable change, reinforced concrete became central to Forbes's policy of material advancement. "All government buildings and bridges," Forbes wrote, "should always be of reinforced concrete; the roads should be built upon strong foundations with durable surfaces . . . our wharves should be built of materials that will resist the destructive insects of the seas."[31] Though it was far more expensive than other forms of construction, Forbes defended the widescale use of concrete as a sound investment, arguing that expense should be calculated based on "the most economical construction on a basis of at least fifty years of use."[32] This relative permanence, Forbes argued, was "nothing more nor less than accumulated or stored-up labor—labor put into . . . lasting form."[33] Though he was speaking of accumulation in general terms, it is not difficult to see how reinforced concrete became a key means of realizing his pat theory of capital.

By building structures immune to the catastrophic losses wrought by termites, earthquakes, and typhoons, concrete would spare native laborers hours and days they would otherwise devote to maintaining their bamboo houses. Beyond this, indestructible buildings instantiated both insurable value and credit against which money could be borrowed, thus providing capital for banks and a material basis on which to establish an insurance industry. The Insular Life Assurance Co., the first Filipino life insurance company, was established only five years after Forbes's arrival. While advertisements like the one below invoked the strength and security of concrete as a means of illustrating the less tangible benefits of life insurance, concrete in fact played a highly tangible role, by guaranteeing the viability of the life insurance company itself (figure 1.3). Beyond providing a form of material insurance by enabling the accumulation of labor time, concrete freed up temporal capital for the construction of an innumerable variety of communally beneficial services—the construction of roads, community centers, and markets, for example. By specifying concrete, Forbes believed he was not only developing a market for the consumer product, but was taking concrete steps toward the reproduction of the conditions that fostered capitalism itself.

The Racialized Characteristics of the Anglo-Saxon Manager

Forbes's gospel of material advancement was, for him, not only a logical path to capital accumulation, but the fulfillment of a racially bound duty, a duty valorized in a variety of literary forms—in the essayistic musings of Forbes's maternal grandfather, Ralph Waldo Emerson; in Forbes's own paean to finance, *The Romance of Business*; and in theoretical texts in the growing field of social science, perhaps none as influential as *Anglo-Saxon Superiority, to What It Is Due*. Despite its obscurity today, this book by the French pedagogue and sociologist Edmond Demolins was a "striking success" at the time of its publication in 1897.[34] Among its many readers were Daniel Burnham and Theodore Roosevelt, the latter of whom had read the book on the train with his Rough Riders

SPENDTHRIFT—Shiftless
No Preparation for Tomorrow

CARELESS—Forgetful
Tomorrow—a Vision

THOUGHTFUL—Thrifty
Tomorrow—Planned For

THE STORY OF THE 3 LITTLE PIGS

One played — one procrastinated — one worked hard and planned for the future.
What will happen to them when adversity comes?

WHAT IS GOING TO HAPPEN TO YOU?

THRIFTY PEOPLE OWN LIFE INSURANCE

THE INSULAR LIFE
ASSURANCE COMPANY, LTD.
INSULAR LIFE BUILDING, MANILA

FIGURE 1.3. Insular Life Insurance Company, Ltd., advertisement in *Philippine Magazine*, December 1936, showing "spendthrift," "careless," and "thoughtful" houses.

to Florida (their departure point for Cuba), no doubt galvanizing his resolve as he prepared for battle against the decadent Spanish empire.[35] Meanwhile, Burnham gifted Demolins's book to Jacob McGavock Dickenson, who was then serving as the general counsel for the Illinois Central Railroad Company. A thank-you note to Burnham was dated only a few months after Burnham submitted his "Report on Proposed Improvements at Manila."[36] A mere five years later, Dickenson followed Burnham's footsteps into the realm of "public service," arriving in the Philippines on official business as President Taft's new secretary of war.

What Demolins argued was that Anglo-Saxon superiority over all nations (as made evident by US and English economic and especially colonial success) was due to the Anglo-Saxon's excellence in "independence, enterprise and practical judgment,"[37] as proven by the Anglo-Saxon's prudent management of the coal and rail industries—the unprecedented scale of which, he argued, organically led to the organization of those industries as joint-stock companies. The discovery of coal and the subsequent rise of industrial capitalism in England gave way, Demolins argued, to "financial undertakings and speculations [of]... unheard-of-proportions." The discovery of coal was "fortuitously" placed in the able hands of the Anglo-Saxons, whose ability to manage large cooperative undertakings was explained by their racial inclination to cooperation. Unprecedented accumulations of wealth that were the result of coal and rail are, Demolins argued, "essentially *unstable*" if held as private property. The only force capable of stabilizing the transformative energies unleashed by coal is, per Demolins, the distinctive moral character, managerial excellence, and organizational inclinations of the Anglo-Saxon.

Demolins's theory frankly demonstrates, as Cedric Robinson put it, the tendency of Western capitalists "to exaggerate regional, subcultural, and dialectical differences into 'racial' ones."[38] In this case, Demolins attributes to Providence that the race best able to handle coal just happened to be the first to use it on an industrial scale. The reception of Demolins's book is important to track here, as the book, though written for a French audience, found an especially enthusiastic readership among Anglo-Saxon colonizers like Burnham, Roosevelt, and Dickenson, who viewed it not only as a scientific explanation of Anglo Saxon superiority, but for whom it also served as a convenient pretext for the pursuit and perpetuation of an explicitly racial capitalism. Those nations that fail to adopt "the law of intense personal labour" that is the primary character attribute of the Anglo-Saxon are, Demolins wrote, "bound to moral depression and inferiority.... Thus the Red-skin, compared with the European; thus the Oriental, compared with the same European; thus the Latin and German races, compared with the Anglo-Saxons."[39]

The Racialized Characteristics of Filipino Labor

The origins of "race development" emerged out of the same milieu as Demolins's work—the still nascent academic discipline of social science.[40] The aim of race development, as its founder Stanley Hall defined it, was, however, slightly shifted in that the aim was not to make "third-class white men" out of colonial subjects (as seemed to be Demolins's suggestion). Rather, a new American approach to colonialism was one specifically aimed at *preserving* indigenous art forms, cultural ways, and the genetic stock of "stone-age men," who, he cautioned, were facing unprecedented levels of "extinction" both within the United States and in the colonies.[41] Hall's project to "preserve race" was tied to the development of distinct destinies defined in terms of a specific set of identified racial aptitudes.[42] This was a white supremacy that not only naturalized racial difference, but aimed to both utilize and amplify those strengths toward particular ends. This project, Hall points out, was not introduced by the *JRD*, but was one identified by the *JRD*'s founders as a program already being executed by the US colonial government. Not only did the 1903 Philippine census identify 25 linguistic groups and five skin colors, offering the race developer a trove of data to work with, colonial functionaries like Beardsley took careful account of native aptitudes (deftness of hand) and native physiques (average height of 5′3″ and weight of 116 pounds), identifying where each could be improved, and identifying how particular strengths could be applied to specific useful ends. For example, after he had gathered "several hundred measurements of matured men" Beardsley was able to compare the Filipino laborer's effectiveness to the "average efficiency of . . . American labor," which he concluded was "about one-third, ranging from a high average where quickness and deftness are required to about one-sixth where physical strength and weight are necessary." Beardsley came to these conclusions not by observing factory work, but by watching traditional occupations like "rice cultivation and harvest and hemp stripping," which required a dexterity that would translate well to any work that required "deftness of hand . . . as in drafting and typewriting, and . . . operat[ing] machines." Though the average Filipino was still less adept than the average American in every measured respect, these relatively low rates of efficiency could be improved, Beardsley assured, by "substituting nitrogenous foods for the prevailing characteristic diet of rice and dried fish."[43] Though it is not stated outright, one can easily assume that any other loss of efficiency was recouped in the form of the reduced cost of labor in the colony.

Assumed native deficiencies were not limited to biological metrics, but also extended to native character. As Beardsley wrote, the Filipino was incapable of succeeding "in lines requiring independent action and personal responsibility," a deficiency that "requires competent supervision based upon a knowledge of their character and local dialect."[44] It was necessary, in other words, for the colonial manager to acquire a knowledge of Filipino culture, habits, and character in order to effectively manage native labor. Relatedly, this "knowledge" was used to make specific arguments against native rule. Beardsley warned that on account of the Filipino's "exceptionally temperate" personalities Filipinos were "easily led by vicious [presumably elite native] demagogues who fatten on false patriotism": this same quality however meant that they were just "as easily influenced towards good citizenship by those in whom they have confidence and who are familiar with their customs."[45] For related reasons Beardsley's descriptions preclude the possibility that any native behavior, especially "indolence," or "unreliability," could be read as related to any kind of *political* sentiment, such as a resentment of poor pay or labor conditions, or even as a rejection of work as such. Both general and specific objections to colonial rule were routinely delegitimized by attributing those retaliations as reflections of racial character, and were often used to confirm the stereotype of the "lazy native."

Beardsley's approach to the Philippine labor problem was connected to the broader project of "developing" Native American, Black, and immigrant populations in the United States into effective laborers and tamping down organized resistance to these practices. In Manila, an internationalist labor movement that was also explicitly anti-imperialist had dogged the Philippine commission from nearly the beginning of US civil colonial rule. Almost as soon as the Spanish-American War concluded, Filipino wage earners in Manila began to unionize.[46] In 1901 the journalist and activist Isabelo de los Reyes organized autonomous unions among barbers, tobacco workers, printers, woodworkers, carpenters, and clerks under a single society known as the Unión Obrera Democrática (UOD). This movement peaked with a massive anti-imperialist rally in front of Malacañang, where the UOD's battle cry was "Kamatayan para sa Imperiyalismo" (Death to Imperialism!). The rally took place on May Day 1903, a nod to the Second International, which in 1899 declared May 1 International Worker's Day.[47] In preparation for the protest, then governor-general Taft evacuated Malacañang and stationed two hundred soldiers with fixed bayonets in front of its gates. Attempting to limit the threat posed to his still nascent colonial project, Taft arrested Dr. Dimonador Gomez, the leader of the renamed Unión Obrera Democrática Filipina (UODF), and ordered a raid and seizure of the UODF's printing press.[48] Though unions continued to mushroom in the Philippines, the colonial government vigorously suppressed what they viewed as radicalized organizations of labor.

That craftsmen in the building trades were beginning to organize in the Philippines was, for obvious reasons, of direct concern to colonial officials.[49] In the United States, where the building trades were increasingly militant, well-organized, and internationalist, concrete was increasingly specified because, as one prominent contractor observed, "the work in a building could be done almost entirely by unskilled labor." Reinforced concrete construction offered an "alternative method of construction . . . [that] in these days of strikes and attempted restrictions of trade . . . [found] favor with employers."[50] Knowledge of concrete construction was furthermore guarded from the workers themselves. In the Philippines this was especially true where proprietary reinforcement systems arrived as an alien kit of parts. When tasked with building a large project, labor was divided such that one crew scarcely understood how their work related to the work of others. These barriers to learning the methods of the trade were exaggerated, especially in the early years, by the fact that none of the workmen spoke English, relying heavily on American or English-speaking Filipino foremen for their piecemeal instructions. In other words, concrete not only enabled the substitution of less skilled and therefore cheaper labor in the place of more highly paid skilled labor, a process referred to as "deskilling," it also introduced a gap between the managerial and unskilled labor that on either end developed as distinct practices and were therefore more difficult to bridge. As Adrian Forty argues, concrete affects the "entire composition of the building industry, shifting the balance between skilled craft labor, unskilled labor, and professional experts."[51] In places like Britain and the United States where the traditional trades were mostly unionized, the use of concrete was seen, Forty points out, as "a chance to bypass the traditional trades altogether . . . making it possible to build without any need for them at all."[52] In the Philippines where unionization was only beginning to take hold, concrete was used as a means of preempting the development of conventionally organized skilled trades altogether through the introduction of a method of building with already integrated hierarchical divisions of labor. Concrete, then, was wielded as a weapon of colonization, a process aimed at producing, as Aimé Césaire argued, "relations of domination and submission which turned the colonizer into a classroom monitor, an army sergeant, a prison guard, a slave driver" at the same time that they transformed "the indigenous person into an instrument of production." Colonization, in other words, was an attempt to reduce colonized persons into concrete, that is to say, measurable, and mastered, *things*.[53]

2

———

STABILITY

I have struck a city—a real city—and they call it Chicago. The other places do not count. San Francisco was a pleasure-resort as well as a city, and Salt Lake was a phenomenon. This place is the first American city I have encountered. It holds rather more than a million people—with bodies—and stands on the same sort of soil as Calcutta. Having seen it, I urgently desire never to see it again. It is inhabited by savages. Its water is the water of the Hooghly, and its air is dirt. —RUDYARD KIPLING, *American Notes*

When Rudyard Kipling recorded his impressions of Chicago in 1889, it was just a year after he had visited Calcutta (today Kolkata) for the first time. He saw in these two cities striking and abject similarities.[1] Both, for example, defied ancient tenets of siting. Whereas Vitruvius had declared "high land" to be the best and healthiest, Chicago and Calcutta were located next to marshy lowlands deemed hostile to human settlement.[2] Chicago's flat, flood-prone terrain lay only slightly elevated above the surface of Lake Michigan, while

Calcutta's alluvial wetland sat nearly level to the Bay of Bengal. The Chicago River was indeed like the Hooghly, which passes through Calcutta, polluted by the effluvia of so many bodies, and even more cows—though in Chicago these were not sacred herds, but rather countless cattle crammed into the endless grid of the city's famous Union Stockyards. And dirt was an accurate description of the air—thick with the aerosolized dung and carbon smoke of industrial progress. Despite the muck, fetid atmosphere, and cholera outbreaks, both cities throbbed with people—a million rude capitalists and commercial traders— "savages" as described by Kipling. Hoards submitted to living on these compromised surfaces—"docked, wharfed, fronted, and reclaimed"[3]—not on account of beauty, or for the purposes of health, but for profit.

Once emplaced, reinforced concrete is an apparently stable material, valued for its remarkable ability to resist fire, rot, and earthquakes. Though its long-term stability remains an open question,[4] since the end of the nineteenth century it has been used not only because of its perceived stability, but for its ability to fix the contours and compositions of unstable environments—setting the shape of rivers, retaining eroding hillsides, and holding buildings upright in marshy ground. Sites previously considered barely habitable—swamps, flood plains, and (at least for white settlers) the entirety of the tropics—suddenly presented themselves as mere engineering problems. In that sense, concrete is not only a universal technology (i.e., available nearly everywhere), but also a universalizing one (making it possible to build virtually anywhere).

Capital of an Inland Empire

Before Chicago became a city, it was a "portage"—a rise of soggy land between the Great Lakes and Mississippi River valley systems. The Council of Three Fires (the Odawa, Ojibwe, and Bodéwadmi) had long valued the area as an important site of exchange. Following the seasonal thaw, the entirety of the Chicago Portage became a navigable waterway, linking Turtle Island's vast continental interior to a world beyond the Gulf of Mexico and the Eastern seaboard. In 1673, when Louis Jolliet first laid eyes on it, the portage appeared to him as a simple engineering problem: a canal cut into the earth only "a half a league" long could permanently transform a seasonal waterway into the pumping, year-round heart of a new inland empire.

It took until 1833 to build the Chicago canal—a feat that first required the coerced signing of the Treaty of Chicago.[5] Its completion instantly accelerated its rate of growth, which was, however, still encumbered by Chicago's flood-prone terrain. The city's exploding population miserably coped with out-breaks of cholera, persistent flooding, and generally insalubrious conditions until February of 1855, when the Chicago Board of Sewerage Commission organized to address the problem, hiring Boston's then-current city engineer, Ellis Sylvester Chesbrough, to design the US's first comprehensive sewerage system. Undertaking a public works project of unprecedented scale, Ches-brough transformed the entirety of Chicago's uneven plane into a rationally designed, flat surface. He began by establishing Chicago's new city datum—setting the surface of Lake Michigan as elevation "0." He placed sewers above the city's datum and down the center of the city's gridded streets. Fill was packed around the sewer vaults and spread in a thin layer on top of the sewer itself, creating a new and neatly crowned roadbed. All vacant lots were filled to meet the city's new level. Existing buildings, both lighter wooden frame build-ings and multistory brick masonry blocks, were either demolished or raised to the new level—a Herculean task—that for the heaviest buildings required hundreds of jackscrews to lift structures between four and fourteen feet. All fill was sourced from the Chicago River, which—in order to accommodate the new sewage load—was being dredged to widen, deepen, and straighten its me-andering course. The result was a new, dry, and carefully graded surface that sloped gently toward Lake Michigan's unbound horizon.

Chesbrough's system, which freed the city from limitations imposed by its as-found condition, was, in fact a form of colonization, characterized not only by the discovery of advantageous conditions, but by the removal of an indig-enous population on the one hand and the management or elimination of envi-ronmental contingencies on the other. Chesbrough's reformation of Chicago's mud enabled industrial capitalists to occupy and develop a site that—despite being unparalleled in terms of geographic advantages—was unfit for perma-nent settlement. Chicago's canal, however, did not only solve a local problem of settlement; it established a physical link between Eastern capital and Western potential by unifying the continent as a single economic unit with comple-mentary needs.[6] Indeed, the Great Fire of 1871 simply provided yet another opportunity for investment. A plan for a taller, better, and more rational city emerged amid its still-smoldering embers. Among the most eager to build were Peter and Shepherd Brooks, brothers from one of the wealthiest families in Massachusetts, whose father had earned a massive fortune in the marine insur-ance industry.[7] Taking on risk was in their blood—though for them Chicago was not a place to live in, but to profit from. Rarely leaving their bucolic estate in Medford, Massachusetts, only Peter had ever visited the city, and he did so only once. Quite likely imagining the tangled knot of railroads that converged on the city, he once wrote to his real estate manager, Owen Aldis, that "tall buildings will pay well in Chicago, and sooner or later a way will be found to erect them."[8] In 1880, Aldis approached Burnham and Root, the partnership of architects Daniel Burham and John Wellborn Root, to find that way. A year later, the young firm delivered the Grannis Block, which at seven stories tall was one of the first in Chicago to take on the perilous prospect of height in the postfire era. Experimenting with new fireproofing techniques, the young architects sheathed the building's cast iron columns in twenty-one inches of terra cotta, roofing the building in the same material. As votes of confidence, five insurance companies rented office space in the building, while Burnham and Root occupied the top floor. The building burned down only four years after its completion. Its unprotected wooden floors provided all the tinder necessary for the building to incinerate in an Icarian flash. The loss did little to deter the Brooks Brothers, who were already planning their next—and taller—project with Burnham and Root. Doubling down on fireproofing technology, Burnham and Root sheathed the Montauk's ten stories of steel with a thick layer of protective masonry—this time covering the floor in terra cotta tiles.[9] Though it managed to avoid destruction by fire, the Montauk stood for a mere 19 years, falling victim not to fire, but to the tremendous real estate pressure exerted onto the site. Burnham made no objection, since his firm was commissioned with the design of its seventeen-story replacement: the First National Bank of Chicago.

Building vertically in the most challenging of environments, Root began to grasp the contours of what he called, in the title of a lecture he delivered to the architecture class of the Art Institute of Chicago in early 1890, "A Great Architectural Problem." Root's lecture offered a detailed account of the various technical issues associated with constructing the modern "tall office building," and included exhaustive descriptions of advances in fireproofing, costs per cubic foot of a "general plan," notes on positioning of piping and shafts, standards for the spacing of windows, suggestions on the placement of burglar proof vaults, and (most importantly) a "general theory of foundations."[10] Though this information, which Root described as related to those "portions of the building with which the public at large can have but little interest," it was knowledge that formed the basis of what he called nothing less than a *material revolution*. Rendering technical expertise as an autonomous and apolitical concern—one isolated within the specialized legal category of code—Root suggests the inevitability of the public's alienation from deeply consequential forms of knowledge.[11]

The Floating Raft

When glaciers receded from the Great Lakes region 26,000 years ago, they left behind an uneven landscape of moraines and shallow ridges that formed the topmost strata of what was once described as Chicago's "great jelly-cake," a composition divided into three distinct layers: a "crust" of hardened clay, or "hardpan," between ten and sixteen feet thick; a four-hundred-foot-thick middle layer of unconsolidated glacial till and outwash (the "jelly"); and a final underlying layer of limestone bedrock.[12] Though the crust seemed strong enough to support the first few versions of urban Chicago—the timber frontier town and the low-rise brick city that succeeded it—the Great Fire revealed some disturbing information. As buildings were being demolished, engineers were able to systematically observe foundation performance. What they found was that, had the fire not catastrophically destroyed Chicago, its poorly designed foundations would have led to its slow demise. Working with an unprecedented amount of data, the engineer Frederick Baumann devised a uniform system of foundation design, which he called the "method of isolated piers," which introduced conservative values for allowable soil pressures, in addition to specifying that loads across the building should be as even as possible.[13] Baumann's observations in the aftermath of the Great Fire allowed Chicago builders to start the "Great Rebuilding" afresh, atop a solid and standardized foundation of empirical knowledge.

Nicknamed the "Chartres of tall office buildings," a number of architecture historians have claimed that the Montauk, Burnham and Root's first "tall office building," was the first to be called a "skyscraper."[14] This despite the fact that preexisting buildings, some more than a decade older than the Montauk, had already exceeded its height of 130 feet. Those East Coast buildings, all anchored into a solid bed of Manhattan schist, edged each other out in a competition of increments that lent Manhattan's towers an air of inevitability. The Montauk, by contrast, rose like an obelisk above what appeared to the human eye as a vast and uninterrupted plane—a horizon that Root defied after he came to a simple realization: one did not build on Chicago's surface, but into it.

Baumann's method was used for virtually all buildings in Chicago until the Montauk, where it reached an almost absurd limit. Though Root lightened the load on the foundation by replacing some of its structure with steel, the required foundations—a series of monumental pyramids 14′ square at the base and 14′ tall—were massive and took up most of the basement's volume. In addition to this, the tops of the piers, which tapered to 1′ tall, sat a full 3′ above the ground level's finished floor, obstructing the free flow of traffic on the ground

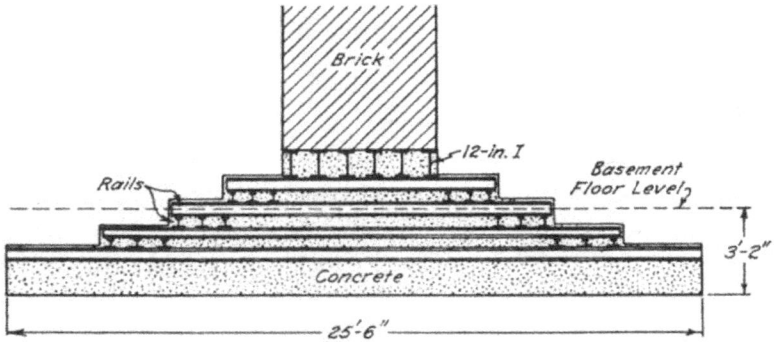

FIG. 7. SECTION THROUGH RAIL-GRILLAGE FOOTING OF MONADNOCK BLOCK

FIGURE 2.1. An example of a floating raft foundation. From Ralph B. Peck, *History of Building Foundations in Chicago*, report, *University of Illinois Bulletin* 45, no. 29, (1948): 23.

floor. When Root first presented plans to Aldis, the property manager balked at the size of the piers. Committed to including every modern amenity, he exclaimed, "we must make room for the dynamos!" Root, who had drawn up the calculations for the foundation piers himself, headed back to the office, only to return two days later with a radically different solution. Root replaced Baumann's pyramids with a shallow 20′ square layer of crisscrossed steel rails encased in a concrete slab which he called the "floating raft" foundation (figure 2.1).[15] Working according to the Archimedean principle of displacement, the raft distributed the weight of the structure over the entire surface of the slab — ensuring even settlement. The building is held afloat by a buoyant force equal to the weight of the volume of soil displaced. Root's invention instantiated a new relationship to the ground by providing a stable base in even the most challenging of conditions.

The White City: An Internal Colony

By the time planning began for the World's Columbian Exposition of 1893 — widely considered to be Daniel Burnham's greatest achievement — Burnham and Root had fine-tuned their techniques for building in Chicago's mud, gaining confidence as each project's height eclipsed that of the last: the eleven-story Phoenix (1887) was followed by the twelve-story Rookery (1888) and the twenty-one-story Masonic Temple (1892). When it was time to select a site for the exposition, Burnham, working closely alongside Frederick Law

Olmsted, selected a muddy patch of undeveloped waterfront on the far southern edge of the city, known as Jackson Park. Members of the Senate-appointed National Commission, charged with approving Olmsted and Burnham's selection, balked. They preferred the newly renovated Washington Park, located just one mile inland. The commissioners, Root would later recall, were rather disgusted with Jackson Park, considering the "swampy wilderness" an inappropriate site for "Chicago . . . to receive the world."[16]

Determining that the commissioners "judged blindly from present conditions," Root argued that it was impossible for non-experts to envision what was only visible to the "mind's eye," emphasizing that it was "difficult for one not experienced in technical consideration of such matters to rightly view this subject." Flexing his technical knowledge, Root drew up a report with Olmsted in which they illustrated Jackson Park's advantages, the two most important being Jackson Park's position on the waterfront, along with the fact that, while the recently finished landscape of Washington Park would require a costly rehabilitation following the close of the Exposition, Jackson Park presented itself "like clay to the hand of a sculptor, with which anything within the artist's capacity may be accomplished."[17] Root's vision was one shaped by years of working with and in Chicago's mud. He was intimate not only with the possibilities of the land's reformation, but increasingly with the ability of dredgers, drains, pile drivers, and sewers to separate mud, a single foul substance, into two desirable parts—dry ground and picturesque water.

Root did not live to see the exposition rise on his chosen site, dying suddenly of pneumonia only six months before site work began, rather unceremoniously, with load tests (figures 2.2 and 2.3). Burnham and Root's engineer, E. C. Shankland, stacked pyramids of iron rails on a small timber platform, and found that under a load of 1 ton per foot, the settlement across the entire site averaged a "respectable" 1/8″ to 1–1/4″, with the exception of a crescent-shaped swale, probably the bed of an old creek, where the earth settled between 14″ and 38″.[18] Olmsted positioned the White City's famous Grand Basin at the center of the curve (such that surface water drained toward it). Shankland then stabilized the remainder of the swale with timber piles. For the rest of the site, Burnham specified large raft foundations, which Shankland noted saved about $6,000 per acre over using piles. Whether or not that is true, standardizing the site's maximum acceptable load (at 2,500 pounds per square foot) greatly simplified the process of designing the Exposition's buildings.

Burnham and Olmsted viewed water as far more than an amenity— navigable water was, after all, the very reason for the city's existence. A unique aspect of Burnham and Olmsted's site planning was that every major building

FIGURE 2.2. Load testing, Jackson Park, Chicago. The original caption reads: "Foundation Test Government B'l'd'g, Load 2 tons per sq. foot. Total Settlement ½ inch. Sept. 17, 1891." From Columbian Exposition Photographs by C. D. Arnold, 1891–1894, Ryerson and Burnham Art and Architecture Archive, Art Institute of Chicago.

was accessible by both land and water. And it was only from the water that the visitor could comprehend the White City in its totality—a fluorescing neo-classical apparition that heralded a new kind of territorial occupation. Though the white architecture ritualized and dramatized this occupation, it was only a temporary sign of a deeper, geological transformation. The infrastructure that undergirded the White City eased the incorporation of the once swampy hinterland into the continuous fabric of Chicago itself. What marked the exposition as a kind of colonization is that it was peripheral: built in relative isolation from the metropole, at a distance from its frenzied center and gated off from its rapidly encroaching limits.

The exact distance did not matter so much as the fact that the White City could, as Alan Trachtenberg put it, "enforce its lessons by contrast."[19] As a gated and freestanding city, the exposition presented itself by virtue of the comprehensiveness of its infrastructure and the beauty of its reformed landscape as something so different and new, it appeared as an almost unbelievable "dream"—

FIGURE 2.3. Load testing, Jackson Park, Chicago. The original caption reads: "Foundation test M'f'r's B'l'd'g Load 3161 lbs. per sq. foot. Total Settlement 3 [+ illegible fraction]
feet, Sept. 17, 1891." From Columbian Exposition Photographs by C. D. Arnold, 1891–
1894, Ryerson and Burnham Art and Architecture Archive, Art Institute of Chicago.

as a complete and *planned alternative* to the city it stood both metaphorically
and physically apart from. As a bounded territory managed by a private corporation, the exposition was just one example of a broad effort led by leaders of
American corporations to stake out distinctively private spheres exempt from
the regulating powers of the state.[20] The exposition offered a fresh start to ward
off the symptoms that plagued the nation at large including the failures of Reconstruction, xenophobic reactions to large waves of foreign immigration, a
looming loss of identity following the close of the frontier, violent labor unrest,
and an international Long Depression that lasted from 1873 to 1896, caused not
by financial speculation but by chronic overproduction (which triggered dramatically falling prices). Thus, even in the shadow of the churning machines
and gleaming white architecture of the exposition, a public sense of crisis deep-
ened, especially outside of its gates.[21] Within this heavily secured, semiautono-
mous territory, the manifold benefits of a corporately managed industrialized
economy were placed on prominent display, unaccompanied by the voices that

challenged it. This was by design. By excluding the voices of dissent, if only temporarily, Burnham provided concrete evidence of the potential benefits of their forceful suppression—providing an object lesson that could be generally applied beyond the exposition's boundaries.

This is all to say that the exposition was never intended to remain a firmly bound project. Burnham's almost immediate turn toward city planning, which allowed him to unleash onto the figure of the city *at large* many of the legal, institutional, and managerial forces developed on what was at first designed to be the separate—one might say utopian—corporate territory of the exposition. The exposition's territorial sequestration allowed Burnham to closely monitor his labor force, his budget, material supply, revenue generated, and profits earned. This creation of an effective subterritory of Chicago was something unprecedented in American jurisprudence. Though temporary and territorially limited, the elimination of legal, social, and even geological contingencies suggested a new role for the state: to rid the world of the protracting and sometimes destabilizing processes of a messy democracy.

All of this was made possible by the foundational work of Chesbrough, Baumann, and Root, who, in freeing the Chicago Portage from its environmental limitations, eliminated any doubt that US empire could be achieved. A populace united by this confident image helped to change the nation's attitudes not only about the settlement and development of the West, but of faraway shores, an adventure now made possible by a set of universalizing techniques that enabled the nation to occupy virtually any land, anywhere.

Exporting Stability

When Daniel H. Burnham arrived in the Philippines in December 1904, building there was a problem already solved. Manila's marshy soil, its poor sanitary conditions, and its lack of a modern sewer system were obstacles that seemed no more daunting than those of Jackson Park. Whether the archipelago could be successfully settled by American colonists was, however, an open question. In the late nineteenth century, most medical authorities and social theorists believed that the geography within which an individual could stay healthy and comfortable coincided with the region in which his race had long been situated—a theory of acclimatization first proposed by Aristotle.[22] The American economist and racial anthropologist William Z. Ripley, whose published works spanned from the study of the financial organization of railroads to sociological studies of the races of Europe, argued that acclimatization was of "concrete importance for the economist and the statesman," despite being a problem that primarily pertained "to the sciences of physiology and of anthropology."[23] Whether European bodies possessed "immunity in the face of the perils of tropical colonization," Ripley warned, had serious consequences for the global balance of power. In other words, if the US's imperial ambitions were to extend across the globe, the limiting factor of climate still had to be solved. Assuming this biological limit as fact, US colonial officials sought new technologies of amelioration.

Fittingly, the first building to arrive in the Philippines atop Root's floating raft was in effect an enclosed artificial environment: a massive ice and cold storage plant that was only the second ever to be built in Asia.[24] The consumption of ice and fresh comestibles imported from the temperate zone was viewed by many as the best available means of protecting the vulnerable American (especially Anglo-Saxon) body from the enervating effects of the tropics.[25] Annihilating the distance between the American diet and the American body abroad, the ice and cold storage plant provided at least a partial solution to the limits proposed by acclimatization theorists. Beyond producing ice, the plant also stored large cargoes of fresh beef and mutton. Though canned meat was widely available and used in military rationing, the import of fresh meat (only recently made possible with overseas continuous refrigeration) was seen as essential to maintaining not only an American "way of life," but American life itself—not just a series of customs, but the maintenance of a biological state. In a sense, it was not until the completion of this building—at the time almost certainly the farthest terminal of a global cold chain network centered around Chicago's immense stockyards—that the United States had actually arrived to the Philippines. Its construction, which consumed the vast majority of Philippine tax revenues for that year (mostly derived from customs duties) was criticized by some as pretentious and "unnecessarily huge"—an unjustifiably large expenditure of funds that had been promised for the exclusive benefit of Filipinos.[26] For most colonists, however, it was an infrastructure that by enabling the management and stabilization of colonists' internal temperatures allowed the United States to seriously consider a colonial occupation of the tropics.[27]

Foundation and land reclamation technologies were used to address a number of other threats to colonial stability. Shortly after Burnham's departure from the Philippines, and even before William Cameron Forbes, then commissioner of commerce and police, would receive Burnham's Manila Plan, Forbes began planning for the construction of a large parcel of land to be reclaimed in front of Intramuros (the old Spanish walled settlement)—an entirely new commercial district on what had been, before the arrival of the Americans, menacing shoals in front of Manila's shoreline. This area—a place, as Forbes put it, for "land (to) meet deep water conveniently" would be formed from fill retrieved by dredging the entirety of the harbor behind two new breakwaters. The project transformed Manila Bay "from an open and turbulent roadstead into a closed and pacified harbor."[28] The main purpose of the district was to provide a landing pad for huge warehouses intended to complement the cold storage plant with a massive capacity for dry storage. The program posed a particularly difficult engineering problem, as the floor would have to carry loads of about 2,500 pounds per square foot. The Bureau of Supply believed, however, that the advantage of having storehouses located near the water-front more than offset the extra costs of reclaiming land. Construction explo-ration began with bearing tests in which large heavy timbers were placed on various combinations of fill in five-ton increments. Some of it was dredged from the bottom of Manila Bay, and included shell, silt, earth, and sand. To this mix they added refuse stone from a nearby basalt quarry in Talim. Aim-ing for a load of one thousand pounds per square foot, the Bureau of Public Works toyed with several different foundation designs incorporating hybrids of native and imported technologies. This included gravel tamped into mud (too weak) and unreinforced concrete raft poured into a sawali form (failed immediately).[29] Concrete piles were considered but immediately rejected on the grounds of cost. Finally, a steel-reinforced concrete floor on timber piles was able to pass the test.

In 1912 the Insular Government piled eight thousand sacks of rice on the just cured concrete surface of an enormous warehouse sited on a large new commercial district adjacent to Intramuros. The reclaimed land on which it sat was dredged from the heavily silted bay, part of a massive port improve-ment project that, Forbes crowed, transformed Manila from the "worst port for freight in the Orient . . . to . . . one of the best."[30] The sacks of rice were pur-chased in anticipation of a possible interruption of food supply brought about by war conditions. Fittingly, a photo of this spectacular test was published just months after the outbreak of World War I, in the October 1914 issue of the *Quarterly Bulletin, Bureau of Public Works* (figure 2.4). There is something about the photo that exceeds the dry language of the engineering report that it accompanied. The "load test" was nothing less than a monument to American stability—spectacular proof of the new colonizer's ability to resist the uncer-tainties of the tropics and the threat of war. In the Philippines, these loads were not only tests of structural soundness, but also signaled the viability of the colonial project itself. The massive stores overwhelmed any fears of potential failure, any knowledge of the history of famine, any theory that suggested the impossibility of the Anglo-Saxon's potential for acclimatization. Foundation

Nine hundred and six pounds per square foot.

FIGURE 2.4. Rice "piled 30 sacks high" in a warehouse near Intramuros, Manila, as a load test demonstrating the foundation's soundness. Engineers calculated the sacks to weigh 906 pounds per square foot. From "A Floor Test," *Quarterly Bulletin, Bureau of Public Works* 3, no. 3 (1914): 39.

technologies became a means through which Americans could protect themselves from the risks endemic to their anchorage abroad.

Though much of this chapter is about stability in the most straightforward, physical sense of the word, this focus allows me to forge a connection between physical stability and stability in a much broader sense. The Columbian Exposition, which ran from May to October 1893, presented a verisimilitude of a stable and abundant future staged amid what was the most calamitous financial panic yet experienced in the United States, a panic which lasted from May until November of the same year.[31] These crashes and panics also took place in 1873, 1884, and 1890, 1899, and 1901. What the exposition demonstrated—on a limited though spectacular scale—was that islands of stability and prosperity could be achieved even when suspended within an ocean of economic chaos. The promise of the exposition was that its spectacular abundance could exert stabilizing effects on its surroundings, shoring up many of the anxieties that plagued a still developing country.[32] The potential of this project foreshadowed the proposals of prominent theorists of the American economy like Brooks Adams and Charles Arthur Conant, who argued for the necessity of colonial activity as a means of stabilizing an unmanageable American economy. In their view colonial activity, or US expansion into "virgin territories," was a potential answer to the economic instabilities that were the result of industrial overproduction and speculative overdrive, or what Theodore Roosevelt characterized as "the overflowing abundance of our own natural resources . . . skill . . . business energy, and mechanical aptitude."[33]

Indeed, it was Thomas Edison's "aptitudes" that led to the destabilization of the Portland cement industry. His invention of the rotary kiln played a central role in the rapid expansion of the industry, which because of oversupply and huge variations in the quality of the American product experienced a crippling dive in prices at the turn of the century.[34] The specification and consumption of huge quantities of Portland cement in large-scale infrastructural and defense projects, including the Panama Canal and all of the concrete projects built in the Philippines addressed throughout this book, helped to stabilize its global price. These interventions revealed the dynamic utility of infrastructural and other public works projects as tools of economic regulation. And it was at precisely this moment that the regulation of the economy revealed itself to be one of the central imperatives of a rapidly evolving federal governance.[35] This new function is perhaps seen most clearly in the colonial context, where the traditional function of government (i.e., to govern in a contractual relationship with citizens) was replaced with the administration of an economy. In Forbes's words:

> Capital demands a stable Government. Capital is not particularly interested in the color or design of the flag. It wants just and equitable laws, sound and uniform policy on the part of the government, just and fair treatment in the courts. . . . No capitalist need feel alarmed as to the security of his investment provided it has been made in such a way as to fulfill the conditions imposed by law. The United States stands pledged to the establishment and maintenance of a stable government in the Philippine Islands. . . . My policy will be to hold out the hand of welcome to all people desiring to engage in legitimate enterprise.[36]

Forbes put it another way in a speech delivered at the annual banquet of the Manila Merchants Association. Turning, as he often did, to a sports analogy, he explained that "the surface of the field is to be kept smooth by the Government; it is the merchants who play ball."[37] What Forbes obliquely described was not a laissez-faire order (or an interventional minimalism), but rather a strong role for the state (minimally encumbered by democratic processes) in supporting capitalist development. It bears remembering that there was an entire population of colonial subjects who Forbes considered as mere spectators of this game. This was not, for Forbes, an exclusively colonial strategy—the colony allowed him, rather, to execute "big plans" in the colony as a large-scale demonstration of the advantages of the progressive antidemocratic State. Men like Burnham and Forbes valorized the rational application of scientific expertise to the development of land, economy, and people (above and against the volatile whims of unenlightened subjects—not only colonial subjects, but a rapidly transforming metropolitan citizenry that included partially enfranchised populations of immigrants, formerly enslaved persons, and women). Perhaps Forbes understood, better than anyone, the amount of physical work required for smoothing this surface. Indeed, the reconstruction of not only the Philippines, but the world, implied an ambitious infrastructural program—a physical means through which the government could ensure the security for the "free play" of capital. Though mostly out of sight, and thus often taken for granted, herculean efforts were required to build this carefully engineered ground, the new foundation for US empire.

3

SALUBRITY

CHOLERA AND THE "HOUSING QUESTION"
IN THE TROPICAL COLONY

By the beginning of the twentieth century, increasing confidence in germ theory had led to vigorous sanitary campaigns aimed at eliminating the visible media—mud, dirt, excreta, rats, natives, and the poor—in which colonists and sanitarians believed germs lingered. Impermeable surfaces, rounded corners (easily cleaned), white paint, strong light, and countless other spatial remedies became mainstays of modern hospital design, and modernist design more broadly. Concrete was used liberally in the Philippines for the purposes of sanitation, especially at sites where natives and colonists were most likely to mix. In the Philippines' traditional markets, for example, bamboo tables and dirt floors were replaced with concrete versions that could be hosed down nightly.[1] It was just one of several measures introduced in an attempt to curb a series of deadly cholera outbreaks that struck Philippine cities and towns during and in the aftermath of the Philippine-American War, the most comprehensive of which was the division of the entire city into two separate, materially defined districts:

ANOTHER EXAMPLE OF THE CLASS OF HOUSES THE BUREAU OF HEALTH IS ATTEMPTING TO HAVE REMOVED.

FIGURE 3.1. Nipa houses. The original caption reads: "Another Example of the Class of Houses the Bureau of Health Is Attempting to Have Removed." From Heiser, *Annual Report of the Bureau of Health for the Philippine Islands, July 1, 1908, to June 30, 1909* (Manila: Bureau of Printing, 1909): 196.

namely, "strong materials" districts where only stone and concrete construction were permitted; and "light materials" districts where bamboo, nipa, and other ephemeral materials were allowed. Though it is disputed whether the Insular Government's extreme measures, herd immunity, or some other factor led to the eventual end of the cholera outbreaks, many of the spatial, social, and material effects—some planned, some unforeseen—were lasting. This included, most significantly, the segregation of the city into two nearly opposing material conditions.

In its annual report for 1909, the Bureau of Health published several photographs of rundown nipa houses (figure 3.1). The caption appearing below the images reads "class of houses the Bureau of Health is attempting to remove." The purpose of the images was clear: to present the nipa house as a sign of native backwardness—a public danger on which the Bureau of Health blamed the spread and protraction of the seemingly endemic cholera epidemics suffered by both American and native populations in the colony.[2] The disease had become a major source of embarrassment for the US colonial government and especially for the Bureau of Health, whose draconian measures—which included strict land quarantine, the use of powerful drugs and disinfectants, and the forced placement of natives in cramped camps for "contacts"—all failed to control the epidemics.[3]

A Modern Sewer for Manila

It did not help matters that an outbreak of cholera in 1902 intersected with the official close of the Philippine-American War—a conflict that in some parts of the archipelago intensified, despite the capture of the leader of the insurgent forces of the First Philippine Republic, Emilio Aguinaldo, in March of the previous year. Resentment and suspicion lingered among Manila's masses, who distrusted medical officers as much as they did US Army troops. The confusion was reasonable, as both Reynaldo Ileto and Warwick Anderson have argued, in the overlapping context of war and epidemic the duties of sanitary officers, military surgeons, cavalrymen, and troops were completely collapsed. Indeed, "medical officers" carried out their mission with an often senseless brutality usually explained away as sanitary "vigor."[4] Despite the intensity of the measures taken, the epidemic persisted for two years, eventually claiming over 5,000 lives in Manila alone, and over 100,000 lives throughout the archipelago—a number exacerbated by the intensified mobility, mixing, assembly, and concentration of populations that result from wartime conditions. Though the Bureau of Health took credit both for depressing the number of cases during the epidemic and for ending the epidemic altogether, the causes of its eventual conclusion were contested. Some believed Manila had reached a state of herd immunity, while others argued that a particularly strong typhoon had cleansed the diseased waterways.[5] Whatever the case, the colonial government's resounding claims of victory over the disease were a source of embarrassment when cholera reemerged in 1908.[6] Adding to the embarrassment was the inconvenient fact that the 1908 epidemic followed the completion of Manila's fifty-two-mile-long modern sewer system—appraised by the colonial government that built it as an engineering marvel—one that negotiated Manila's flat topography with a modern pumping system. Though usually a hidden amenity, the Manila sewer was proudly announced by the distribution of handsome sewer pumping houses across the city.[7] Modern sewer systems were still rare in the Far East and, where they did exist, served only a fraction of the population. For example, the construction of the Tokyo sewer, which began in the late nineteenth century, served less than 6 percent of the population until the late 1950s; the same was true of Hanoi, where a modern sewer system built in the late 1890s served only the city's French Quarter. The Manila system, by contrast, served almost every quarter of the city.[8] This was not, as will be seen, evidence of a service rendered to all of the city's residents, but a means of maintaining a separation from the city's poorer residents amid a comprehensive and radical change of Manila's urban order.

Manila's new sewer system linked San Miguel, one of Manila's oldest and wealthiest neighborhoods outside of Intramuros, to Tondo, a district of contrasting characteristics. On the one hand, as Manila's main commercial district, Tondo featured handsome bank facades and store fronts; on the other, it was Manila's most densely populated district. Behind the bright façade of shops lining Tondo's main thoroughfares were crowds of shift workers, small vendors, and a rapidly growing number of factory employees. In its northernmost parts, a fishing village of densely packed nipa houses huddled on the edges of the shore, while inland nipa homes clustered together on the edges of old haciendas. These groupings were remnants of the old Spanish feudal order, in which hacenderos (many of Spanish or mestizo origin) received rent and extracted labor from the poorer classes residing on their land. This arrangement shaped a mixed pattern of settlement, where the oldest and wealthiest families in Manila lived in relatively close proximity to what some Americans described as the city's "dirtiest and most crowded part."[9] This urban arrangement, in which poverty was adjacent to a commercial district heavily trafficked by Americans and more well-to-do Manileños, was considered a nuisance to public health, and became a site of intense scrutiny during the 1902–4 epidemic. Making matters worse was that a large area of Tondo—the Farola (lighthouse) district—was located on a shallow tidal plane with poor drainage.

The first two recorded cases associated with the 1902 epidemic lived in Farola. Though no one could prove what particular cargo had been the source of the disease, the chief quarantine officer pointed out that, at the time of the cholera outbreak, cholera "was more or less epidemic" in Canton. Some shipments had reached the Philippines before vegetables from Canton had been banned. Recent experiments had determined that the cholera bacilli could live up to five days on unwashed cabbages, and it was assumed that the bacilli had come via a contaminated head or two.[10] Though the epidemic claimed victims even in the wealthier quarters of Manila, the most extreme and notorious measures for controlling the epidemic were reserved solely for the residents of Farola. After a strict land quarantine placed on the district failed to contain the disease, the Bureau of Health forcibly removed all of its residents to an isolation camp on the grounds of the San Lazaro Estate—the site of an old hospital run by Franciscan Friars—in early April of 1903. A few days after the evacuation of the Farola district, Dean C. Worcester, the secretary of the interior, along with Colonel Maus, the public health commissioner, oversaw a noxious spectacle—a bonfire of 125 nipa homes, drenched in kerosene and carbolic disinfectant.

It was just a few months before the fire that the engineer Owen L. Ingalls began his study for the sewer system, which included a section in Tondo. As is the case with any sewer system, Ingalls's design accounted for the growth of the city's population, which was projected to almost double (from 223,000 to 441,000) over the next fifty years.[11] What was curious about the Tondo section was that it accommodated only twenty thousand people, a number that the area already exceeded by almost double.[12] That is to say, Tondo's de-densification and gentrification—its development as real estate—was an unstated goal of the sewer project. That the system was designed to exclude certain of Manila's residents is further demonstrated by the fact that the calculated "maximum flow" of the system was based on per capita estimates set at "one-half the amount that has been generally considered a fair allowance by American engineers for cities in the States." Ingalls never cited any study that suggested that Manileños produced half of the human waste produced by Americans. He, however, explained away the huge difference between per capita accommodations made for American cities and those for Manila by pointing out that the per capita estimate in Manila is "considerably greater than has generally been allowed by English engineers in designing sewer systems for certain cities located within the tropics, which . . . are said to be working very satisfactorily."[13] For Ingalls this served as proof that the "prejudices and habits . . . [of colonized natives] are in many ways so different from [those of] American people." Anticipating a different approach to native sanitation, Ingalls continued, "What may be found wholly satisfactory in the States is not necessarily best for the natives of this tropical country."[14] In other words, Ingalls justified his insufficient design on the grounds of a sensitivity to native "customs and practices." Here a "consideration" of native difference overrode what was at the time largely accepted as universal standards of hygiene. That is to say, despite claims that US colonialism would be qualitatively distinct in its approach, the sewer re-created a classic racial divide between colonizers and the colonized.[15]

The Sanitary Barrio: "A Variance on the Universal" and the Housing Question in the Colony

The accommodation of "native customs and practices" came in the form of a new approach to housing. This is remarkable in part because one of the most common criticisms of Burnham's grand plans, and of City Beautiful planning in general, is that as a movement, its focus on public facilities—parks, monumental civic buildings, and broad boulevards—displaced housing as the object of urban reform.[16] This was not a mere oversight on Burnham's part. The "housing question" was largely responsible for animating the urban reform movement of the 1870s and 1880s.[17] Chicago, on account of the work of Jane Addams and a well-organized labor movement, was in fact an epicenter of the housing reform movement. Though Burnham did, almost as a side note, express in his comments on the 1909 Chicago plan that "thoughtful people are appalled ... at the toll of lives taken by disease when sanitary precautions are neglected; and at the frequent outbreaks against law and order, which result from narrow and pleasureless lives,"[18] he never aimed to address the actual living conditions of the city's poor. Rather, he offered his plans of cultural zones, administrative centers, and patches of urban green as respite from poverty's drudgeries.

Though large-scale construction of public housing did not begin in earnest in Chicago until the late 1920s, in the Philippines the sanitary barrio provided an early and large-scale publicly subsidized project to "improve" the housing of Manila's poorer residents. The colonial state's involvement was motivated less by the need for housing as such, than by cholera. In this respect, Manila was not a unique case. Housing reform in both Europe and the United States was motivated by and tied to a history of sanitary reform, a movement to house poor populations that, as Friedrich Engels points out, only began when it was scientifically established that "cholera, typhus, typhoid fever, and ... other ravaging diseases" could develop into epidemics and "spread beyond their breeding places ... into the more airy and healthy parts of the town inhabited by the capitalists."[19] Exposing the self-interested motivations of what was often framed as capitalist benevolence, Engels shows that housing reform began (in England) only when and where "the bourgeoisie itself was most immediately threatened."[20]

This was also the case in the Philippines, where housing reform first appeared as part of a "new and sweeping solution to Manila's unsanitary conditions," known as the "sanitary barrio." George Guerdrum, an engineer working for the Bureau of Public Works, developed the scheme as an immediate response to the 1908 cholera epidemic. One major aspect that set the sanitary barrio apart from housing reform in England is that it was conceived and developed not along the lines of a universally applicable science, but rather along lines of assumed differences between Manila's poor (mostly native) population and wealthy (mostly mestizo, Spanish, American, and foreign) population. It is on account of these differences that Guerdrum noted that "it had become necessary to develop a form of sanitation in certain outlying sections of Manila which in some ways is *at variance* with sanitation as practiced in occidental and temperate zone cities."[21] This "tropical" form of sanitation was a solution that Victor Heiser, the Philippines' director of health from 1903 to 1914, wrote would be "*the foundation upon which all future work in the sanitation of Manila will be based*."[22] This "foundation" did not consist of a single unified plan, but rather a bifurcated one—a total division of the city that in turn led to a comprehensive and ostensibly permanent double standard. In Guerdrum's words, the sanitary barrio was "not applicable to the business and better residence sections of the city where the new sanitary sewer is in operation and municipal sanitation is much the same as in American cities."[23] That is to say, the sanitary barrio was developed because he considered the native city and that of the colonizer as irreconcilable.

"Strong Materials" versus "Light Materials"

The major problem Guerdrum faced, as he saw it, was that many of the "better residential districts" contained dozens of nipa huts, which sanitary officers and engineers viewed as a menace to the health of their wealthier neighbors. In Heiser's words:

> Nipa shacks in the strong-material districts must go, and repairs to the old nipa shacks, which perpetuate this problem, must be prevented. These nipa districts exist by sufferance within the strong-material districts, dilapidated shacks crowded together in the most insanitary manner, where there are excellent public closets, patronized only by a select few. The majority still find it easier to deposit or throw their dejections upon the swampy ground. These districts are the natural homes of cholera and from there the people who are trying to live decently are infected by the *muchachos*, cooks, or *cocheros*, who spend their time in these plague spots.[24]

Heiser does not mention that there were no viable alternatives to throwing "dejections upon the swampy ground," as modern sanitary facilities were not made available to those living in "nipa shacks." Heiser's "solution" to what he presented as a native behavioral preference was to segregate the city—to expunge it of older patterns inherited from the hacienda system so that it would better conform to urban divisions more typical of nineteenth-century European colonization. This would result, as Heiser himself implied, in separating "*muchachos*, cooks, and *cocheros*" from their places of employment. Sanitary officials, indifferent to the ways in which this inconvenienced workers, advocated for the passage of a new set of ordinances to effectuate their plans. Perhaps the most important of these was Ordinance No. 158, which included a specification that divided the whole of the city into two types of districts, according to their use of "strong" or "light" materials.[25] The ordinance stated that in "strong materials" districts, the only form of acceptable construction was either masonry or reinforced concrete. Bamboo and nipa construction would be permitted"[26] only in "light materials" districts (but there, too, the use of "strong materials" was encouraged and even mandated to a certain degree).

At the same time that those districts were being defined, laws were passed to restrict the construction, repair, and/or improvement of preexisting nipa structures within strong materials districts. The passage of this law soon resulted in the disheveled appearance of nipa structures throughout the "better areas" of the city, which was, in fact, the law's desired effect. The criminalization of repair proved an effective strategy for phasing the buildings out, as poor maintenance made it relatively easy to prove the "unsanitary" nature of nipa structures. As the Bureau of Health understood, the nipa shelter was not a stable object, but rather the perpetually renewed outcome of a set of practices that entail continuous building and maintenance. As Heiser himself noted, if repairs of nipa structures were prohibited the "nipa-shack problem . . . would solve itself." The resulting disrepair was photographically documented by the Board of Health and published in its annual report, as evidence of the necessity of their removal.

There were several contradictions embedded into the sanitary barrio system, perhaps the most glaring being that if the nipa house itself was deemed unsanitary when within strong materials districts, why was it considered sanitary outside of it? Guerdrum answered the question simply if unsatisfactorily, arguing that with "a mild form of building supervision this style of construction has been rendered quite sanitary."[27] Heiser, meanwhile, described the type as "very desirable," allowing for excellent ventilation and the penetration of sunlight. Carroll A. Fox, who served as acting director of health in 1911–12 while Heiser was on leave, went even further, arguing that "if nipa houses are properly constructed they are the most sanitary houses that can be built"—even *more* sanitary, he implied, than buildings built out of strong materials—adding that if not for nipa structures, the "detrimental effects [of overcrowding] . . . would be more apparent."[28] Whatever the case, the selective valorization of the nipa house enabled colonial officials to specify native materials even as they generally advocated for the replacement of nipa structures.

"Surplus Populations" at the San Lazaro Estate

Preparations for the first sanitary barrio, built on the old San Lazaro Estate (formerly Augustinian friar lands), began when city officials hired locals to build drainage ditches leading to an adjacent estero. As would be the case with all sanitary barrios, the estate was then divided into "sanitary blocks" through a system of streets and alleyways. Each block was furnished with public closets, public baths, a laundry, and public hydrants. Each block was then subdivided into lots, each of which was crowned with lightly compacted earth and assigned a unique address. The nipa huts built atop these newly prepared lots were essentially identical to those removed from the strong materials districts, with the exception of a hole cut into the bamboo slat floors. Cement lined basins were placed at the crown of each lot, such that the waste drained toward the cement canals placed at the lot lines. The lot lines were then paved over with one-foot-wide concrete surface drains which led to larger surface drains that ran down the center of each alley and street. At San Lazaro, these larger drains led to an open sewer that eventually emptied into a concrete "bacterio-lytic tank," which treated the sewage before its final delivery to San Lazaro's adjoining estero. In other sanitary barrios, which did not share the advantage of being located next to an estero, untreated sewage was left to be collected in open sewers for manual cleaning, thereby exposed to both the "purifying effects of the sun" and the examining eye of sanitary inspectors, who routinely gathered samples from these heaps to check for or to verify the presence of cholera within each barrio. This system, Heiser noted, would be tolerated despite its "insanitary features" due to the exigencies introduced by the 1908 cholera epidemic, as well as the supposedly different needs of the "oriental."[29]

As detailed in the Bureau of Health's annual report, as the final preparations of the new site were reaching completion, more than seven hundred of the "most unsanitary hovels" were removed from Manila's strong materials districts. All of those evicted from these districts were relocated to the newly organized San Lazaro sanitary barrio, where they joined those who were displaced as a result of the preparation of the sanitary barrio itself—over a thousand residents who, Heiser wrote, lived in "several collections of miserable shacks." The San Lazaro Estate alone contained forty-five blocks consisting of a total of 1,648 lots intended to house a total population of 13,184 people. An adjacent piece of land, which would be administered by the church, was prepared in much the same way and contained close to ten thousand more people. In the end, the "experimental" San Lazaro Estate provided a "sanitary solution" for a population about a third the size of the planned total capacity of the municipal sewer system.[30]

FIGURE 3.2. The San Lazaro Estate before and after its transformation into a "sanitary barrio." From Heiser, *Annual Report of the Bureau of Health for the Philippine Islands, July 1, 1908, to June 30, 1909* (Manila: Bureau of Printing, 1909): 197.

Although it remained the largest of all the sanitary barrios, San Lazaro contained only a fraction of the total inhabitants of the sanitary barrios that would be built throughout the city. At less than 5 pesos (hereafter ₱) per lot, the cost per person is astonishing, considering that the municipal sewer system cost almost ₱4 million. It was in this way, Heiser wrote, that Manila's "congested *surplus population* . . . can be gradually cared for . . . and conditions in general improved."[31] An additional benefit of this ordered concentration of these "surplus populations" (what Karl Marx referred to as a "reserve army of labor") was that it would have been a welcome sight for visiting potential investors who might peek from a passing train or from one of Burnham's boulevards a well-ordered barrio of potential native laborers (figure 3.2).[32]

Following the completion of the San Lazaro Estate, the Insular Government set out to expand the sanitary barrio program. Without exception, all strong materials districts were more affluent neighborhoods, while all light materials districts housed the city's poor. Not all "light materials" districts, were (yet) sanitary barrios—any area that housed mostly poor people and where the preponderant building material was already nipa was considered a light materials district. However, as these areas were not yet laid out according to the standards of the "sanitary barrio," they were simply referred to as "insanitary barrios," whose defining characteristic, the Bureau wrote, was the crowding of several structures onto a single lot. At the time "insanitary barrios" included the large districts of Tondo, Santa Clara, Ermita, and Malate.[33] It was suggested in the Bureau of Health's annual report that all of the residents of these areas would eventually be relocated to sanitary barrios once sites with appropriate capacities were identified.

The cost effectiveness of the sanitary barrio was enhanced by the fact that, as a "self-help" housing scheme, the construction of the individual houses cost the colonial government next to nothing. In "The Housing Question," Engels argues that self-help housing schemes are particularly popular among capitalists because they make use of the free labor of those who will live in the houses, and place the responsibility of housing (otherwise assumed by municipalities, by the state, or by capitalists themselves) back onto labor.[34] In addition, self-help housing had the double effect of relieving the colonial government of any need to provide more robust forms of state assistance, while placing responsibility for sanitation solely on the shoulders of colonial subjects. That is to say, whereas sanitation was viewed as an amenity for the inhabitants of Manila's wealthier quarters, it was viewed as the personal responsibility of Manila's poorer inhabitants. Indeed, the construction costs of the nipa houses, which residents were expected to build themselves, rarely exceeded ₱50; but, because these costs were limited to the negligible cost of sourcing the readily available and renewable resources of bamboo and nipa, they were expected to be absorbed by the residents themselves. Furthermore, not only was the sanitary barrio an affordable solution for the colonial government, it was also organized as a new source of revenue. After offering future residents free rent for six months (a means of recruiting new residents to live there) the government charged residents a "nominal ground fee." It was thus also a means of more reliably extracting tax revenue from Manila's poor, who had hitherto been difficult to track. The only expenses to the rent-seeking colonial government were the low cost of the labor used in the ground preparation, the cost of the Portland cement used to line surface drains, and the administrative costs associated with rent collection and other policing and managerial tasks.

One of the more common criticisms of modern housing projects is a lack of sensitivity toward local customs and context, a problem essentially eliminated by the self-help scheme, which instrumentalized vernacular, or traditional, forms of building. In figure 3.3, nipa houses and the lots ready to receive them are sandwiched between electrical poles on one side and railroad tracks on another. Here "variances on the universal" are woven tightly into the cloth of a globalizing modernity. These modern infrastructures appear more permanent

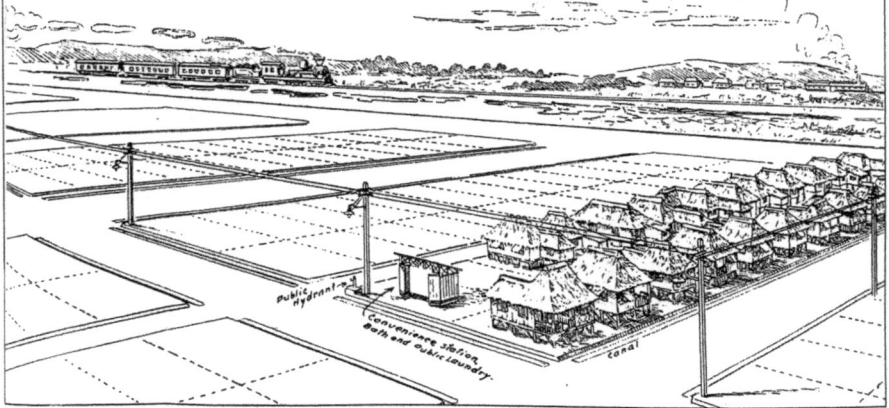

FIGURE 3.3. Bureau of Health for the Philippine Islands, Division of Sanitary Engineering, "Plan in Perspective of a Sanitary Barrio," July 2, 1912. From *Philippine Habitations* (Manila: Bureau of Printing, 1912), 3.

than the nipa houses that were the "basis" of the barrio itself. Following the patterns of the development of the American West, tracks were laid speculatively with the expectation that a real estate market would be generated in its wake. In the meantime, the nipa structures kept Manila's wealthier residents free from the fear of disease, while the lightness of the sanitary barrio's infrastructure guaranteed that these settlements could be swept aside once the best price for the land was realized. Indeed, despite being an affordable means of providing housing for Manila's poor and laboring populations, none of the sanitary barrios were maintained in the long term. Little is mentioned of them in colonial records after the cholera emergencies had subsided. The sanitary barrio on the San Lazaro Estate (the largest of such barrios), for example, was razed in 1912 to make way for the Manila Jockey Club's new hippodrome. Though there is no record of what happened to populations living in sanitary barrios, it is fairly safe to assume that they were pushed into ever tighter and more marginal spaces within the city.

Concrete Parterre and Cordon Sanitaire: Origins
of the Divided Colonial City

The Manila Plan, like all of Burnham's urban plans, was patterned after Pierre Charles L'Enfant's plans for Washington, DC, and Georges-Eugène Haussmann's renovation of Paris—both characterized by radial axes that divided the city into well-defined districts. In Manila these districts came to serve as a readymade hygienic infrastructure, functioning both as germ barriers and as an easily navigated network from which sanitary inspectors could police both the strong materials neighborhoods (where some landlords were found to harbor light-materials structures as well) and the sanitary barrios themselves. The areas trapped between the radial system of axes—the parterres (a term borrowed from landscape design)—in effect created a patchwork of permanent cordons sanitaires. Where concrete roads were not possible, compacted earth was spread with lime to keep the road's surface both firm and clean. As in Washington, DC, the interiors of the Manila parterres were organized with a colonial gridiron pattern. The intersections of the axes and grids were particularly effective from the standpoint of sanitation. From the boulevards, sanitary inspectors mounted on motorbikes could visually penetrate the neatly gridded barrios. The gridiron that organized the sanitary barrios meanwhile facilitated supervision by providing a rational grid of roads to inspect the barrio's surface drains, which further subdivided the sanitary barrio into an even finer mesh. The organization of the drains (really just collection basins) made it such that—when samples were found to contain cholera—inspectors could, at least in theory, trace the bacteria back to a single residence. Disease, then, was not localized to a body exhibiting symptoms, but to particular places within the sanitary barrio itself. Each neatly demarcated plot of land was viewable as an extension of the native body. Houses deemed improperly maintained were treated as suspect—susceptible to, if not already symptomatic of, disease. In the sanitary barrio, then, cholera was not a disease of the human body, but rather an infection that targeted the externalized concrete bowels of a native settlement. The sanitary barrio could thus be treated like an infected person would be. If cholera was ever detected, pressure hoses had a wide and clear berth into which disinfectants could be sprayed with a power hose, eradicating disease from the collective bowels of the barrio.[35]

The definition of Burnham's network of lines was of central importance, as sanitary barrio sites were often adjacent to developing strong materials districts, as was the case with the Vito Cruz barrio, where "a number of objections [had] been raised" on account of its location "on the path of construction of strong material houses and . . . within that part of Manila which is at present enjoying the greatest amount of construction of the higher class of residences." However, despite the fact that the sanitary committee thought it "seemed undesirable to insert a nipa barrio in the middle of a highly developed residential district . . . [and] that the land in that district is too expensive for a sanitary barrio," the owners of the property were set on using their land for this purpose and the committee could not lawfully object to owners who wished "to rent [their property] for that purpose."[36] Though this made little sense to the sanitary committee (who viewed land through the naturalized lens of real estate speculation), what they encountered were, as I have already pointed out, the remnants of an essentially feudal hacienda system. Some hacenderos were slow to transform themselves into industrial capitalists, or even real estate speculators. They were even more loath to relinquish what had been a steady source of income for generations. The sanitary barrio, in fact, allowed hacenderos or other large landholders to rationalize their rental properties and regularize income with minimal risk and little investment.

What the sanitary barrio demonstrates is the flexibility of Burnham's plan. As a general diagram that facilitated both circulation and control, the plan was able to not only accommodate a number of ad hoc schemes, from the sanitary barrio to polo grounds to college and factory campuses, but was also able to accommodate massive changes within the overall scheme. Entire districts could be changed without threatening the plan's overall organization. However, despite their early importance, Burnham's boulevards are only occasionally recognizable today, the most notable perhaps being the curving bay shore boulevard now known as Roxas Avenue. In the end, the sanitary barrio has had a far more durable effect on Manila than Burnham's plan itself. Its legacy can best be seen in the "informal settlements" that make up increasingly dense portions of Manila's vast urbanscape of uneven development. Indeed, what the history of the sanitary barrio reveals is that "informal" settlements, which have replaced sanitary barrios as the predominant form of housing for Manila's laboring classes, are not informal at all, nor are they "postcolonial"; to the contrary, they are structural residues of the colonial city as *planned*. Though sanitary barrios barely occupy a blip in the histories of Philippine urban planning, as a model of development they persist as the variable patterns of light and strong, rich and poor that still characterize Philippine urban space to this day.

4

REPRODUCIBILITY

THE BURNHAM PLAN AND THE ARCHITECTURE

OF AN "EFFICIENT MACHINE"

In the first decades of the twentieth century, what was meant by "standardiza-tion" varied widely and could refer to anything from the specification of stan-dardized parts to buildings replicated in their entirety (figure 4.1). Though the use of standard doors and windows was a widely accepted building practice, the idea of a fully replicated building still unnerved most architects. Beyond threatening the profession and destabilizing what Michel Foucault termed the "author function,"[1] the replica also violated an architectural value system that held unique responses to place and context as sacrosanct. Architectural cop-ies were not new, nor was a preoccupation with the potentially destructive effects of industrial reproduction (which dominated architectural discourse beginning in the mid-nineteenth century).[2] By 1920, however, modernists, mostly in Europe, had begun to write forcefully about the potentials of stan-dardization, viewing the advent of industrial production as a new horizon of possibilities—one particularly useful in addressing the desperate need for mass

FIGURE 4.1. Identical
municipal buildings in (*top to
bottom*) Tabaco, Davao, Con-
cepcion, and Lopez. From
*Bulletin, Bureau of Public
Works* 15, no. 1 (1927): 24;
18, no. 1 (1930): 29; 19, no. 1
(1931): 32, 43.

housing that followed the explosion of urban populations—itself the result of industrialization. The advantages that issued from industrial reproducibility were, however, never fully extended to the monument. For some architects and theorists, industrialization (as a positive project) was coextensive with the death of the monument as such. Assuming modernism's rejection of historical forms, Lewis Mumford once declared, "[t]he notion of a modern monument is veritably a contradiction in terms. If it is a monument it is not modern, and if it is modern, it cannot be a monument."[3] Other modernists, among them Sigfried Giedion, argued for the monument's continued importance. Advocating for a "new monumentality," Giedion maintained that the monument's direct appeal to emotion was a fixed and "eternal need" that nevertheless required a radical rethinking.[4]

It was no different in the Philippines, where industrialized building products and processes enabled the US colonial regime to realize ambitious and archipelago-wide projects quickly, cheaply, and easily.[5] Rapid construction techniques played a major role in delivering potable drinking water, sanitary modern markets, and an archipelago-wide system of public education that enjoyed widespread popularity. That schools and market halls looked identical from town to town raised little concern among local populations. This ease with architectural replicas, however, reached its limit at the monument, a discomfort detailed by Ralph Harrington Doane, the final American to serve in the Philippines as consulting architect:[6]

> Just as a person has individuality and individual taste in the matter of clothes and personal adornments, just so communities have a collective individuality and desire individuality in their public works. Instances can be recalled where a municipality . . . has lost entire interest in a town hall project simply because it was ascertained that it was to be, when completed, identical to one in an adjacent town. Public spirit can be marshalled to improve public works in a manner to give the community distinctness but becomes apathetic when required to construct architectural replicas.[7]

If the Filipinos' rejection of replicas was not an indication of a universal and "eternal" desire, it was evidence of an already deeply ingrained cultural value. During Spanish times, Doane wrote, Philippine natives regarded their religious monuments with "the utmost pride and appreciation." Filipinos' relationship to these monuments, Doane pointed out, was, however, complicated, as at the time of their construction, Spanish churches usually enlisted the labor of the entire town while they "absorb(ed) almost the entire communal wealth."

"It was no wonder," he concluded, that "when the Spanish government was overthrown . . . reactionaries attempted to destroy many of these edifices, the results of forced labor and oppression."[8] Aiming to distinguish US colonialism from an exploitative Spanish regime Doane attempted to produce an honorific architecture that was not only more affordable, and built under a system of free labor, but was also, by virtue of its unique beauty, able to "marshall . . . public spirit." With the exception of affordability, Doane failed at his tasks, making liberal use, as did his predecessors, of both corvée labor and a robust system of prison labor while resorting to the fully replicated monument.[9]

Before Burnham

Daniel Burnham was not the first American architect to arrive and work in the Philippines; that distinction belonged to a young unknown practitioner by the name of Edgar Ketchum Bourne. He began his work in the Philippines by familiarizing himself with the Philippine "context" by purchasing a small reference library on Spanish styles, which included Max Junghändel's giant folio, *Die Baukunst Spaniens*, Owen Jones's *Details and Ornaments from the Alhambra*, and Andrew H. Prentice's *Renaissance Architecture and Ornament in Spain*. Extending his self-education by surveying the existing skilled labor on the islands, his first report as consulting architect included several elaborate examples of local wrought iron work, executed by both native and Chinese blacksmiths. Bourne's buildings—far humbler than the baroque examples illustrated in his sourcebooks—borrowed from the simplicity of both local precedent, as well as the Mission style popularized on the American West Coast. The most significant difference between Bourne's buildings and those of his Spanish predecessors was the material used to construct them. Though both Spanish and American buildings were finished in stucco, Spanish structures were built using local volcanic rock or brick, while Bourne specified the Western lumber (mostly Oregon Pine and California Redwood) then flooding the Philippine market.

Following the lead and pattern of the American frontier, the use of soft woods allowed Bourne to build quickly and design flexibly.[10] Among his most important buildings were the Government Laboratories Building, and the rather clumsily designed Insular Ice and Cold Storage Plant. Though variable in terms of architectural merit, most of his projects revealed a concerning lack of technical expertise. Most projects, for example, failed to account for both the poor bearing capacity of Manila's alluvial soil and the voracious appetite of the *anay*, or Philippine termite. There were, however, other motivations behind his eventual dismissal. Complaints about Bourne began to pile up as the pace of construction picked up in Manila, reflecting a dissatisfaction that surfaced alongside a clearer picture of the US colonial project.

In July 1903, Bourne was brought before the Office of the Secretary of Public Instruction on vague charges of "incompetence." As noted in an article published in the *Manila Times* on July 17, 1903, the plaintiffs, a group of contractors, pleaded for Bourne's removal "by reason of his arrogance and . . . arbitrariness." Though there were few clarifying details, it was clear the disagreement lay in the process of construction. Whereas American contractors arrived to the Philippines with standardized methods and construction systems in hand, Bourne pushed craft-oriented details that contractors viewed as little more than taxing obstacles. By the time of the lawsuit, the building industry had become one of the more profitable commercial activities to gain a toehold in the archipelago, and its development was emerging as a central objective for US colonists.

William E. Parsons, Producing "an Efficient Machine"

Bourne, who for the most part faded into historical obscurity,[11] was famously replaced by Daniel Burnham, who, along with his Beaux Arts–trained assistant, William Pierce Anderson, arrived in December of 1904 to survey existing conditions in Manila, as well as the site of a new summer capital in the highland province of Benguet. From the moment of his arrival he worked closely with William Cameron Forbes, then the commissioner of commerce and police, who had been previously acquainted with Burnham through a family connection.[12] Sharing a relationship marked by both deep respect and casual familiarity, the two men discussed the future of the colony on road trips, at site visits, and over elaborately catered banquets of imported American food.[13] Though Burnham spent a mere five weeks in the Philippines (compared to Bourne's three years), his "big plans" set the stage for the near total transformation of the archipelago. Back in Chicago, Anderson drafted the plan, while Burnham searched for an executor to take up residence in the Philippines. Though he initially struggled to find a suitable architect, he found one at last in William E. Parsons.[14]

Born in Akron, Ohio, Parsons had received his BA from Yale, followed by a BS at Columbia University, where he received the prestigious McKim prize on graduating, which earned him admission to the École des Beaux-Arts, where he trained for three additional years. When he accepted the job in the Philippines, Parsons was working as head draftsman at the San Francisco office of John Galen Howard. In a letter to Forbes, Anderson enthusiastically endorsed

Parsons, who was "strongly backed by those who know him best ... [and] carr[ied] a very tenacious purpose under a very mild and self-deprecatory manner." Beyond his agreeable character, he possessed a commitment to pragmatism that Burnham and Forbes considered essential. He was, Anderson assured Forbes, "a man ... less interested in the mere matter of the aspect of things than in the real solutions of the practical problems of architecture—a man whose desire is to produce an *efficient machine* capable of doing its work besides carrying a little over-load."[15]

Arriving in Manila in November 1905, Parsons began organizing an office of both American and Filipino draftsmen. Parsons's early buildings in the Philippines were, like those of Bourne, executed in a Spanish Mission style. This is perhaps surprising, as by that time Burnham was closely associated with the industrially reconstructed Neoclassicism popularized at the Columbian Exposition. Working in the local colonial idiom was, however, Burnham's direct mandate. As with Bourne, it did not seem to matter that the Spanish Mission style was associated with a defeated colonial power. Presenting contextuality as common sense, Burnham wrote in his Manila Report that "[i]n any given locality the things already existing as a result of long experience in the city are likely to prove the best. In Manila," Burnham emphasized, "this general rule seems to apply with especial force."[16] Turning toward specifics, he described how the overhanging second stories of Manila's domestic architecture accommodated the tropical climate by shading the sidewalks below. Elevations of continuous sliding wood screens, meanwhile, enabled maximum ventilation on humid days. Burnham lamented the recent prohibition of these overhangs on account of the difficulty they posed to the erection of telegraph and telephone poles. Reconciling context with modern needs, Burnham made the simple suggestion that, in lieu of poles, one could string concealed lines from rooftop to rooftop. Similarly, Burnham believed that stone's "pleasing effect" could be similarly achieved in an earthquake-proof and economical reinforced concrete.[17] Apparently committed to historical verisimilitude, he rejected the "invasion of galvanized iron," which was quickly replacing Manila's "beautiful roofs of Spanish tile."

Though Bourne and Parsons worked in the same stylistic idiom, Parsons's architecture was designed around wholly different parameters. Following Burnham's directives, Parsons's aim was not to design distinct buildings, but to introduce new methods of construction and management—a shift in practice that enabled him to think not in terms of discrete sites, but about the colonial project as a whole.

Despite this, historians have tended to focus on Parsons's aesthetic sensibilities. To the extent that he has been celebrated at all, it is for his proto-modernist inclinations toward abstraction and truth to materials.[18] By his own account, a disciplined simplicity was necessary to offset the florid beauty of the tropics. However, to judge Parsons's work on the terms of a modern aesthetic sensibility would be to ignore his primary achievement—quantity. Parsons was responsible for an astonishing amount of construction during his tenure as consulting architect, overseeing not only dozens of monumental and institutional structures in the capital, but also for the construction of hundreds of buildings throughout the archipelago. Toward these ends, Parsons allowed contracting companies great leeway, enabling them to specify details at their discretion. Minimally designed elevations and plans, and few deviations from standard details, reduced both cost and margin for error. The early introduction of proprietary reinforced concrete systems like the Kahn system (which dominated the Philippine market) greatly simplified both design and engineering. The use of regular bays and a consistent scale—not only within but between buildings—at once slashed costs and eased the process of overseas sourcing.

In this way, Parsons's achievements throw Bourne's insufficiencies into stark relief. Parsons's desire for efficiency made him popular among contractors in the Philippines, with whom he developed cooperative rather than antagonistic relationships. What set the two architects apart was their differing conceptions of an "architectural whole." Bourne's was a conventional understanding of architecture as the practice of designing discrete buildings, whereas Parsons, following Burnham, treated buildings as mere parts, viewing the colony itself as a single, systemic "big plan." Burnham himself viewed the work in the Philippines as demonstrative of the benefits not only of big plans but also of the executive leadership required to fulfill them. In the speech from which his famous "big plans" quote was pulled, Burnham made a point to praise the executive labors of "that superb young commissioner, W. Cameron Forbes, now governor general of the Philippines Islands."[19]

The Manila Hotel and Economic Reproduction

Burnham's Manila Plan, like the 1902 McMillan Plan for Washington, DC, was presented as what Manfredo Tafuri described as "an ideology realized in terms of urban images"—a highly configured symbolism defined against the developmentally driven urbanism of Detroit, Chicago, and New York. Unlike Washington, DC, in Manila, the symbolic heart of the plan—a civic center where executive, legislative, and judicial buildings gathered around an all too familiar rectangular lawn, remained for decades, little more than a fanciful graphic.[20] That is not to say that construction did not begin immediately—it did, though on a city created and adapted to business. This was an order drawn into the plan that operated alongside its highly configured symbolic features. The nerve center of this clandestine order was the government-owned Manila Hotel, the first major building built that was a part of the Burnham plan. Designed to rival the Astor in the British concession in Tianjin (1863), the Hotel Continental in Saigon (1880), the Raffles in Singapore (1887), and the Hongkong Hotel (1893), the Manila Hotel was built not only as luxurious accommodation for tourists, but like the aforementioned hotels was to serve as a gathering place for foreigners with disposable capital. Forbes was explicit about the role of foreign capital in the colony. During his inaugural speech as governor general, he opined that though " it might be possible in the course of several generations to develop the latent resources of the Philippine Islands without the assistance of outside capital and finally to accumulate enough to develop the domestic business from within. But why wait?" It was better, he emphasized, to "attract for our use the accumulations of wealth already made in other countries, sure that the advantages which flow from them will far more than offset any possible disadvantage due to the fact that some of the profits will leave the country or that the owners of the capital will endeavor to influence the administration of the Islands or their political status."[21]

Despite its inconspicuous location on Burnham's plan, off axis and behind the hulking mass of Intramuros, the Manila Hotel is in fact sited on what was perhaps the city's most valuable piece of real estate—surrounded by the new port works to the north, the newly landscaped "Burnham Green" to the south, Intramuros to the east, and Manila Bay to the west (figure 4.2). Its position was determined by its economic function as an accelerant to development—wholly integrated into the working city, even as it set itself apart from the plan's ideologically driven formality (figure 4.3).

Preparations for the hotel began almost immediately after Burnham's plan was approved. In April of 1906, as the land for the future site was being reclaimed, Parsons invited construction bids—specifying that it would be one of the first buildings on the archipelago to be composed entirely of reinforced concrete.[22] The winner of the contract, the Eastern Engineering Company, worked closely with Parsons to manage the hotel's construction. Specifying the Kahn trussed bar, Eastern Engineering received thousands of prefabricated pieces, which arrived by rail and steamship from Julius Kahn's new steelyard in Youngstown, Ohio. Despite the company's youth, by the time the Manila

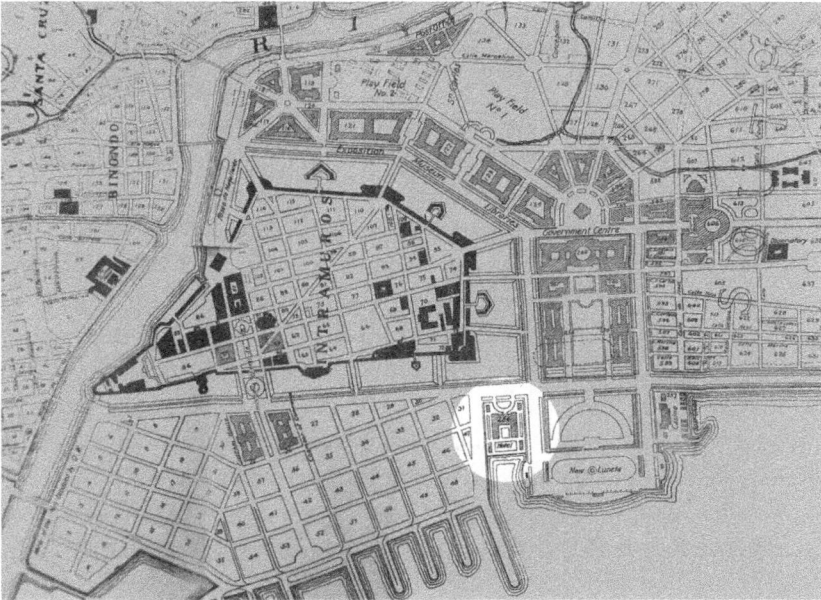

FIGURE 4.2. The location of the Manila Hotel on Daniel H. Burnham's "Plan of Proposed Improvements" for the city. From Daniel H. Burnham and William Pierce Anderson, "Report on Proposed Improvements at Manila," 1906.

FIGURE 4.3. Aerial photograph of Burnham Green showing the Manila Hotel on the far side of the green, 1933. From the collection of John Tewell, http://www.flickr.com /photos/johntewell/5200263761/.

Hotel began construction, over fifteen hundred buildings had been built using the Kahn bar in the United States, where it was preferred for its remarkable ease of use. Its components were competitively priced, standardized, and highly adaptable. As a single rigid armature of metal, the entire bar could be placed as a unit inside a formwork, precluding any variation in reinforcing and enabling construction even in the absence of skilled steel workers or rod setters (as was required, for example, by its main global competitor, the Hennebique system). Not only were associated labor costs lower, the Kahn bar was also significantly cheaper than most other systems of reinforcement due to the simplicity of its fabrication: rolled out as a single plate of steel, with diagonal "wings" scored and bent to achieve its characteristic profile.

Though reinforced concrete construction was at the time most strongly associated with factories and warehouses, it was easily adaptable to any number of programs and to a limitless variety of styles. For example, in keeping with the Spanish colonial style specified by Burnham, Parsons wrapped the hotel in twelve-foot-deep arcades reminiscent of the monasteries of the old walled city. Few noticed that the barrel vaults used by the Spanish were replaced by the straight profiles of reinforced concrete beams, but it hardly mattered. Parsons was able to approximate a semblance of Manila's colonial charm—with all the comforts, safety, and convenience of a modern building. Every finishing detail, from its polished wood finishes of native narra, camagon, and ipil to the locally made rattan furniture and potted Philippine palms, infused the hotel with a relaxed colonial air—even a nostalgia for a departed Spanish regime (a historicism that disguised the otherwise uninterrupted cadence of industrial reproduction). Natives were also a part of the scenery—a brown-skinned waitstaff in starched white livery stands poised to serve (figure 4.4). Their omnipresence suggested, as the hotel manager once remarked, that the hotel was also a site to develop labor. In his words, his Filipino staff were "excellent material out of which to evolve servants," only needing, he continued, "proper instruction."[23]

Thick with a mañana ambience, the atmosphere at the Manila Hotel belied its industrial manufacture, a modernity that resurfaced in its up-to-the-minute amenities: Otis elevators, the first interconnected telephone system in the Far East, private bathrooms equipped with American plumbing, and push-button butler service. To assuage the fears of foreigners with delicate stomachs, cooled and distilled water was piped throughout the hotel, while a seven-hundred-square-foot refrigerator stored imported perishables from the United States and Australia (which arrived to Manila's shores under continuous refrigeration). For entertainment, guests retreated to the roof garden, where under potted palms they waltzed on a springy dance floor of "elastic conolite," serenaded by

FIGURE 4.4. Postcard showing the main lobby of the Manila Hotel, ca. 1913.

native musicians and surrounded by a sweeping panoramic view that encompassed both medieval monuments and symbols of modern progress.[24] From the highest point in Manila, guests could look down on the Luneta, a neatly clipped ellipse of lawn where wealthy Manileños ritually circumambulated to the rhythms of a daily afternoon concert, or at the adjacent six-lane Cavite Boulevard, a bayside drive that hugged the curve of Manila Bay, where after dusk electric lights illuminated new model-Ts, streetcar rails, and fresh macadam. Later renamed after Admiral Dewey, Cavite Boulevard was a gateway to an extensive network of modern roads that penetrated deep into Luzon's interior, providing access to a bounty of export crops, from coconut groves and fields of sugar cane to tobacco and abaca farms. Drives out to the countryside concluded with a preprandial restorative on the hotel's veranda, which offered diners a front row view of Manila's famous sunset, a brilliant eventide spectacle that unfolded behind a massive construction site of docks and other port works. In short, the hotel bracketed a sequence of experiences carefully curated to give the potential investor a complete impression of the archipelago's commercial possibilities.

Wrapped in the languid sidestreams of Flor de Filipinas cigars, over lavish meals of roast midwestern tenderloin, new potatoes Rissole, California celery, and mango frappé au Porto (familiar classics, seasoned with just enough tropical flair),[25] American commissioners issued contracts to mostly American capitalists to build railways and roads, buildings, ports and bridges—all of which were already incorporated into Burnham's plan. Just the first in a series of amenities aimed at attracting capital to Philippine shores, Burnham's plan also included an extended area of "city clubs . . . [with] ample grounds for gardens and outdoor games" grouped with "official residences, hotels, and clubs in parkway boulevards and gardens along the waterfront" designed to accommodate "an attractive social life that will bring many influential people to Manila and count for much in the prosperity of the islands."[26] These spaces, where leisure and business were barely distinguishable from one another, were those in which men like Forbes and Burnham felt most at ease. As Burnham put it, "the delightfulness of a city is an element of first importance to its prosperity, for those who make fortunes will stay and others come if the attractions are strong enough to insure continuous good times."[27] Burnham described these leisure programs as "semipublic," by which he meant that these were places where profit-seeking investors could meet in well-appointed comfort under the auspices of an expansively defined public interest.[28] The central importance of the clubs and hotels reveals the integration of private capital into a plan that attempted to formally sublimate capital's appearance as the driver of the colonial project. Indeed, the construction of the symbolic heart of the plan—a lawn around which the legislative, executive, and judicial branches gathered—was contingent upon the sale of the hotel to a private investor. That money would then be used to acquire the property necessary for the development of the government center, located on a site adjacent to Intramuros, on sacred ground where José Rizal was martyred.[29] In this way, Burnham's monumental Manila plan, designed to invoke a model democracy, in fact, functioned to conceal a project of economic development already implied in the actual destruction of democratic values.

Standardization Takes Command

Though Parsons's work in the Philippines was divided between "semipublic" projects like the Manila Hotel, which catered to the comfort of investors, and fully public projects aimed at Filipinos (schools, prisons, markets), both types of projects were conceived as integral parts of a single colonial mission. Clubs and hotels attracted outside capital, while schools, prisons, and markets played an important role in producing and maintaining a viable labor force. This is what Pierce Anderson meant when he described Parsons as desiring to "*produce* an efficient machine." Previous scholarship misreads Parsons's work as the

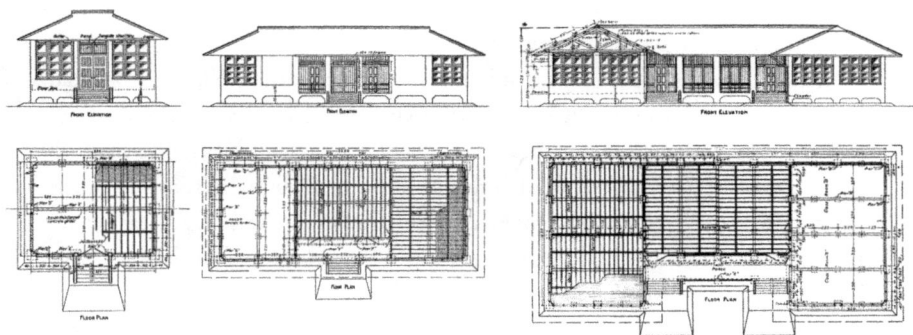

FIGURE 4.5. Standard plans and elevations for (*from left*) a one-room, a three-room, and a five-room school. From *School Buildings: Plans, Specifications, and Bills of Material for Standard Revised School Buildings of the Bureau of Education* (Manila: Bureau of Printing, 1912), 18, 36, 58.

outcome of an aesthetically driven desire to stylistically hybridize modernist, local, and historicist forms, when his architecture is best understood as the outcome of a drive to economize—an imperative sometimes obscured by his inclusion of locally produced architectural elements.[30] Parsons's specification of capiz shell windows, for example, enabled him to exploit locally abundant material (and very cheap labor) while saving money on plate glass—an expensive and difficult-to-ship commodity. Like Bourne, he appreciated the "soft, pearly light" that filtered through capiz shells, but their beauty was equal, if not secondary, to their economy.[31] That is to say, pleasing effects were wholly compatible with the production of a "machine."

Designed for rapid deployment across the archipelago, Parsons's architecture enabled the immediate execution of a number of colonial project types, including markets and artesian wells (which protected laboring bodies from disease), prisons (which beyond serving a disciplinary function became important mustering stations and educational sites for cheap, industrialized labor), and most importantly schools (where English was taught)—which William Howard Taft considered the main feature of the colonial administration (figure 4.5).[32] For each program Parsons developed modular plans in a range of sizes, specifying room dimensions, formworks, reinforcement schedules, windows, doors, hardware, furniture, blackboards, and so on. As described in the *Architectural Record*, Parsons restricted his use of decoration, confining "his efforts to the proper functioning of the utilitarian side of the problem, without resorting to the use of extraneous ornament for effect"—reducing construction costs to a "minimum consistent with durability."[33]

These programs, especially schools, markets, and artesian wells, were popular among Filipinos living in the cities and towns in which they were built. Education, especially in the sciences and the liberal arts, had during the Spanish colonial period been mostly denied to Philippine natives, who received in the main a catechistic education provided by the Catholic Church. At least as far as education went it seemed that the United States did in fact deliver on its "benevolence." However, as several scholars have pointed out, whether or not those involved in developing a system of colonial education in the Philippines viewed their work as benevolent, education was also deployed as a tool of social engineering, and as a means of producing and integrating an industrial labor force, among various other more tailored colonial purposes.[34]

The popularity of the schools and markets notwithstanding, Parsons considered a standardized approach inappropriate for monumental structures. This was especially the case for provincial capitol buildings, which played a symbolic role similar to that of the capital's government center. They were arguably of even greater symbolic significance, as the construction of each capitol building was intended to ceremonially mark the local conclusion of a process of military "pacification." As such, the planning for each provincial capitol took place as soon as insurrectionist activity was considered extinguished in that province, signifying the political incorporation of each province into the Union.[35]

Each capitol was placed in front of an open public green, an organization of civic space that referenced both the government center in Manila and the typical "plaza, cathedral, cabildo complex" that was the spatial expression of the combined spiritual and political power of the Spanish colonial state. Though approximating the Spanish layout, there were clear differences. First, there was no church—the provincial capitol building provided a single spiritual and political reference to an "enlightened" political power. Second, unlike the plaza, a field of mixed civic and commercial activity, the lawns that fronted the capitols was strictly symbolic—a clearing that visually and spatially emphasized the eminence and local presence of colonial governance.

According to A. N. Rebori, a critic writing for the *Architectural Record*, it was in the provincial capitol buildings that Parsons demonstrated "his ability to full advantage." Their "design, general proportion, exactness of detail, and handling of material," Rebori wrote, exposed "the hand of the competent architect." Parsons's "competence" was not measured by any individual design, but rather in his ability to produce diverse results by varying certain basic parameters to create "interesting relationships between openings and solids" (as opposed to simply adding "moulding or applied decoration"). Careful to qualify his praise for Parsons, Rebori wrote that he did "not mean to imply that a new architecture is to be found in Mr. Parsons's method of expression," nor did his work possess "any great amount of originality." Nevertheless, it did show a marked improvement over the "stereotyped classic architecture perpetrated in so many American public buildings" and provided a means of "local betterment" by introducing "a permanent construction suited to the needs of a tropical country."[36] Rebori's halting praise demonstrated that Parsons's accomplishments in the Philippines were not judged according to the same criteria usually applied to work addressed in a publication like the *Architectural Record*. It was rather shaped by a colonial approach that attempted to redeem an economically rationalized industrial construction with a semblance of individuality.

Rebori's conflicted description of Parsons's provincial capitols was, in fact, generous. Little more than dismal, minimally decorated cubes, the buildings were the outcome of a managerial process that optimized cost over all else—and it showed. Systematically conceived, the provincial capitols are best understood when read *across* the type, rather than on the basis of any individual specimen. Using Spanish *presidencias* (city halls) as a starting point, Parsons further simplified the type by replacing stucco-covered masonry construction with reinforced concrete. For example, the provincial government buildings in Pampanga and Capiz (figure 4.6, center and bottom) were essentially the same clumsy rectangular volumes with minimal decoration, the only difference being the shape of the punched openings and the number of structural bays. The general proportions and hipped roofs were taken from the provincial government building in Iloilo (figure 4.6, top), a structure originally built by the Spanish in 1872 on which Parsons placed a second story of reinforced concrete. In general, the embellishment of each building accorded with each region's economic importance, as can be seen in the treatment of Iloilo, which specified larger window openings, more ornament, and an open loggia. These simple calibrations allowed Parsons to introduce variety without sacrificing economy or efficiency. Furthermore, more decoration suggested a kind of hierarchy—Capiz, for example, was not as wealthy a province as Iloilo, a difference reflected in its level of ornament. In contrast to Capiz's barely relieved walls and punched rectangular windows, at Iloilo, Parsons specified freestanding Tuscan columns, recessed panels and applied rondels, decorative wrought iron railings, and even a porte cochere—elaborations intended to induce a

FIGURE 4.6.
Provincial capitol
buildings designed
by William E.
Parsons: (*top to
bottom*) Iloilo, 1910;
Pampanga, 1907;
and Capiz, 1911.
From H. F. Cam-
eron, "Provincial
Centers in the
Philippine Islands,"
*Quarterly Bulletin,
Bureau of Public
Works* 2, no. 4
(1914).

sense of pride, and even competitiveness, as well as an incentive to politically and economically assimilate.[37] The uniqueness and relative fineness of each structure would, at least in theory, allow the United States to ritualize the pacification of each province, and to present their economic assimilation as historic events.

The Neoclassical Turn: Ending the "Period of Suppressed Nationalism"

Between 1906 and 1910, Parsons's provincial capitol buildings were each executed in the modified Spanish Mission style prescribed by Burnham; but toward the end of his tenure, Parsons made a sharp turn to neoclassicism. Though he offered no explicit reason for turning away from the mission style, he did argue in favor of neoclassicism's suitedness to the Philippines, writing that although classical architecture was "foreign" to the island, its origins "in the near tropics" made it eminently suitable to the local climate.[38] Specious climatological arguments aside, neoclassicism was undoubtedly easier to execute by this time, aided by the return of a handful of Filipino architects who had just completed their architectural training in the United States. This included Carlos Barreto (Drexel, 1908), Antonio Toledo (Ohio State, 1911), Tomás Mapúa (Cornell, 1911), and Juan Arellano (Drexel, 1911), all of whom were products of Taft's Pensionado Act program.[39] They were joined by George Corner Fenhagen, an architect with a Beaux Arts pedigree that rivalled that of Parsons. A graduate of the University of Pennsylvania and of the American Academy in Rome, Fenhagen had most recently been working at the office of the Philadelphia firm of Pell & Corbett. In short, by 1911 the consulting architect's office was fully staffed with Beaux Arts–trained professionals.

The first of Parsons's neoclassical structures was the Paco train station (figure 4.7)—which in both program and style stood as a powerful symbol of a distinctly American civilization (recall Burnham's own monumental Union Station).[40] Though more complex than his previous designs, the austerity of his earlier work was still apparent, a simplicity driven on the one hand by what he viewed as the limitations of reinforced concrete itself, and on the other by a lack of skilled native labor which he described as both "scarce and difficult to train."[41] As a first test of locally available labor Parsons confined ornament to the central portico, while limiting the actual applied decorations to a few easy to cast forms—four eagles supporting stiff festoons, a dentil course, and a shallow frieze of alternating triglyphs and rondels. Though for Parsons this was a greatly increased use of ornamentation, its primary monumental effect

FIGURE 4.7. William E. Parsons, Paco train station, Manila, completed 1914. From US National Archives, 350 MR Collection.

was still due, according to his own assessment, "for the most part, to straight-forward design."[42]

Around the same time that construction began on the Paco train station, Parsons prepared to begin construction on University Hall, the first building of the University of the Philippines (figure 4.8). A more complex structure than the train station, Parsons at first struggled with reconciling economic efficiency with the aesthetic demands of the new style. Following two rounds of bidding, Parsons failed to find a contractor willing to meet the brief, which included a tight budget of ₱250,000 and a 300-day timeline for completion. The lowest bid came in at ₱273,000, though the contractor insisted on an extension of 100 days. Frustrated, Parsons resolved to build "by administration" (wherein the Insular Government acted as its own contractor). He did not take the decision lightly, as the development of the building industry had become an important focus of the colonial government. Parsons, however, took the opportunity to prove a point. On completion, the *Quarterly Bulletin, Bureau of Public Works* published a meticulous account of University Hall's construction that read like a set of repeatable instructions specifying the order of operations, the machinery needed, concrete admixture proportions (to the barrel), and concrete mixing times (to the minute). Most importantly he wanted to demonstrate that the budget he specified was accurate (to the last peso). Exactly 300 days after construction began the building was complete, at

FIGURE 4.8. William E. Parsons with Antonio Toledo, University Hall, University of the Philippines Manila, completed 1914. From *Facts and Figures About the Philippines* (Manila: Bureau of Printing, 1920), 46.

a cost of ₱251,794—just ₱1500 over budget, a cost that *Quarterly Bulletin* was quick to blame on the congestion of the steel market.[43]

"Building by administration" allowed Parsons to closely manage labor conditions at the jobsite, a task he viewed almost exclusively in racial terms. At University Hall construction managers tried out various arrangements of Japanese and Filipino "teams," arguing that when one Japanese carpenter was paired with two Filipino helpers, the Filipinos "generally looked on at the Japanese working," rather than themselves executing work. Managers found it "more economical" to compose teams of one Filipino carpenter with one native helper for the initial stages of construction, and for finishing work (like the hanging of doors and windows) it was best to create teams of 3 Japanese carpenters with one native helper.[44] It did not seem to occur to labor managers that Filipinos "looking on" might be anything beyond proof of the "lazy native."[45] When the refusal of work was racialized, managers did not view it as an objection to the higher pay and more favorable treatment of Japanese labor, for example; or as motivated by resentment accrued on account of counterrevolutionary war and successive laws of dispossession that separated native laborers from their means of subsistence.[46] To acknowledge any motivation behind a reluctance or refusal of work would be to point out the inherent contradictions of the US colonial project—to question, in other words, the liberating effects of market mechanisms, "free labor," and industrial production. It is not by chance that Parsons avoided discussions that were overtly political in nature: He regarded Filipinos not as political subjects to be governed, but as economic subjects to be managed.

When finished, Parsons's neoclassical buildings emphasized, whether he wanted them to or not, the conflict between neoclassicism's association with Enlightenment values and the racialized logistics of architectural production in the colony. The contradictions presented by Parsons's turn to neoclassicism were amplified by the symbolism that played an outsized role in the political subject formation of Filipinos. The advent of neoclassicism happened to coincide with the tail end of what Philippine nationalist historians have referred to as the "period of suppressed nationalism," a time associated with laws prohibiting a wide range of actions considered seditious, including pro-independence writing and speeches, and the flying of the Philippine flag.[47] These laws were (predictably) a failure. Rather than suppress nationalism, they significantly contributed to the spread of nationalist sentiments, to an upsurge of anti-American discourse, and to a renewed celebration and circulation of nationalist symbols, each of which served to galvanize an imagined Philippine community.[48] Elite Filipinos and an increasingly large percentage of the general Philippine population understood and used these ideological contradictions as rhetorical ammunition to further their own demands for recognition and independence. The turn to neoclassicism then, can be seen as a sort of legitimation of a nationalist politics (officially legalized in 1907 with the first democratic elections of the First Philippine Assembly). Just one effect of this legalization of nationalist political activity was that the attention of the leaders of a once active and radical labor movement (most prominently, Dimonador Gomez and Isabelo de los Reyes) was "diverted from union to political activity."[49]

Reproducing Monuments

Parsons completed only three neoclassical buildings—the Paco train station, University Hall, and the provincial capital of Laguna. He resigned in February 1914 (a year following Woodrow Wilson's inauguration), citing "the scuttle policy of the administration."[50] Fenhagen, who took control of the office of the consulting architect, designed just one provincial capitol building, in Sorsogon, before he left for similar reasons. When Doane took over the office of the consulting architect, he made a full commitment to Beaux Arts neo-classicism, taking as his model Fenhagen's capitol building for Sorsogon, with which he was particularly impressed, considering it a vast improvement over Parsons's first neoclassical work—clumsy designs marked by unrelieved repetitiveness and awkwardly wide intercolumniations (reflecting the greater spans possible by reinforced concrete). In Doane's words, at Sorsogon Fenhagen was able to achieve "a building architecture of style and quality, not yet seen in the Philippines."[51]

Though Doane admired Fenhagen's work, it would prove a difficult standard to maintain. New pressures placed on the Bureau of Public Works by the Jones Law (see chapter 7) meant that "for every schoolhouse there is the demand for . . . ten others; for every municipal building . . . [an] immediate need for . . . five simultaneous constructions."[52] Unable to efficiently divide his attentions, Doane chose to focus his office's efforts on a few select projects, leaving the vast majority of others to *maestros de obras* (foremen). For these delegated projects Doane replicated Fenhagen's Sorsogon capitol for the capitols of Negros Oriental and Marinduque (figure 4.9). Copies in Western Samar and Batangas soon followed—though in those provinces, additional wings were added. Not only were these buildings constructed on the same plan, the same private contractor (B. F. Millis) had used all the same molds for the pillars, capitals, and other classical details, reluctantly realizing what Doane argued was "obviously the only practical procedure under these conditions." Attempting to ward off his own anxieties, Doane made a point of forcefully condemning the very practices he permitted, emphasizing that "while standardization of architecture may be necessary during formative periods as now exists in the Philippine Islands, as a policy to be perpetuated it is never desirable."[53]

Doane's concerns reflected the long reckoning of the profession with industrial modes of production and the feared loss of ennobled craft traditions. This loss, as John Ruskin famously argued, was abetted by the revival of classicism. Greek temples—an architecture, Ruskin points out, built by slaves—are composed of identical parts and as such were consonant with industrial production and reproduction. This certainly was the case with concrete neoclassicism. As such, neoclassicism itself, or so Ruskin argued, condemned those who labored on it (even in systems of free labor) to a "verily degrading kind of work" that "makes [workers] less than men."[54] By contrast, in Spanish-era churches built across its colonies from Acapulco to Goa to Manila, native and indigenous themes were incorporated into an ornate and eclectic global baroque. At the late eighteenth-century Miagao church in Iloilo, for example, broad-leaved banana and papaya trees stand among the carvings of saints in native dress.

FIGURE 4.9. Identical provincial capitol buildings: (*top*) capitol of Sorsogon, Sorsogon City, designed by George Corner Fenhagen; (*center and bottom*) capitol of Boac, Marinduque, and capitol of Negros Oriental, Dumaguete City, both built under the direction of Ralph Harrington Doane. From *Quarterly Bulletin, Bureau of Public Works* 5, no. 3 (1914): 37; *Bulletin, Bureau of Public Works* 13, no. 1 (1925): 17; 17, no. 1 (1929): 24.

In these buildings stone carvers might recognize their own hand in the mix of indigenous themes and nativized Christian saints. It is in the recognition of a dehumanizing reproducibility that replicas fail, in Doane's words, to rally "public spirit." In other words, the ideological goals of the US colonial regime were poorly served by his own resort to an industrially produced neoclassicism.

It is precisely this inability of the replica to arouse enthusiasm that interested Walter Benjamin, who understood the immediacy of the power to recognize the replica as replica. Benjamin proposed that replicating monuments disembedded them from tradition and ritual, rendering them "completely useless for the purposes of Fascism" or in this case for the purposes of US empire.[55] In other words, this failure to conceal the cheapness of empire's facture had the potential to dissolve the mystifying power of the monument. Though neoclassical architecture was intended to present US occupation as formally consonant with "timeless" enlightenment principles, their reproducibility plainly exposes the economic forces that set the colonial project into motion, opening up, as Benjamin suggested, a new possibility for the production of historical consciousness.

And yet it is worth entertaining the idea that the image of neoclassical architecture itself was enough to transcend these disenchanting effects. Reproduced monuments may even preserve meaning across what art historian Christopher Wood described as "a chain of mutually substitutable artifacts," amplifying ritual value not because they are unique, but on account of multiplying formal links to both classical and Enlightenment principles.[56] Fenhagen's provincial capitol buildings are not even replicas, but multiples. As such, no single building can make a claim to its primary importance. The manner in which the first instance is produced is the same for the second and twentieth. The abstract idea of a liberal democracy here stands in the place of a concrete original, embedding ritual meaning in a strangely enchanted seriality.

5

SCALABILITY

ALTERING THE

ARCHIPELAGIC INTERIOR

"Business is Business," the Big Man said,
"But it's something that's more, far more;
For it makes sweet gardens of deserts dead,
And cities it built now roar;
Where once the deer and the gray wolf ran
From the pioneer's swift advance;
Business is Magic that toils for man,
Business is True Romance. —ANONYMOUS, "Business Is Business"

The hero of the poem "Business Is Business," published in the April 1917 issue of the Bureau of Public Works' *Quarterly Bulletin*, was not a particular person but "Business"—in particular, "big business": a force, the poem reveals, capable of transforming entire landscapes.[1] Theodore Roosevelt racialized this capacity to convert what he called (borrowing from John Locke) "the world's waste spaces" into productive land, by emphasizing that this kind of transformation had only been achieved by the "English-speaking" conqueror, characteristically omitting the contributions of exploited Black, Chinese immigrant, and native labor. As Roosevelt tells it, this is what distinguished the Anglo colonist from other previous conquerors like the Dutch, who preferred "immediate gains" like those "derived from . . . trade with the Spice Islands" over the more arduous work of developing inland colonial interiors like those of North America, Australia, and New Zealand into productive land.[2] As such, though much of the initial interest in the Philippines was commercial, the most dramatic differences could be seen in the development of its interior. This conquest was, however, not attributable, as Roosevelt would have it, to the "work" of the white conqueror, but to the organizational capacities of corporations and the availability and use of modern technologies, both of which accelerated a transformation presented as an improvement of the entirety of the colony's land. Forests were transformed into frontier towns, mountains were made into mines, and great prairies were planted with waving oceans of grain. None of this would have been possible (or necessary) without the tandem development of the factory system, inland shipping routes, modernized roads, and the astonishing growth of the US rail network. It did not take long for US colonial administrators to realize the nation's strengths lay not only in the transportation of goods from port to port, but in cultivating internal connections between urban markets and rural development.[3] Indeed, Daniel Burnham's Manila, even if fully realized, would be a mere terminus for a colonial project conceived on a global scale—a totality designed to bring the colonial interior's minerals, tropical hardwoods, and a wide variety of agricultural products to the world market.

Concrete enabled the construction of this totality. Its world-altering capacities were placed on prominent display starting in 1904, when the United States took over a failed French attempt to construct the Panama Canal. Five million cubic meters of concrete and 250,000 tons of rebar were used to construct the manmade channel. Though no single infrastructural work in the Philippines consumed as much cement, the entire archipelago was transformed by modern concrete, which spread across its islands in tentacular networks of roads, irrigation systems, and vast urban surfaces. Concrete became so ubiquitous in the Philippines, in fact, that to describe it in terms of discrete projects would be to miss its most significant consequence—a totally transformed relationship between the land and those who lived on it.

Irrigation, "Land Reform," and the Corporation

One of William Cameron Forbes's first actions as governor-general of the Philippines was to fund the irrigation of lands belonging to the Barcelona-based Compañia General de Tabácos de Filipinas, or—as it was more popularly known—the Tabacalera. Founded in 1881 by Antonio López y López, a wealthy Spanish entrepreneur, the Tabacalera was a multinational joint-stock company and one of the world's most important enterprises in the late nineteenth and early twentieth centuries.[4] Though the irrigation canal was technically public, the Tabacalera was given prioritized access to it, on account of having provided easement for the canal's construction. As Forbes explained, it was because the Tabacalera owned the entirety of the land to be irrigated that he prioritized its construction as the first of 216 irrigation projects planned by the Bureau of Public Works (BPW). Revealing his preference for working with corporations, Forbes reasoned that the Tabacalera's singular control over the land "obviated the legal difficulties" that often faced irrigation projects with multiple small landholders. Indeed, the Hacienda Luisita (named after López's wife) was and still is the largest hacienda in the Philippines—40 percent larger than the area covered by the city of Manila, and still the epicenter of contentious land reform struggles in the Philippines.[5] Working directly with Philippine corporations, Forbes believed, would more quickly place them on equal standing with their US counterparts, a goal that he argued would ultimately benefit all of the peoples of the Philippines. Whether that would be the case or not, the construction of the irrigation canal diverted waters of nearby small landholders positioned downstream on the O'Donnell River, prompting a group of affected landholders to file suit against Hacienda Luisita in 1915. Demonstrating its reliably pro-corporation stance, the Supreme Court ruled in the Tabacalera's favor, and as a result many of the farmers were absorbed into tenancy on the Luisita estate.[6]

In the Philippines, Forbes aimed to perfect pro-corporation initiatives recently passed by the US Congress. Most directly, his irrigation plan seemed to be modeled after the Reclamation Act of 1902, which provided for the US government to enter the field of direct promotion of irrigation, eventually leading to the establishment of the Bureau of Reclamation (which oversees all federally funded irrigation projects).[7] The act was passed in the interest of encouraging Western settlement (especially the "waste" land of the arid American West), which had slowed in the face of climatic conditions inhospitable to smallholder farmsteading. Congressional intervention, in other words, began to extend beyond the legal work of land distribution, to take on the infrastructural work of "reclaiming" arid lands for the purpose of agricultural cultivation. The 1902 Reclamation Act built on earlier acts including the Desert Land Act of 1877 and the Carey Act of 1894, which among other things gave private irrigation companies easement rights through public lands. Forbes's irrigation projects went further by committing both financing and convict labor to develop land owned by private corporations. According to Forbes's plan, the irrigation system was built under the agreement that the Tabacalera would pay the government a fixed annual irrigation fee of ₱29,000. These fees included the cost of operation and maintenance, an amortized payment to recover the capital invested in construction, and a contingency charge to take care of unforeseen major repairs. Following a predetermined twenty- or forty-year period, during which the government's initial investment was recovered, ownership and operation of the system was to be turned over to landowners. Payments collected from landowners were to be used in the construction of other irrigation projects.[8] This arrangement outlined how, based on a centralized model of capital accumulation, the colonial state planned to underwrite and subsidize a corporate occupation of the land.

In early 1910, large crews descended on the worksite, cutting huge furrows into Tarlac's loamy earth, lining the newly cut ditches with an even layer of concrete (figure 5.1). Photographs of the worksite echoed, in miniature, photographs of the astonishing, simultaneous progress being made on the Panama Canal. In the images, native workers are diminished as tiny, albeit integral components of a massive industrial-agricultural machine operating on a global scale. Though an "extraordinary flood" in July 1911 destroyed the dam when it was 90 percent complete (greatly discrediting the irrigation division of the BPW), it was redesigned and completed by late 1913. By 1926, Forbes reported, the Luisita estate had produced 250,000 bushels of rice and 65,000 tons of sugar cane, a scale of production that enabled the Tabacalera to build one of the "largest and most modern sugar mills in the world."[9] Diverting waterways once freely accessible to small landowners, sharecroppers, and tenant farmers, the irrigation works also concretized a corporate claim on the land that was nearly impossible to reverse.

Images of public works projects published in the *Quarterly Bulletin* rarely included recognizable faces, emphasizing instead each body's integration into the featured project. Similarly, in images of the San Miguel irrigation works, faceless bodies are subsumed into a large and efficient machinery. It is in these images that one could see, perhaps most palpably, what Forbes envisioned as an indivisible capitalist system. Here Forbes's insistence that "capital and labor

FIGURE 5.1. Construction of irrigation works in Tarlac, Central Luzon, 1910. From *Quarterly Bulletin, Bureau of Public Works* 1, no. 2 (1913): 39.

are one" is given concrete form by operating in concert as a single, large assemblage.[10] The photograph below, taken on the project's completion, is particularly suggestive in that the composition (and the design of the spillworks itself) approximate a neoclassical temple front, an impression emphasized by the placement of the spill gate operators who stand like allegorical figures in the space of an implied pediment (figure 5.2). It was a powerful image that demonstrated what was made possible by combining modern engineering, financial planning, industrialized construction practices, and corporate consolidations of land and capital.

Roads, Prison Labor, and Counterrevolution

In Forbes's view, it was not enough to render the interior productive; the goods it produced had to be conveyed to the "best market," wherever in the world that might be. Put simply, developing the interior was pointless without roads.[11] As Director of Public Works James Beardsley noted, though the "development of coastwise transportation and of railroads connecting the centers of trade" was valuable, it was of "far greater importance to the development of an agricultural country" to build the archipelago's highways in order to service and connect

FIGURE 5.2. Head gates of the San Miguel Irrigation System. From *Quarterly Bulletin, Bureau of Public Works* 7, no. 2 (1918): 8.

its "interior areas."[12] Accordingly, the first act of the Philippine Commission, passed in September of 1900, appropriated $1 million for roads. In turn, US-trained civil engineers flooded the Philippines, taking positions as either Division Engineers (stationed in Manila at the BPW, where they produced standard designs for concrete bridges, culverts, and road sections), or as District Engineers, assigned to provinces to survey existing provincial roads (where they tested new methods of construction with local materials). Extensive systematic studies were conducted to determine the distribution and location of roads, as well as the class of roads to be built,[13] taking into account, among other metrics, the square area of country to be developed, the total population it would serve, the valuation of agricultural goods produced, projections of future revenue based on available agricultural land, and potential value of mineral and oil sections.[14] Once the projected traffic (or load) was determined, each road was allocated an amount of broken rock, gravel, or coral, at a depth calculated to sustain the number of wheels known to pass over it. Cement boxes were placed at even intervals and filled with deposits of approved road material.

The "class" of road built was based on a single, rigorously applied formula that set the "justified cost per kilometer" as less than or equal to the average number of wheels to pass over the surface multiplied by the assumed value of 2 centavos to users of the road for 1 kilometer per day multiplied by the total value of 1 kilometer of road to traffic per 360 days minus the estimated cost of maintenance per annum, capitalized at 4 percent. This formula accounted not only for the likely size of the provincial budget, but also (by taking into account the projected traffic) the required bearing capacity of the roads—which were divided into three classes, with third-class roads being of compacted aggregates, and second-class roads having deeper sections and a crown of macadam asphalt "formulated especially for the tropics by Standard Oil." This concoction was also placed atop first-class roads, which were strengthened by a subgrade of reinforced concrete.[15]

As with many of his projects, Forbes took advantage of his broad charge as commissioner of commerce and police. It was during his tenure in that position that commerce and policing were fully developed as complementary objectives. For example, for the road between Tabaco and Ligao, which was necessary to "tap a region productive of Manila Hemp," Forbes addressed labor shortages by "reliev[ing] the overcrowding in the Bureau of Prisons." For the project, Forbes organized "road-building camps" for "well-behaved prisoners . . . to work under guard provided by the army,"[16] a "method of construction" that, Forbes wrote, produced "one of the most beautiful roads on the archipelago." The same method was used for the notoriously precipitous Benguet Road, and subsequently for countless public works projects built throughout the archipelago.[17] For Forbes, this was not only a cost-efficient means of sourcing labor; it was an effective disciplinary and counterrevolutionary tool, aimed at reorienting the prison population (mostly incarcerated for their insurrectionary activity) toward productive activities.[18]

"Caminero Forbes"

Though the prisons were a significant source of labor, Forbes's ambition required the mobilization of nothing short of the archipelago's entire population. As such, the vast majority of road labor was secured by Forbes's reintroduction of an unpopular Spanish system of forced labor, known as the *polo y servicio*, which required every able-bodied man on the islands to give five days of labor each year on road construction or maintenance (or to pay a sum equivalent to the local cost of labor).[19] As Forbes understood, roads and reinforced concrete structures were only as permanent as they were carefully maintained. Thus, though it was "human nature to like to build new things" he emphasized the importance of "the less interesting, but even more necessary restoration of slow grinding wear of roads already built."[20] Toward this end Forbes organized the "*caminero* system," a system with which he was so closely associated that his nickname was "*caminero* Forbes" (also a play on his middle name). Based on a Spanish colonial system,[21] each *caminero* was assigned a small section (the length of which varied according to the road's traffic) and issued a red uniform with a brass badge riveted to the cap, along with a copy of the *Road Book* (1909), which introduced in simple though lofty terms the importance of the *caminero*'s work to civilization. It began:

> Road improvement immediately results in the improvement of the condition of all the people. Money spent on road improvement produces more real and useful results than money spent in any other way. Better education, better food, better houses, and better health conditions follow good roads. For these reasons all civilized countries are constantly improving their roads. . . . A country develops when the people can travel easily and move products to market easily. This can be done only when the roads are kept in good condition. . . . Good roads make it possible to sell at profit many things which it would not pay to haul to market over bad roads.[22]

Moving abruptly between the scale of the colony and that of each *caminero*'s small section, the *Road Book* detailed the responsibilities of the *caminero*, who was expected to walk over his section daily, filling every small crack; raking every loose stone; fighting water "all the time and by every means"; keeping account of materials; maintaining ditches, drains, and a perfect crown; and managing the tropics' ever-invasive vegetation—all while exercising police powers (mostly to prevent the use of bull carts or other vehicles that might impede the speed of modern traffic).

If properly executed, the *caminero*'s work might seem almost trivial, as his job was to address problems before they were apparent to those driving over the road. To emphasize the importance of the *caminero*'s work, the *Road Book* provided 32 illustrations of moralizing side-by-side scenarios dramatizing the destructive consequences of neglect (figure 5.3). In one scene, a tiny crack opens into an impassable gorge, while in another a carefully tamped road gives way to a puddle deep enough for a mother to bathe her child in public (signaling a breakdown in social order). Just as the smallest unit was significant to civilization, so would the smallest crack lead to civilization's collapse. In this way

FIGURE 5.3. Illustration demonstrating the importance of vigilant maintenance of roads, and the breakdown of social order that results in the absence of maintenance. From Bureau of Public Works, *Road Book* (Manila: Bureau of Printing, 1909).

the *caminero* system was shaped as a disciplinary practice. Cracks were seen as nothing short of moral failures—the beginning of a rapid devolution of a civilization gifted to the Filipinos by their benevolent colonizers.

Never viewing his work as limited to the colony itself, Forbes took pleasure in pointing out that the *caminero* system cost about a third of what it cost for a gang of laborers to repair a road when damage became intolerable (as was typical, Forbes emphasized, in "these backward United States").[23] The roads were not local projects, but conduits to a world market. The success of the insular road program was demonstrated, the BPW claimed, by an increase of traffic as high as 1000 percent, a phenomenal rate of growth that the BPW argued reflected the success of the system in terms of the "increased agricultural products which are now finding their way to market." The value of these goods in turn "increase(d) the value of the property near the road," benefitting, the *Road Book* claimed, not only landowners but "all classes of people." More settlement and more development of agricultural land followed, which in turn "justified a continuance" of road building and, presumably, the endless growth of the system.[24]

Pastoral Sequelae

If the story of Philippine roads sounds familiar, it is not by coincidence. It is what Ralph Waldo Emerson once prophesied as an American "sequel." In his words: "I hear the whistle of the locomotive in the woods. Wherever that music comes it has its sequel. It is the voice of the civility of the Nineteenth Century saying, 'Here I am.' It is interrogative: it is prophetic: and this Cassandra is believed: 'Whew! Whew! Whew! How is real estate here in the swamp and wilderness?'"[25]

William Cameron Forbes, who happened to be Emerson's grandson, aimed to fulfill this prophecy. Though inspired by Emerson's aestheticization of capitalism, Forbes's work in the Philippines was in more significant ways prefigured by the careers of his paternal grandfather, John Murray Forbes, perhaps the nineteenth century's most important railroad financier,[26] and by his father, William Hathaway Forbes, who—as president of the Bell Telephone Company—played a role in expanding the nation's next great network. William Cameron Forbes would settle for nothing less than identifying the next engine for American expansion. Believing he had found it in the Panama Canal, Forbes applied to the Canal Commission, but was passed over for military men and engineers. In that same year, however, Theodore Roosevelt appointed him to be the Philippines' commissioner of commerce and police. In that position, and later as governor-general, Forbes's aggressive infrastructural program was designed to integrate the colony, as quickly as possible, into a capitalist world economy. This was *the* colonial project as Forbes envisioned it. Devoted to the ideal of a free market, he argued that though the government could not itself "make prosperity . . . it can assist" by ensuring "the least possible obstruction to legitimate enterprise."[27] Though Forbes's characterization of his work suggests a sort of interventional minimalism, or even the *negative* work of removing "obstructions," in actuality his work entailed the construction of the largest and most ambitious infrastructural projects the archipelago had ever seen.

The scale at which Forbes operated is difficult to appreciate in the dry graphs, tables, charts, and reports published in the Bureau of Public Works's *Quarterly Bulletin*. Mixed in among that material, however, were brief poetic passages and dramatic photographs of the landscape—content that exceeded the *Bulletin*'s otherwise calculating tone. The inclusion of this self-consciously romanticized imagery of progress mobilized a landscape aesthetic that attempted to resolve the tensions between a tropical unknown and what was, even for the average American, a familiar image of the land's sublime transformation. Railways, roads, and bridges were entrenched parts of the visual culture of the

FIGURE 5.4. George Inness, *The Lackawanna Valley*, ca. 1856. Oil on canvas, 33 ⅞ × 50 ½ in. (86 × 127.5 cm). National Gallery of Art, Washington, DC.

American frontier, as perhaps most clearly illustrated in paintings like George Inness's *The Lackawanna Valley*—a now iconic painting with humble origins as an advertisement (for the Delaware, Lackawanna, and Western Railroad) (figure 5.4). As Leo Marx noted, the painting strikingly presented "machine technology . . . [as] a proper part of the landscape," providing an image of a distinctly American Arcadia that aestheticized an environment in harmonic balance with the advance of capitalism. The organic unity of nature and technology as represented in *Lackawanna Valley* was, by the opening of the Spanish-American War, a way of seeing deeply embedded in the American psyche. Starting around the middle of the nineteenth century, the inclusion of infrastructure became increasingly popular in both American landscape painting and in the transcendental literature of Thoreau and Emerson, where the machine existed not as an intrusion into a virgin landscape but as an inseparable cultural symbol of improvement, a pastoral cultivation eased by machines.

Whether he consciously invoked this aesthetic or not, the unnamed photographer of the Sabang Bridge (see figure 5.5) composed this image to present the road and bridge as extensions of the lyrical path forged by Inness's locomotive. Inness's composition, in Leo Marx's words, embraces new territory, assimilating antithetical images of nature and machine into a unified American composition bound together by the elegant curves of infrastructure. This pastoral image

FIGURE 5.5. Sabang Bridge on Batangas-Ibaan Road, Batangas, 1910. Library of Congress, Washington, DC, LC-USZ62-118734.

was, however, only a symbolic snapshot of a global system of circulation. The roads were conceived as only a part of a massive machinery that also included irrigation, sewage, and—of primary importance to Forbes—ports.

Mammoth, Portworks, and the American Sublime

Billed as the world's largest steel piledriver, Mammoth was a giant and sublime American thing. Brought to the Philippines in 1921 to construct what would be the longest covered pier in the world, Mammoth dwarfed in both size and power the mostly native force that manned it. In the carefully staged photograph in figure 5.6, what looks to be at least a hundred laborers pose atop Mammoth, diminutive against its massive scale. Though the Pacific was often referred to as the US's new "frontier," the image of Mammoth was an ill fit with the muscle-powered axes, shovels, plows, and hammers that were the symbolic lexicon of the often-invoked myth of the American frontiersman. US pioneering in the concrete age was enabled by an arsenal of fuel hungry, automated machines of steel—tractors, cranes, rock crushers, steam rollers, coal-powered

FIGURE 5.6. The pile driver "Mammoth," 1921, with its large crew. From *Bulletin, Bureau of Public Works* 9, no. 1 (1921): 23.

dredgers, automatic mixers, building systems, and giant piledrivers, all of which were, like Mammoth, poised to transform the colony into a fully integrated part of the modern and global economic engine.

Mammoth was only part of a massive machine assembled to construct Pier 7 in Manila (figure 5.7). Construction began at a temporary outdoor casting plant located at an adjacent site. Imported rebar and cement were cast into slender, 110-foot-long piles. Once cured, one of the "largest and finest cranes ever built" lifted the piles into open rail cars that then carried them to the construction site, where another pair of large cranes attached to Mammoth guided and loaded the piles under its steam-powered hammer. Once loaded Mammoth's hammer drove the piles into Manila Bay's unstable sea floor. When completed, Pier 7 possessed a capacity three times that of Manila's existing piers

FIGURE 5.7. Pile casting plant for Pier 7, Manila, 1921. Following the completion of the pier, the pile crane was used in the operation of the pier itself, handling cargo weighing as much as 80 tons. From the *Quarterly Bulletin, Bureau of Public Works* 8, no. 2 (1920): 18.

combined—capable of berthing the world's four largest vessels simultaneously. Claiming the title of longest covered pier in the world, it would enable, as Forbes had longed hoped, the Philippines to become the cornerstone of commerce in Asia.

The Filipinos who worked on the pier were folded into its image as Lilliputian figures manipulating a giant metal Gulliver. The project's "splendid progress," as celebrated in the *Far Eastern Review*, was the result of not only modern machinery, but a well-managed force of skilled mechanics, artisans, carpenters, and workers, who "as a whole . . . create[d] a smooth working organization of more than a thousand individuals."[28] Humans had become an attribute of the machine, scrambling atop mobile and exposed steel frameworks to form an open-air industrial spectacle the likes of which had never been seen in Manila. The leaders of the Insular Government were acutely aware of the importance of this dramatic image, and of the importance of the spectacle as viewed from the city itself. The dining veranda of the Manila Hotel offered a front row seat in a theater of modernization that unfolded before a captive audience of foreign investors.

Pier 7's construction reproduced an American system of belief in a national greatness induced by the individual's experience of immense public projects. As David Nye argues, by the early nineteenth century, large public works projects had already become inseparable from an American conception of self. This identification was enhanced by the fact that these technological objects and landscapes had not only radically transformed the environments in which they were situated, but—in even more significant ways—forever altered everyday lives, bringing electricity to American homes, water to their taps, more dependable crops, and a seemingly limitless variety of products from far-off places to local store shelves. The 300-mile-long Erie Canal, for example, completed in 1825 and built in only eight years, more than doubled the volume of east-west trade in its first year of operation. It also stimulated urban development along its banks and accelerated westward migration. It made western agricultural produce available to eastern cities and acted as a powerful political link that permanently and materially bound the Great Lakes region to the East.[29] It was a feat repeated and expanded by streams of westward rail, by telegraph, interstate roads, and so on. Pier 7 was yet another node in this serial history, inserting itself into already existing East-West and intra-Asian shipping lanes. As with the Erie Canal, this was not just a symbolic link, but one that structurally and materially unified the United States with a Far-Eastern colonial unit that was just one part of the US empire's ever-expanding hinterlands.

When the pier was complete, it assumed a very different public appearance than the one presented by Mammoth (figure 5.8). Designed by Tomás Bautista Mapúa, the Beaux Arts pierhead recalled Warren and Wetmore's Chelsea Piers project in New York City, built just a decade earlier in 1910. As with the earlier design, Mapúa's neoclassical pierhead eased the disjunction between the industrial construction of the pier itself and its public, urban face. A sorting device that separated streams of passengers and flows of goods, the pierhead was just tall enough and wide enough to conceal the machines that lay behind it— tower cranes that lifted the interior's extracted material loads onto ships bound for global distribution.

In the same year that Mammoth arrived in the Philippines,[30] Forbes published *The Romance of Business*, a book in which he presented "the whole story of our business development." The book's frontispiece, a drawing by Aiden Lassell Ripley, a little-known Boston artist, presents an aesthetic that differs markedly from Inness's naturalization of the machine (figure 5.9). Ripley depicts a family dressed in loincloths, huddling around a fire in front of a primitive hut. The male leader of the family stares across a foreshortened ocean. In the distance, a skyline—seemingly without foundation—floats above the clouds,

FIGURE 5.8. Tomás Bautista Mapúa, Pier 7 bulkhead, completed 1926. From *Bulletin, Bureau of Public Works* 15, no. 1 (1927): 22.

dwarfing the landscape that unfolds before it. American technology appears here not as a coal-powered machine, but as an imposing and powerful opposition between an expansive nature and the looming metropolis that threatens to overcome it. The caption reads, "half-naked creatures in crazy shelters of grass, mud and leaves." Here the native is offered a choice—between the insanity of their "crazy" shelters, and the vertically extruded frontier, presented here as both an inevitable and more civilized modernity. To choose the metropolis in the air was depicted here not only as the logical choice but as the overwhelming reality of American power. We cannot see the man's face—nor do we need to. The sublime takes root in a universal human capacity for astonishment, crowding out the ability to imagine any expression other than awe or terror.

The city depicted is not an industrial city—there are no smokestacks, no silos, and no scaffolds. Rather, the skyline reflects an accumulation of financial capital. Heavy industry takes the form of a distant memory, vaguely represented by a billowing and restive steam that mysteriously emanates from several layers of middle ground. Though hazily rendered, that middle ground—a flat prairie cut through by a serpentine river, rolling hills, and a perfectly conical mountain—depicts an unmistakably American landscape. Here, Ripley offers the culminating experience of a storied American capitalism. Indeed, the title of Forbes's book is not *The Romance of Industry*, but *The Romance of Business*. Native submission is depicted here as a positive affirmation of capitalism's "vast

FIGURE 5.9. Aiden Lassell Ripley, frontispiece of William Cameron Forbes's *The Romance of Business* (Boston: Houghton Mifflin, 1921).

increase of power."[31] The classical architecture that eventually came to symbolize US colonial rule in the Philippines bears little relation to the colossal concrete mass approaching the generic native family (are they Filipino or Native American? It hardly matters). The city approaches, longing to close the gap between itself and the native transfixed by its arrival.

The realities of modernization in the Philippines looked nothing like the fantasy of development depicted in Forbes's *Romance*. Settled centuries before Spanish arrival in 1571, by the time Dewey's fleet arrived in Manila it was a cosmopolitan metropolis of approximately 200,000 people, some of whom had already elaborated on their own visions of modernity. One such vision, that of Isabelo de los Reyes was published in the newspaper *El Renacimiento* in January 1903. Nearly two years before Burnham's arrival, Reyes described a modernized city that in many ways anticipated Burnham's Manila plan, including the razing of Intramuros's walls; wide shaded boulevards; electric streetcars; and sidewalks populated with lively bazaars, newspaper stands, and places for refreshment.[32] His ideas were drawn from experience. De los Reyes lived in Barcelona following his release from Montjuïc, where—just before the outbreak of the Spanish-American War—he was held on charges of fomenting revolution. In the company of anarchists and Republicans, he grew familiar with Barcelona's Eixample—the city's modern extension.[33] Traveling around Europe, he observed the modernizations of Paris, Bordeaux, and Madrid, and in those cities, the daily interactions between the working class and the rising bourgeoisie. In the article, de los Reyes asks if this modernity is not the kind of improvement that Filipinos should expect from the United States. The subtlety of his anticipatory criticism is easy to miss. Reyes's desire and demand for modernization scrambles commonplace narratives about the direction of development, countering sublime images of American power with a native claim to a right to the city—a city that was not merely the result of market forces (the end point of a system that exports the extracted riches of a dispossessed countryside)—but also a source for the pleasures of social interaction, of new possibilities for a citizenry not bound to a fantasy of the unchanging nature of indigenous life, but rather open to new possibilities.[34] Though de los Reyes's specific vision was born out of an exceptional life experience, it demonstrates that Philippine natives did not (as Ripley's illustration suggests) view themselves as captive to an overwhelming modernity. Rather, they increasingly saw themselves as agents within it.

6

LIQUIDITY

AN INTERLUDE ON
PORTLAND CEMENT

Portland cement was not manufactured in the Philippines until 1914—a remarkable fact given that almost as soon as Daniel Burnham left the archipelago in late 1904, reinforced concrete was being used for permanent government projects, "to the practical exclusion of other building material."[1] The reason for the delay in building a cement manufactory in the Philippines was simple: Cement was, by the time of Burnham's arrival, already widely available in the region and affordably priced. Beating those prices was unlikely, as nearby sources—Japan, which began manufacturing cement in 1873 (the same year as the United States); the British concessions, which operated a plant in Macau since 1886; and French Indochina, which opened a cement plant in the port city of Haiphong in 1899—all held significant comparative advantages when it came to cement production, enjoying access to cheaper fuel, cheaper labor, or both than the Philippines had.[2] Though not a regional supplier, Germany (which produced roughly twice as much cement as it consumed) also exported significant quantities of cement to the Philippines, where the German product was favored for its high and consistent quality (largely the result of state-controlled standards) and for liberal credit arrangements.[3] Remarkably, the United States did not export significant amounts of Portland cement to its colony, furnishing just eight barrels of Portland cement to the Philippines in 1913.[4] Regional prices were difficult to outdo, even though US cement entered Philippine ports free of the 60-centavos-per-barrel tariff placed on all "foreign" (i.e., non-US) cement—a tax that would have been a considerable source of revenue for the colonial government, considering how much foreign cement was imported. In addition to this tax benefit to the colony, a strong domestic market for US cement, existing supplier relationships, the availability of regional product, and an up-to-10 percent loss of product in shipping kept US cement at bay.[5] Though creating a market for US manufactures was in general a motivating force for retaining the colony, margins on Portland cement were negligible if compared, for example, to higher-margin steel reinforcement systems like the Kahn bar (which dominated the Philippine market).[6]

Just a year before the first cement plant opened in the Philippines, Woodrow Wilson had been sworn into office, as the first Democratic president since Grover Cleveland. *Nacionalistas* rejoiced—an anti-imperialist stance had been part of the Democratic Party platform since 1901. Though Wilson did not pass legislation to recognize Philippine independence until 1916, he and Francis Burton Harrison, his appointee as the governor-general, began to lay the groundwork for a transition toward national sovereignty by, on the one hand, preparing the fledgling nation for political independence (a history of "nation building" addressed most substantively in chapter 8), and on the other hand by developing its economy (addressed in this chapter and chapter 7). The push to open a cement plant and other industrial factories was part of Wilson's drive to accelerate what we now refer to as "economic development." To a certain extent, economic development (as the keystone of a more broadly defined race development) had always been central to the colonial project in the Philippines. William Cameron Forbes and other retentionist Republicans, however, believed that direct sovereignty over the Philippines yielded better advantages toward this end. Forbes's position was, however, far easier to maintain in 1909 than it was in 1914, when the US's moral objection to German imperial aggression made the retention of an overseas colony untenable. More importantly, by this time, leaders in the United States began to realize that the economic advantages rendered by colonialism could be achieved without the significant ethical liabilities or fiscal expenses of maintaining an overseas colony. This realization did not happen all at once, but was the result of years of learning from colonial practice, as demonstrated by the regional cultivation of the Portland cement industry in which the United States exerted extra-colonial influence over a broad geographical area—all without entangling itself in the contradictions of a colony ruled by a liberal democracy.

Though cement was not produced in the Philippines, the US colonial government was deeply invested in regional production, strongly motivated by the key role the material played in achieving US colonial objectives. In 1906 the Bureau of Science established a cement testing laboratory to, on the one hand, test the effects of local sand, aggregates, and water on concrete admixtures (figure 6.1), and on the other, to test the quality of imports of Portland cement, which at the beginning of the twentieth century was a highly variable product, with no global production standards to speak of.[7] It was out of necessity, then, that American scientists evaluated the quality of every shipment of imported cement—chemically analyzing, sifting, and steaming samples, and subjecting test ingots to a variety of load-bearing trials.[8] By 1918 ten thousand samples of Portland Cement were tested every year. Not long after testing began, the Bureau of Science found that product consistency was especially a problem with cement from French Indochina and British Macau. Walter C. Reibling (head of the Bureau of Science's Division of General and Inorganic Chemistry) decided to address the increasingly expensive problem in two ways. The first was to visit and inspect regional manufacturers, and to offer "practical suggestions" (what we might today call technical assistance) to improve product quality. The second was to create a "bonus system for the purchase of Portland cement"—in which the Insular Government would "set a standard specification below which no cement should be accepted"—while at the same time rewarding cement "which is far superior to the specification" with a price "in proportion to its superiority."[9] This unusual regulatory tactic was Reibling's attempt to bring regional producers into alignment with US standards in the absence of legal recourse. This was just one example of the ways that US colonialism spread beyond the geopolitical framework of the colony itself, exerting its influence on the development of the region. In this way, the "colonial" work of the Philippine Bureau of Science prefigured extra- and supra-sovereign forms of "postcolonial" governance.

Ultimately unsatisfied with the pace of regional development, the Bureau of Science intensified an often tabled pursuit of developing a Portland cement industry in the Philippines. Preliminary investigations actually dated back to 1908, when the bureau conducted extensive studies of cement "field relations"[10] on three potential manufacturing sites: one on the centrally located island of Cebu; one in the town of Binangonan in the Rizal province, just 30

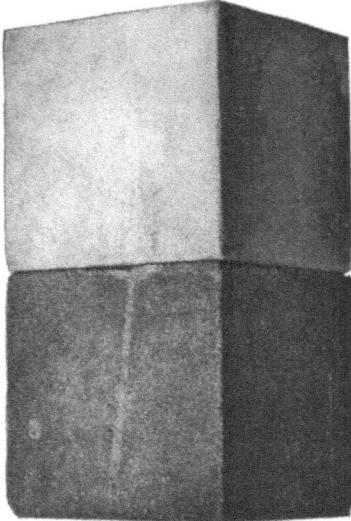

Fig. 1. Sand-lime brick made from Talim basalt quarry débris.
Beautiful, polished, strong, dense "artificial marbles"
can be made from this material.

Fig. 2. Sand-lime brick made from Maytubig beach sand.
A compressive strength of 3,840 pounds per square inch
was obtained without grinding any of the sand.

FIGURE 6.1. Concrete bricks using different local sands: (*left*) "Sand-lime brick made from Talim basalt quarry débris. Beautiful, polished, strong, dense 'artificial marbles' can be made from this material." (*right*) "Sand-lime brick made from Maytubig beach sand. A compressive strength of 3,840 pounds per square inch was obtained without grinding any of the sand." From Alvin J. Cox, *Eleventh Annual Report of the Bureau of Science* (Manila: Bureau of Printing, 1913), n.p.

kilometers southeast of Manila; and one on the island of Palawan at the Iwahig penal colony. In Cebu, the Bureau of Science found large deposits of an "impure coralline limestone," the natural composition of which "approaches very closely to that of a raw mixture for Portland cement" (figure 6.2). This "exceedingly soft" limestone was located adjacent to existing railroads, natural harbor facilities, and clay deposits, and just a few miles from "undeveloped deposits of coal . . . (that) could be successfully used for burning Portland cement in rotary kilns."[11]

The site in Rizal was considered a promising one for a factory (albeit still inferior to Cebu). There, a "practically pure crystalline limestone" (harder and more difficult to mine) was found close to a deposit of andesitic tuff. Coal, meanwhile, would be shipped upstream from Manila. The principal advantage of the third site, at Iwahig, was a readily available large and cheap labor force,

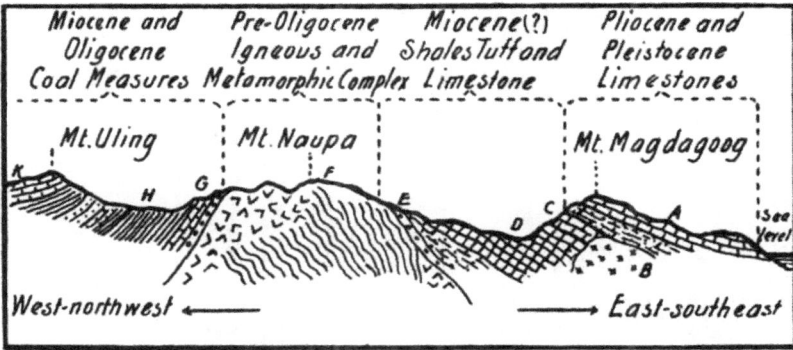

FIGURE 6.2. Cross section showing coal and limestone deposits on the island of Cebu. From Wallace E. Pratt, "Geology and Field Relations of Portland Cement Raw Materials at Naga Cebu," *Philippine Journal of Science* 9, no. 2 (1914): 153.

in addition to large deposits of fine coralline sand that could be mixed with the local clay (from which prisoners were already manufacturing brick). In locating and drawing up reports for each site, the Bureau of Science (which also kept meticulous records of domestic demand) acted as a prospector, providing for the potential investor everything they needed to know to set up a cement plant.[12] All that was missing, it seems, was capital.

Taking advantage of the report, Augustinian Recollects, under the leadership of Father Juan Labargo, opened a factory on the Binangonan site with financial backing from the Vatican. Incorporating in December of 1911, the Rizal Cement Company purchased the quarries and factory sites and sent (most likely on the recommendation of the Bureau of Science) two representatives to Germany (generally regarded as producing the best quality cement) to investigate cement-mill machinery. The mill machinery contract was awarded to Friedrich Krupp, with several other German manufacturers awarded contracts for barrel-making machinery, an aerial cableway (to transport the limestone from the quarry to the plant), electrical equipment, and a power plant.

In July 1914—the same month that Austria-Hungary declared war on Serbia—the Rizal Cement Company produced its first barrels of cement (figure 6.3). This coincidence ultimately led to the company's demise, as it was almost wholly on account of World War I that the Rizal Cement Company failed after less than five years of operation, going into receivership in March 1919 and completely halting production just four months later.[13] Though fingers were pointed at both laborers, who were "given to strikes on the slightest

Fig. 1. Raw materials from Naga, Cebu, and the Portland clinker, cement, and concrete produced.

PLATE II.

Fig. 2. Raw materials from Naga, Cebu, and the Roman clinker, cement, and concrete produced.

FIGURE 6.3. First Portland cement manufactured from Philippine raw materials: (*left*) "Raw materials from Naga, Cebu, and the Portland clinker, cement, and concrete produced." (*right*) "Raw materials from Naga, Cebu, and the Roman clinker, cement, and concrete produced." From W. C. Reibling and F. D. Reyes, "The Efficiency of Portland Cement Raw Materials from Naga, Cebu," *Philippines Journal of Science* 9, no. 2 (1914): pl. 2.

provocation," and managers, who were accused of improper treatment of labor, the largest factor was undoubtedly the astronomical surge in the price of coal, the availability of which, political economists argued, "constituted a sine qua non for carrying on the war."[14] In February 1917, when the United States cut off diplomatic ties with Germany, the price of coal rose from ₱11 per ton to ₱60,[15] a market "disturbance" that affected every industrial enterprise across the globe, including the Rizal Cement Company.[16] Although the price of Rizal cement rose along with the global market price, and despite the fact that demand for Portland cement in the Philippines remained high, there was simply not enough coal available to run the plant efficiently or cost effectively.

As a direct result of the high cost and scarcity of cement, during the war the Bureau of Public Works (BPW) spent on average ₱3 million a year in excess of its annual budget. Though dramatically high, the exorbitant cost of construction was not an indication of the colony's overall economic performance. In fact, the war brought unprecedented prosperity to the islands. Abacá (made into rope), sugar, coffee, tobacco, and coconut charcoal (used in gas masks) were all in high demand. Revenue from Philippine exports surged by 5.6 percent between 1915 and 1917.[17] Both a boon and a burden for the archipelago's economy, the war revealed just how globally integrated the Philippines had become. However, dependence on foreign cement and coal was of particular concern to Governor-General Harrison for the threat it posed to Philippine security and development. Though he recognized that prices would eventually fall after the war, Harrison determined that the "the Philippines should never again be caught in this awkward position."[18] Indeed, what Harrison meant was that a nation's ability to isolate itself economically by producing its own strategically important commodities—a development strategy now referred to as "import substitution"—was not only a measure of national sovereignty, but a means to secure it. Thus, it was in the interest of shoring up Philippine "independence" that Harrison formed what he called "government auxiliaries" (essentially state-owned enterprises), the first of which would be national coal and cement companies. In the immediate term, this was done to support BPW projects and to save the flailing Manila Railroad Company (which was also nationalized at the time); in the longer term, it was conceived as a means of training native captains of industry. Harrison's dirigiste turn "demanded," he argued, "a good deal of moral courage, because it expose[d] the administration to [the] constant sniping [of] . . . those whose financial interests are affected," which, in the case of the cement company, were "the importers of Japanese cement and the owners of the defunct cement plant [in Binangonan]."[19]

The plan for the cement factory was to approach a "prominent American cement man" to set up a plant "with government money, giving him the right to purchase at the end of a certain date, under a perpetual contract to furnish cement to the Government at cost plus ten percent."[20] This arrangement, Harrison argued, was expected to save the government as much money per year as it had originally invested. Though the Cebu Portland Cement Company (CEPOC) shared certain features of nationally owned enterprises, under the arrangement described by Harrison, the "expertise" of the American businessman earned him the "right" to purchase the cement factory. That is to say, though Harrison's government auxiliaries were presented as being developed in the interest of Filipinos, it was a scheme that did not preclude the accumulation of profits on the part of American capitalists. Thus, though Philippine concrete was presented as thoroughly nationalized (minus imported steel reinforcement), it was a "nationalization" intended first and foremost to sustain the reproduction of American capital.[21]

Incorporating in March 1922, and setting up operations in Naga, Cebu, CEPOC's manufactory was capitalized by the Philippine National Bank and the Philippine Development Corporation (also government auxiliaries established under Harrison), which invested nearly ₱3 million in the operation. C. F. Massey, a Chicago businessman who owned and operated a company specializing in precast reinforced concrete products, filled the role of "prominent American cement man." As already identified by the Bureau of Science, most of the raw materials needed for the factory were in close proximity to the factory site, with the exception of gypsum, which was shipped from Batangas. The Philippine government immediately moved to protect the fledgling industry by raising the foreign cement tariff by 100 percent, from ₱0.60/barrel to ₱1.20/barrel. As specified in the initial arrangement, Massey owned a majority stake in the company until 1924, when he was bought out on account of "administrative difficulties and high costs of supervision."[22] Soon afterward, CEPOC turned a profit, recouping the government's initial investment and earning enough capital to expand and modernize the factory.[23] Its success, however, relied on state sponsorship and protectionist measures, without which the fledgling industry would be unable to compete with long-established foreign firms.

CEPOC's success seemed to pose a problem, though: Permanent state ownership was ideologically incompatible with liberal objectives, and especially with the Republican free-market orthodoxy that had governed colonial policy since at least the establishment of civil government in 1902. Economic autonomy was, however, nearly impossible to achieve without state sponsorship, and foreign capital was unlikely to invest in sites lacking in comparative advantages. This was made evident in 1921, when Republicans attempted to reverse Harrison and Wilson's development strategies by "get(ting) government out of business."[24] Plagued by the uncertainties of the colony's future political status, Republicans—led by Governor-General Leonard Wood—failed to sell a single state-owned enterprise. In fact, CEPOC remained under government ownership for more than seventy years (though the reasons for retaining CEPOC changed over time). Because CEPOC produced reliable dividends, the debate over its sale centered around benefits that accrued to the government rather than an ideological commitment to the "market."[25]

Though CEPOC was eventually privatized, state-owned enterprises (SOEs) have endured as a developmental tool, regardless of a country's ideological orientation—playing just as large a role in market-oriented countries as they do in socialist countries or where interventionist policies have been historically strong.[26] Following protracted controversy over CEPOC's possible sale, the Mexican multinational CEMEX acquired the company in 1999. Though a full account of SOEs in the Philippine context or in the ambit of the larger international financial community is beyond the scope of this chapter (and indeed this book as a whole), the history of CEPOC illustrates the economically functional role that the nation plays in development, alongside global contingencies and transnational dynamics. This complexity is composed of local aggregates extracted with foreign machinery, and is bound together by a globally circulating cement that swirls about the archipelago and its surrounding seas in curling eddies of regional relationships. Parsing the aggregate monolith scrambles the discursive oppositions—the local versus the global, the colony versus the postcolonial nation-state, interventionist versus market-oriented policies, and nationalist versus internationalist ideologies—revealing their entanglements and common origins.

7

ARTIFICE

THE "BASTARD" MATERIAL AND

A LEGITIMATION CRISIS

Reinforced Concrete while structurally excellent is artistically bastard [and] . . . is admitted by the architectural profession to be the least desirable of all masonry materials. Its natural color is gray and lacking in vibrant quality capable of producing pleasurable color sensations. Furthermore, while the natural effect of time upon accepted building stones produces a weathering beneficial to their tone quality, the effect of weathering upon concrete is decidedly detrimental, and results in a more unsightly and depressing aspect than is presented by the newly constructed material. . . . Since the construction of genuine ashlar stone exteriors is impossible at the present time, a synthetic artificial stone has been devised comprising granulated particles of handsome local marbles mixed with cement in such proportions as to make the marble particles completely preponderant. The surface of this product, being tooled to expose the actual marble aggregate, produces a vibrant color tone, by virtue of the exposed particles of marble, and resembles in mass the appearance of white marble or cream warm limestone . . . and responds to the gorgeous colorings of tropical sunlight. —RALPH HARRINGTON DOANE, "Architecture in the Philippines"

On the eve of his departure as the last American consulting architect to serve the Philippine Insular Government, Ralph Harrington Doane summed up his thoughts and experiences in the article "Architecture in the Philippines," first published in the *Quarterly Bulletin, Bureau of Public Works*.[1] There he described the artificial stone he developed for use in the archipelago's monumental civic building programs. Once released from its formwork Doane's stone revealed the same smooth and dull gray finish of the reinforced concrete already omnipresent on the archipelago, indistinguishable from the surfaces of the colony's increasingly ubiquitous water towers, bridges, roads, culverts, sewers, and warehouses. Gray is concrete's natural color, a color not bound to place (though modern cement is named after its resemblance to the stone of Portland, England) but to a standardized process of industrial production. With the aid of a pneumatic bush hammer, Doane chipped away concrete's unrelieved gray to reveal an otherwise concealed ingredient—a Philippine stone of a quality and description comparable, Doane effused, to Botticino marble, a prized Italian variety favored by Palladio (figure 7.1).

Doane's reference to concrete as a "bastard" material was motivated by more than his hatred of its "depressing" appearance. His comparison of concrete, born of an illegitimate union of natural and industrially produced components, to the white marble of civilization exposed both deep general anxieties about the industrialization of architectural production and specific anxieties related to the task laid out for him in the Philippines. Regarding the latter, Doane arrived to the Philippines at the very moment that the US colonial project faced a legitimation crisis. Colonial retention had become nearly as unpopular in the United States as it was in the Philippines. Moral outrage among US citizens over German imperial aggression was difficult to justify in light of the US's own maintenance of a distant annexed territory. Moving to fulfill a campaign promise and eager to rid himself of this contradiction, Woodrow Wilson pushed legislation to relinquish colonial sovereignty over the Philippines. During his first annual message to Congress Wilson declared that "in the Philippines . . . we must hold steadily in view their independence, and we must move toward the time of that independence as steadily as the way can be cleared and the foundations thoughtfully and permanently laid."[2]

Wilson's speech presented a vision of a slow and methodical process, not of disassembly, but of building. Indeed, the US's withdrawal from the Philippines did not result, as one might expect, in a contraction of an American building program. Instead, Doane debuted a revised architectural agenda that was in many ways far more ambitious than that carried out by the prior Republican regime. To the casual observer, the structures addressed in this chapter are barely

FIGURE 7.1. Doane's artificial stone. The left half of the sample is bush hammered to reveal marble aggregate. From *Quarterly Bulletin, Bureau of Public Works* 7, no. 2 (1918): 2.

distinguishable from the simultaneously built replicas addressed in chapter 4. The buildings discussed here are, however, distinguished by their uniqueness, by their conspicuously elaborate ornamentation, and by Doane's use of his specially formulated artificial stone, all part of an attempt to suppress an industrial expression of concrete. Though replication and this more lavish mode of architectural production might be seen as being at odds, they were, by Doane's own admission, economically complementary. As Doane points out, the extra expense to build these structures was not accommodated by a bigger budget; rather, he "appl[ied] funds saved on one building to another."[3] That is to say, though Doane lamented relenting to "standardization," the savings rendered by replication enabled him to address a new representational task, namely, to monumentalize what Wilson designed as a highly ritualized process of decolonization. The significance of this process, and of the crystallization of what I have termed the "pre–postcolony," was not limited to what it meant to Filipinos and within the Philippines. Rather, it was intended to broadcast Wilson's proposal for the world's new postimperial order.

The Last American Architect

A recent graduate (class of 1912) of the Massachusetts Institute of Technology (MIT), Doane arrived to the Philippines in 1916—a full three years after Woodrow Wilson's first inauguration. Wilson's delay in appointing both Doane and dozens of other key civil service positions in the Philippines was due not only to the exigencies of World War I, but also because Wilson was reluctant to make changes in colonial governance without first fulfilling his campaign promise to pass legislation that would initiate the transition toward Philippine independence. Doane's appointment came immediately after the passage of the Jones Law in 1916—the US's first formal commitment to Philippine independence, which had gained Congressional approval under Wilson's persuasive influence (figure 7.2).

The preamble of the Jones Law stated that the goal of the United States was "to withdraw sovereignty over the Philippine Islands and to recognize their independence as soon as a stable government can be established therein."[4] The inherent tension within this transitional arrangement was, as historian Erez Manela points out, that the "civilizing" power had to stay in order to allow it to eventually leave.[5] Under the terms of the Jones Law—which included no timeline for withdrawal—US colonial sovereignty was re-presented as a finite process with an indeterminate duration—the conclusion of which was contingent on the Philippines' meeting a set of requirements laid out by the United States. Operating as a symbolic corollary to the Jones Law, Doane's architecture had to signal a change in colonial status, without signifying the full privileges of national sovereignty. Though intended to be "transitional," Doane's architecture took the form of a positive, permanent, and monumental image—a gesture simultaneously intended to establish a permanent reminder of the US's "benevolence" and to demonstrate through its lavishness the sincerity of the promise enshrined in the Jones Law. That these monuments were actually built made the fulfillment of the promise seem imminent if not partially realized. But how might these symbols of "independence"—made out of the same material as the buildings before it and which are to some degree stylistically similar to those buildings—be substantially differentiated from the architecture of US colonialism?

FIGURE 7.2. *La Gloriosa Ley Jones* (The glorious Jones Law). Graphite drawing by Fernando Amorsolo, ca. 1916. Pictured (*left to right*): Governor-General Francis B. Harrison, Congressman William A. Jones (author of the Jones Bill), President Woodrow Wilson, Manuel Quezon (president, Philippine Senate), Sergio Osmeña (speaker, Philippine House of Representatives), and Manuel Earnshaw (resident commissioner). (*top*) A personification of the Philippines rises above the Ayuntamiento (old Spanish hall of government), holding an olive branch and a cornucopia. Her banner reads "Wilson Victorioso, Filipinias Agradecida" (Wilson Victorious, the Philippines, Grateful). Private collection of Ramon Villegas.

Doane's appointment was unusual in that it defied the stated policies of the Wilson administration, which under the direction of his newly appointed governor-general, Francis Burton Harrison, began the transition to Philippine independence by aggressively recruiting Filipinos into all levels of government—a process referred to as "Filipinization." The process began with the first archipelago-wide elections for both houses of the Philippine Legislature, and was set to conclude with the replacement of all civil service positions with Filipinos.[6] That the role of the consulting architect was reserved for an American demonstrates the delicacy and perceived importance of Doane's task. Certainly, appointing a Filipino would have been possible, as the Pensionado program had yielded several talented American-trained Filipino architects—already working at the Bureau of Public Works (BPW). Whether the appointee would be Filipino or not, the passage of the Jones Law created an awkward task for the consulting architect, who was called on to shape the image not of the United States, nor of the Philippines as such, but of a more nebulous, pre–postcolonial relationship. Tasked with rendering the transition to independence as an intentionally conspicuous process, Doane's architecture aimed to substantiate what the Jones Law described as the US's "always noble" and "never self-aggrandizing" intentions toward the Philippines.

Wilsonianism and Character (Moral and Architectural)

In order to understand the full weight and nature of Doane's assignment, it is useful to examine some details particular to Wilson's presidency and political philosophy, and specifically as they relate to the Philippines. In 1900, when Wilson was still a history professor at Princeton, one of his former students wrote to him, inquiring how the principle of self-government might apply to the Philippines. In a reply that resonated with his racist objections to the Civil War Amendments, Wilson argued that "'the Consent of the Governed' is part of a constitutional theory which has, so far, been developed only or chiefly with regard to . . . established systems of government," and did not apply to "politically undeveloped races which have not yet learned the rudiments of self-control." Thus, Wilson concluded, the "'consent' of the Filipinos and the 'consent' of American colonists to government . . . are two radically different things—not in theory, perhaps, but in practice."[7] Six months later, in an article published in the *Atlantic Monthly* in 1901, Wilson publicized his sentiments, writing, "We should not hand over to the Filipinos complete individual liberty or the full fangled institutions of self-government" which would be, "a purple garment for their nakedness . . . not blessings, but a curse, to undeveloped peoples, still in the childhood of their political growth."[8] As Wilson went on to write in the *Atlantic* in 1902, it was therefore America's responsibility to teach "backwards nations" "the discipline of law . . . [and] love [of] order," because "we are . . . old in this learning and must be their tutors."[9]

The Philippines would follow, Wilson argued, the pattern of the United States, which owed the strength of its character to the tutelage of English colonial rule. This remarkable claim aligned with Wilson's philosophy of history, the central principle of which was that *real* history was constituted not by war or revolution but by "the slow processes by which we grew and made our thought and formed our purpose in quiet days of peace." It is only during these moments of repose that national character develops, though only under the watchful eye of "tutors" and "masters." The American Revolutionary War, Wilson quipped, "had not made a nation, but only freed a group of colonies."[10] In Wilson's view, American independence was a "habit" or temperament passed from England to the United States, and not a political status wrested from England. Wilson's version of American history radically deviated from the still dominant narrative of the United States as a revolutionary republic. By disparaging revolution, and by valorizing English colonial rule, Wilson told the history of the United States from the perspective of those once viewed as its oppressors. This was not only the twisted outcome of his pernicious Anglophilia, but also the rhetorical foundation of a cultural and racial hierarchy that governed Wilson's political thought and action.

Wilson's political philosophy was underpinned by the ideas of Sir Edmund Burke, whose trustee model of representation was born out of Burke's distrust of the uneducated masses. As such, the trustee model (in opposition to a delegate model) relied on the morality and strength of character of government representatives as educated and uncorruptible individuals. *Trusteeism* was especially applicable relative to colonies—that is to say, in the absence of popular representation.[11] Wilson's colonial trusteeism is distinguished from Burke's in that he presented it within an explicitly developmental framework, in his writing in the *Atlantic*. As preparation for eventual independence Wilson proposed a program of character development to "moralize [the Filipinos] by being . . . moral, elevate and steady them by being . . . pure and steadfast." In this way, Wilson maintained, the institutions of liberty and democracy would take hold as an *ethical* standard—"as effect, not cause, in the order of political growth."[12] Extending his argument several months later, Wilson criticized those who demanded "that we give the Philippines independence and self-government now." Granting "independence" was for Wilson more than a political status, but was rather a question of character. "How," he asked, "is self-government

FIGURE 7.3. General Robert E. Lee, his neoclassical Virginia home, and a caricatured Black man. From the illustrated edition of Woodrow Wilson's *A History of the American People* (New York: Harper & Bros., 1902).

'given'? *Can* it be given? Is it not gained, earned, graduated into from the hard school of life?"[13]

In addition to expressing his views in the *Atlantic*, in 1902 Wilson completed a massive five-volume history of the United States titled *A History of the American People*. Though comprehensive in its coverage of politics and society, the entire book was organized around a central theme: the origins and development of American character. Part history, part bildungsroman, Wilson's book dramatized the character formation of the "American People" (by which he means white Americans) against the incursion of "foreign" and "savage" peoples. Though Wilson couches his racism in the elliptical pretensions of his long-winded prose, the book's illustrations make a more candid point. In a manner that recalls Viollet-le-Duc's pairings of racialized men and their dwellings in *The Habitations of Man in All Ages*, which I discuss in chapter 1, dignified portraits of Jefferson Davis and Robert E. Lee are placed next to illustrations of the Confederate capitol building and of Lee's Greek Revival home. These images are in turn succeeded by racist caricatures of Black Americans (figure 7.3).[14] Depicted as vagrants, the subjects of these cartoonish sketches are left unpaired with a distinguishing architecture. As the blunt force of the images demonstrates, ideas of character were more easily *embodied* than they were translated into colonial (or domestic) policy. That is architecture, as something that could itself possess character, was a medium uniquely poised to fulfill Wilson's political aims. To be sure, Doane was not starting from scratch—the discourse on architectural character had been a mainstay of architectural theory since at least the late eighteenth century. Still, Doane's task to characterize the transition to national sovereignty is extraordinary if not unique, and a consideration of his work introduces unexamined dimensions of the architectural discourse on character.[15]

An "Architectural Policy": Soft Power Between "Primitive" Taste and American Character

In taking over the BPW's Architectural Division, Doane inherited a large, complex, and prolific operation. Though outwardly appreciative of William E. Parsons's dedication to Burnham's plan, Doane was a harsh critic of his predecessor's architecture, judging it not according to Parsons's own goals of economy and efficiency, but rather on conventionally aesthetic terms, arguing that the austerity of Parsons's architecture, which Doane described as being "devoid of embellishment," was wholly out of touch with the "native luxuriance of the tropics or the prevalent ease of life in the far East," and with a culture "subject for centuries to . . . lavish Spanish ecclesiastical architecture."[16] Remarkably, Doane's criticism of Parsons included no claims to the universal value of ornament. Rather, he wrote that his "architectural policy" was designed to produce particular "effects," and was "calculated . . . to arouse a popular response to the cause of architecture." This populism, in other words, was not aimed at any *specific* end (save for the "cause" of architecture itself); rather, it was intended to "gain the confidence of the people and their officials in recommendations with respect to the more intangible problems of the future [which] . . . must be considered years in advance of their actual realization." This confidence would be achieved, Doane continued, "by producing a current government architecture impressive enough, and it may even be said ostentatious enough, to arouse widespread and *general* enthusiasm."[17] Doane's transitional architecture, then, was aimed at cultivating the lasting loyalty of a soon to be sovereign nation by means of a spectacular display of American largesse.

This generosity, Doane argued, was the measure of a "real democracy," the genuine character of which was demonstrated by "provid[ing] for the masses" what was "until the nineteenth century reserved . . . for the upper classes." This induction of gratitude was designed to structure an enduring political sway that, it was hoped, would last long after the end of colonial sovereignty. In the anticipated absence of direct colonial control, architectural quality was shaped as a channel for soft power.[18] At this point, one might ask whose character the building represented—that of the colonizer or that of the colonized. In a sense, it was both, as the architecture was to serve as a surrogate for the colonizer in its projected absence and as an example and model of improved character for the colonized to aspire to.

Ornament and Management

Realizing Doane's showcased structures presented some obstacles. With the exception of Spanish churches, the level of ornament specified by Doane was unprecedented. Though like Bourne and Parsons before him, Doane made use of locally available forms of artisanal labor (i.e., blacksmithing, capiz shell crafting, and wood carving), Doane's designs required experience in decorative trades associated with reinforced concrete construction, namely clay modeling and ornamental casting, expertise almost totally lacking on the archipelago at the time. On the site of one of his first projects, a customs house in Iloilo, district engineers complained about the considerable cost and effort that went into instructing local workers in the art of mold-making. Proper supervision and training at the dozens of projects under Doane's purview was, he complained, impossible, forcing him to reckon with what Parsons understood from the outset—the need for centralization. As the Iloilo project reached completion Doane began to assemble a cadre of dedicated tradesmen—a "special corps of fifty or sixty sculpturers and moulderers"—all based in Manila where artists tended to concentrate on account of a density of ecclesiastical institutions. This pattern solidified with the establishment in 1890 of the Escuela Practica y Professional de Artes y Oficio de Manila (Manila Practical and Professional School of Arts and Trades) where many of the sculptors that Doane hired—including Graciano Nepomuceno, Ramón Martínez, and the father and son team of Isabelo and Vidal Tampinco—either taught or received their training.[19] Arranging these artists into ateliers, Doane placed them under the direct supervision and employment of the BPW's architectural division. Within each atelier artists modeled and cast column capitals, festoons, acroteria, and other applied sculpture. When finished these building parts were shipped off to various sites across the archipelago, where they were secured to the plain surfaces of an almost completed building. This was not a new way of working. Dignifying industrial architecture with decorative finishes and applied sculpture was a method already perfected by Burnham's firm at the Columbian Exposition, where legions of artists plied their crafts in workshops cramped with gargantuan plaster bodies, which were developed and finished even as the steel skeleton of the exposition was being erected. As was the case at the exposition, this division of worksites allowed Doane to separate the building into two distinct tasks—the erection of a basic structure, relegated to prison and low-skilled laborers under the management of district engineers or *maestros de obras*; and the skilled labor in the ateliers. Leading architectural critics like Montgomery Schuyler and Lewis Mumford argued that this way of working reduced architecture to a practice of specification in which ornamental plaster was weighted with ameliorating the discomforting expression of architecture's industrial manufacture.[20] What these critics viewed as an architectural death was in Burnham's eyes a pathway to new organizational possibilities. Centralized coordination across multiple sites of work allowed architects to not only work at a distance from the jobsite, and at multiple jobsites at once, but to complete buildings at an unprecedented pace. From his office in Manila Doane worked simultaneously on projects throughout the archipelago without having to leave the capital city.

Doane's centralized ateliers reflected not only a more ambitious architecture, but also the changed goals of the Insular Government under Wilson and Harrison. While Republican administrations prioritized the use of private contractors, Doane focused on architecture as a form of representation. This resulted in designs more intricate than local contractors were willing to build. Accordingly, Doane turned to "building by administration,"[21] an arrangement under which the BPW oversaw all onsite and offsite constructions and sourced all its own labor and materials. The key advantage of this arrangement for Doane was the opportunity to raise the general level of architectural production on the archipelago through the direct management of labor. Another key benefit, from the perspective of labor costs, was the ability to take advantage of a very large labor pool then under the direct management of the American administration—prison labor. At the same time that Doane's cadre of artisans carefully carved and cast capitals and cornices in Manila (figure 7.4), in Lingayen the grading of site grounds, the pouring of foundations, and other low-skill tasks were executed by a "gang of prisoners."[22] Though Doane argued that the United States distinguished itself from Spain by not resorting to forced, coerced, or otherwise exploitative forms of labor, prison labor was used to produce many aspects of the building, including the sparkling artificial stone that Doane specified as a finish for all of his buildings. Though this may seem to present a contradiction, this was wholly consistent with a Progressive project of social reform. Certainly, Doane was not the first to do this. As Parsons put it, "where there is prison labor, good soil, good drainage, and a supply of water in the dry season, the conditions are ideal for completing a provincial capitol building."[23] Though Doane made no such pronouncement, he never explicitly objected to the practice. Whatever the case, despite elevating the work of a

FIGURE 7.4. An Ionic capital for the Pangasinan capitol building, carved in Graciano Nepomuceno's workshop in Manila. From *Quarterly Bulletin, Bureau of Public Works* 7, no. 2 (1918): 6.

few skilled craftspeople in Manila, Doane failed to significantly distinguish his own labor practices from those of his supposedly less enlightened predecessors.

A More Lavish Neoclassicism

Regardless of its mode of manufacture, once a building was complete, it operated on a different register. It mattered little to those astonished by the Columbian Exposition that the White City's steel skeletons were forged in Andrew Carnegie's Pittsburgh factories. Once covered in airbrushed plaster the massive, pillared warehouses belonged to what Carnegie called "the higher realm of artistic development."[24] Though panned by architects and architectural critics, who blamed Burnham for the virulent popularization of a bargain basement neoclassicism, the potency and ideological valence of the style was never totally diminished.[25]

In contrast to Parsons who never rationalized his turn toward neoclassicism, in both his writing and in the architecture itself Doane leaned heavily on the style's rhetorical capacities; positively adopting and embellishing the style to suit and affirm the aims of the Harrison-Wilson administration. Curiously, Doane structured his legitimization of neoclassicism around what had been a distinctly American anxiety—the US's supposed lack of a native architecture. In his words, "America began its history, as the Philippines began theirs, without any native architecture, but has legitimately followed ancient and Renaissance precedents, making such adaptations as were necessary to solve American architectural problems." Presenting this practice of "adaptation" as one rooted not in history, but in "logic," Doane proposed that "the Philippines might well proceed on the same policy, utilizing the best in Classic, Renaissance, and Modern architecture, with the modifications necessary to produce a style eminently suitable to those Islands." By proposing that the Philippines follow the same "legitimate" path Doane gave imageable form to Wilson's culturally hierarchical tutelary scheme. If Filipinos could convincingly adapt the work of their civilizational masters (just as the United States did theirs), it would serve as a concrete measure of their readiness for independence. Only after this benchmark was met could a Filipino style be allowed to "organically" emerge. As Doane put it, "The Philippine Islands must go through a long period, in which the adaptation of European and American science shall be accomplished before the field of original research is reached, and so in architecture, they must proceed far with the adaptation of foreign architecture and methods of construction before a distinctly characteristic Philippine style will appear."[26] Here Doane neuters the ongoing debate between American organicists and historicists by placing both within an evolutionary framework, positing that organicism must follow historicism.[27] In doing so, Doane naturalizes imperialism (and its architecture) as a historical stage to pass through before a native architecture (and by extension, the nation as such) could posit its own legitimacy.

Neoclassicism was positioned as precedent to the emergence of an organic nationalism already envisioned (though in the abstract) by former imperial powers. It was thus, by design, that Doane's provincial capitol buildings avoided any attempt to express an inner spiritual principle of the Philippine nation—this was set aside as the delimited contribution of postcolonial nations. Neoclassicism, as a universally applicable signifier of civilizational progress, is offered as the "logical" structure against which states will *eventually* distinguish themselves through a set of unique racialized national characteristics. As I will

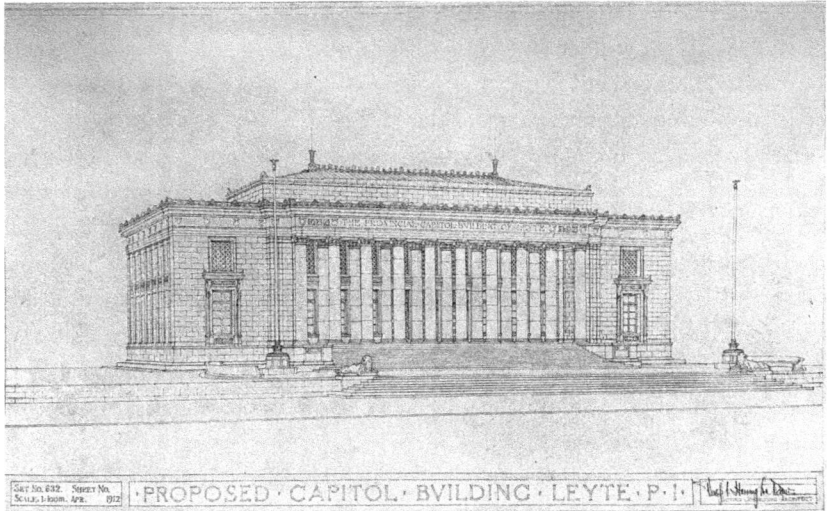

FIGURE 7.5. Ralph Harrington Doane with Antonio Toledo, proposed design for the provincial capitol building of Leyte, 1917. From *Quarterly Bulletin, Bureau of Public Works* 6, no. 1 (1917): 19.

address in "Plasticity," affecting this national identity was taken up by a US-trained native elite as the fulfillment of a national destiny.

Doane's prelude to a national architecture was a neoclassicism that simultaneously emphasized a civilizational pedigree, the advantages of modern technology, and the style's adaptability to tropical conditions. Though it looked like it could have been easily plucked from Washington, DC, the long colonnade of the Leyte provincial capitol (figure 7.5) protected the windows of the building's primary façade from direct sunlight while providing a space of repose during wet seasons. Pangasinan's cyrtostyle elevation, which directly referenced the South Portico of the White House (figure 7.6), faced picturesque Lingayen Bay, inviting sea breezes into the building's interior. The narrow layout of the plans for both buildings facilitated efficient cross-ventilation, while the deep window wells and the mass of the concrete itself kept interiors cool. Doane trimmed each building in the finest work produced by his Manila ateliers. For Pangasinan, which Doane considered his most important project, Graciano Nepomuceno's shop carved seashell acroteria, repeating panels of festoons, two six-foot-tall Philippine eagles, and the capitals for an ornate, foliated Ionic order (see figure 7.4).

When construction began on both buildings in 1917, World War I had reached its nadir, and in April, following a revelation of a German-Mexican

FIGURE 7.6. Ralph Harrington Doane with Antonio Toledo, provincial capitol building of Pangasinan, completed 1918. From *Quarterly Bulletin, Bureau of Public Works* 7, no. 2, July (1918): 29.

conspiracy against the United States, Wilson reluctantly called on Congress to declare war on Germany to, as Wilson famously pronounced, "make the world safe for democracy." Within this context Doane's work aimed to communicate a more "civilized" and constructive means to "democratic" ends. Charged with presenting the very image of US's anti-imperial culture, Doane's architecture was an overture directed at two different audiences. First, as a gesture directed outward, it symbolized an institutional and cultural stability aimed at a community of former imperial powers anxious over the loss of their colonies. And second, as a gesture directed inward it was aimed at a limited community of elite, in other words, "civilized" Filipinos who were promised positions of power at the dawn of a new postcolonial era.

Sparkling Skin, Clean Hands

Though applied ornament played an important role in Doane's architecture, it amounted to little more than jewelry. The true character of the building lay in his development of a new and meaningful materiality. Toward this end his "artificial stone" was an attempt to invoke an enduring convention of architectural "character"—locally sourced materials. As Antoine-Chrysostome Quatremère de Quincy argued in 1788, local materials link a particular architecture to the environment in which it is situated. Not all local materials were equal in this respect. Stone, Quatremère de Quincy wrote (borrowing from Burke), gives architecture the most grand of characters because its hardness suggests difficulty of workmanship.[28] The effort required to extract, carve, and dress stone bonded human labor to the material, imparting character through a mastery of the land and constituting a sort of doubled-up geopolitics in the sense of a politics informed by *both* geography and geology.[29] If stone architecture, as a topological reconfiguration of land, could be construed as a means of legitimizing a territorial claim, then Doane's artificial stone, an admixture of locally and globally sourced materials—a hybridization of human and industrial labor—modifies this claim.[30] By bonding machines, rebar, and US technical assistance to local stone Doane found the perfect material expression for the complex political ground on which postcolonial sovereignty was built.

According to Doane, his idea for the artificial stone struck him suddenly on a site visit to one of his first projects as consulting architect—a customs house in the province of Iloilo, on the island of Panay, about 655 kilometers south of Manila. There he spotted a pile of crushed aggregate "as white as a pile of sugar" being mindlessly mixed into a concrete slurry for a road construction project. Lamenting that its brilliance would languish as uncelebrated macadam, he immediately thought of using the stone as an exposed aggregate for projects across the archipelago. The logistics of distribution at the time were, however, beyond his capacity. Fortuitously, just months before construction began on one of his marquee projects—the Pangasinan capitol building—American speculators discovered "unlimited quantities" of a similar marble in nearby Alaminos, about 40 kilometers from the building site. Though deposits, he pointed out, were large enough to obtain both slabs and blocks, the quarries were "so underdeveloped . . . it [was] impossible to obtain stone ashlar veneers for concrete walls." Doane settled for aggregate, which was extracted and processed in much the same way that all other aggregates on the islands were—with some combination of mechanical rock crushers and cheap or free (most likely prison) labor.[31] Prison labor was also employed in the "artisanal" finishing of Doane's prismatic stone, which despite being conceived as an affordable way to incorporate a more luxurious finish, turned out to be a highly specialized and laborious method involving two separate pours of two different classes of concrete, the bulk of which was mixed with the standard gravel aggregate, while the top three inches, containing a greater density of the marble aggregate, was poured into a special galvanized iron mold in front of it. That finish was then carefully bush hammered on site. Specifying this special concrete for all of his monumental projects, a "special gang of men" was set aside "for this work and used on this work only." Traveling from jobsite to jobsite this "special gang" ensured an even level of quality could be achieved across the archipelago.

Doane's glittering stone reconciled American efficiency with a noble and legitimizing material expression—endowing the United States' pre–post-colonial architecture with a uniquely hybridized character. Indeed, the crystal studded concrete was an astonishingly capacious symbol. By binding the semiprecious mineral with an industrially produced Portland cement, in its very composition, Doane's artificial stone united—to starkly dramatic effect—American industrial development with the Philippines' rich natural resources. When sunlight hit the exposed facets of Alaminos marble, the entire building scintillated with an aura of reflections captured from a sun so lovely, it moved Doane to fulsome and poetic description:

> The tropical Philippine sun is a more gorgeous sun by far than is ever seen in the temperate climes. The low-lying solar displays of the temperate zone, that seem to hug the horizon so close, are tame in comparison. A sunset seen from New York looks as though it was really taking place at San Francisco, but in equatorial regions the sun sets right where one happens to be. Great banks of fluffy white clouds sail up from the immediate horizon high into the heaven, and lighted by flashing golden shafts, and played upon by a galaxy of colors gorgeous beyond description, seem to form a gigantic canopy of nature's most marvelous stuff, shutting out all the cold world beyond and producing effects which are of great importance in architectural design.[32]

By capturing the rays of the Philippine sun, Doane's artificial stone acted not only as a material, but more insistently as a *medium*—one that used a newly discovered natural resource to mediate the archipelago's spectacular solar phenomena. Doane took special pleasure in pointing out the fact that while the stone was native to the Philippines, it was not known to the Filipinos before US colonization.[33] The tropical sun, in other words, never appeared as beautiful as when refracted through the prism of US development. By specifying a material only recently discovered and developed by Americans, Doane found an opportunity to not only dignify concrete construction with a local material of exceptional quality, but also to make an argument that US assistance was needed in order to develop an untapped Philippine asset. Unlike the hopelessly derivative Lingayen eagle or the seashell acroteria, Doane's artificial stone conveyed a deeper understanding of the land revealed only with the help of US technical expertise, a point powerfully illustrated in the Division of Mines' display at the Philippine Carnival in 1918 (about a year into the construction of Doane's provincial capitol buildings). There a painted canvas depicts the sur-

PLATE 1. EXHIBIT OF THE DIVISION OF MINES, BUREAU OF SCIENCE, PHILIPPINE CARNIVAL, FEBRUARY, 1918.

FIGURE 7.7. Cutaway section of mine, from the exhibit of the Division of Mines, Bureau of Science, at the 1918 Philippine Carnival, illustrating the extraction of "native" stone unknown to natives before US colonization. From Philippine Bureau of Science, *The Mineral Resources of the Philippine Islands* (Manila: Bureau of Printing, 1920), frontispiece.

face of a mountain cut away to reveal an open pit mine (figure 7.7). The viewer is asked to imagine themselves walking not upon the earth, but through a new world of resources. Doane's architecture acted as the fulfilled promise of the excavation—a transformation of once unspoiled land into a body enriched by American development.

Though Doane left the Philippines before completing his most important projects, they were, as he had hoped, popular among the local population, having already "inspired the pride and interest of the community in which [they were] located." Furthermore, his projects demonstrated that Filipino character could be redeemed from Spanish indoctrination by showing that "the Filipino people [were] willing to forgo the shoddy gaudiness of Spanish standards for the more substantial and satisfying results of legitimate architecture."[34] Over and above these benefits, the most important function of Doane's architecture was to legitimize the US's role as an international leader. Toward this end, Doane was able to deliver a striking symbol to Harrison and Wilson, illustrating the superior moral character of the United States over the corrupted character of "European conquerors." In Harrison's words:

FIGURE 7.8. The capitol building of Pangasinan, prepared for its inauguration, October 1918. Library of Congress Prints and Photographs Division, LC-USZ62-126689.

The whole of continental Asia south and east of the plateau of Tibet is seething with discontent . . . toward the European conqueror. About seven hundred and fifty million people who inhabit those territories are kindling into fury against the white race on account of the European theory of colonization. While they point to individual instances of injustice and rapacity, the main . . . complaint is that Europe had no right to annex their countries. . . . There is a bare chance that with the rise in the recently low level of international morality, the colonial questions may eventually be settled upon principles of right rather than might. When the day arrives for this momentous change in our modern system, the United States of America, because of her policy in the Philippines, can "come into court with clean hands."[35]

The capitol of Pangasinan was thus intended to be far more than a symbol of local pride (figure 7.8). It was a representation of the postcolonial nation-state as both a moral and stabilizing American creation—part of a civilizing strategy that would hold off what Wilson called, invoking Burke, the "insurgent madness" of a potential revolutionary uprising. As a reflection of Wilsonian policy, Doane's architecture—presented as material truth—allowed the United States to take its mantle as world leader ascendant "with clean hands."

This desire to wash American hands clean of historical forms of colonialism was an attempt to conceal that the process of "withdrawal" from the Philippines was also structured as an expansion of American power. Realizing this, when writing for an American audience, Doane framed his work in the Philippines not as the conclusion of a colonial project but rather as the beginning of one. In his words, "American *colonial* Architecture . . . must unmistakably indicate to posterity the Era when American democracy surplanted [*sic*] the exploitations of Spanish despots. . . . Here lies our *first* opportunity as a great nation to inaugurate a *real* colonial architecture."[36] By "real," Doane meant an architecture that ennobled legitimate US imperial expansion, one that "afford[s] an inspirational field [where] . . . our sympathies have broadened, and our considerations easily reach the uttermost parts of a civilized world."[37] Doane's dazzling cover for the complex transfigurations of imperial power was offered as a promissory gift in lieu of unconditional independence. Embedded with the archipelago's own resplendent light, his buildings were revered not because of the labor required to execute them, nor for any other reason tied to their use or manufacture, but because, as gifts, they possessed both a mystical character and intrinsic value.[38] As the new structure of US imperialism continued to take shape, Doane shaped his architecture to ensure a lasting loyalty to the United States. And just as the masses worshipped at the old and sublime Spanish churches, so too, Doane hoped, would they pay tribute to his palaces of artificial stone.

8

PLASTICITY

CONSTRUCTING RACE,

REPRESENTING THE NATION

Shortly before its planned inauguration in Manila on July 16, 1926, the Legislative Building of the not-yet-sovereign Republic of the Philippines underwent a last-minute change (figure 8.1). An inscription cast into the panel above the portico was quickly plastered over. It had read:

ERECTED BY THE FILIPINO PEOPLE AS
MONUMENT TO RIGHTS WON AND
DEDICATED BY THEM TO THE
CAUSE OF FREEDOM

The order came down from the Governor-General Leonard Wood, best known to history as the leader, alongside Theodore Roosevelt, of the famous Rough Riders—though more (in)famous in the Philippines for leading a military campaign that included the brutal execution of more than one thousand unarmed women, children, and men in an event now known as the Moro

FIGURE 8.1. Legislative Building, Manila, ca. 1926. From *Philippine Education Magazine*, October 1926, 265.

Massacre.[1] Two decades later, Wood ordered the inscription's removal for two stated reasons. The first was supposedly grammatical; Wood argued that the article "a" was necessary before the word "monument." The second reason was that the inscription had been unauthorized. The grammatical correction was trifling—the elimination of punctuations or indefinite articles was not atypical for monumental inscriptions. The lack of "authorization" pointed to the inscription's more complicated context—namely, a complex politics of recognition that also shaped the inscription's calculated rhetoric. For example, there was no specific reference to independence—only to "rights won." Likewise, there was no claim to freedom, only a stated belief in the "cause of freedom." Most poignant, however, was the claim that the monument was erected not *for* the Philippines, but *by* the Filipino people. In short, Governor-General Wood ordered the inscription's removal because he understood the building for what it was—a convincing argument for self-determination.[2]

On the day of its inauguration the Legislative Building appeared before an assembled public without a dedicatory inscription. Instead, a large blank panel served as a striking symbol of the indeterminate future of a not quite independent

Republic. It hardly mattered. The building's heavily loaded ornamental program restated the inscription's case through a relentless iteration of "the Filipino" as its decorative theme. Filipino bodies, both real and represented, adorned every corner of the Legislative Building, providing an exemplary image of how post-colonial nations were compelled to self-racialize in order to claim their place within a changing world order. Perfectly suited to represent the imperatives of liberal internationalism, Beaux Arts architecture provided a platform for national identity, though only within a framework formally disciplined by the classical orders. Here "expression" was presented to native elites as a strictly delimited arena of political agency. The native voice would be included—but only if enclosed within the bounds of a legitimizing "civilizational" structure.

In speeches and articles dedicated to the building and its architect, Carmi S. Thompson, then-President Calvin Coolidge's special envoy in the Philippines, never mentioned concrete, alluding only to the structure's strength and "enduring" qualities. Instead, he focused on the building as the creation of "the Filipino." In Thompson's words:

> This stately edifice, the new legislative building in Manila, was designed by Juan M. Arellano, Supervising Architect of the Philippine government, and himself a Filipino. The constructor was Ramon Arevalo, also a Filipino, who in turn employed Filipino labor. Here is a stronger and more enduring argument as to the capacities of the Filipino race than any that the most enthusiastic of the American friends of the Filipinos can formulate.[3]

In his mind, the building had transcended its base materiality to serve as both proof and symbol of the Filipino race's technical and cultural "capacities," because, as he said, it was "designed by Filipino brains and built with Filipino hands." But this was not a full endorsement of a Filipino claim to sovereignty. First and foremost, Thompson's praise was meant to emphasize the building as a "permanent testimonial to the success of . . . America's Philippine policy," one that demonstrated the positive effects of colonial rule on the Filipino race, paving the way for the successful "Filipinization" of the nation-state.[4] The building, then, was an American construction by proxy—a monument, if not to colonialism, then to an American achievement in "race development."

On the Plasticity of Concrete and Race

Concrete's form, as Frank Lloyd Wright observed, "is a matter of this process of casting rather than a matter of anything at all derived from its own nature."[5] Susceptible, Wright quipped, to the whim of any "parlor architect or interior desecrator," concrete's lack of an inherent form—its plasticity—presented both a danger of "demoralizing influence" and a unique creative opportunity to architects. As plastic matter, concrete enabled architects to foreground a building's form over and even against the meanings fixed to its material constitution.[6] Whereas chapter 7 addressed the amelioration of the displeasing industrial appearance of concrete's default surface, this chapter addresses attempts to obscure the legibility of concrete—as concrete—through manipulations of form. This chapter, then, appears to take a departure from an investigation of concrete's qualities, but only seems to do so, because one of concrete's qualities is formlessness itself.

The Legislative Building gave physical form to the idea of the Philippine Republic, which, though not yet a politically sovereign state, preemptively sought recognition as a nation. Concrete architecture here served as the material embodiment of Filipinization, a policy that, as I aim to demonstrate, was a strictly formal—and thus immaterial—reconstruction of the colonial state.

Though the Jones Law of 1916 (discussed in chapter 7) entailed a formal promise by the United States to grant the Philippines its independence, Woodrow Wilson did not move to fulfill this promise until the very end of his presidency, when his lame-duck status rendered it practically moot.[7] Wilson's policy of Filipinization, however, frustrated the efforts of his retentionist Republican successor, Warren G. Harding, who was left unable to reverse the transition to national sovereignty.[8] It was on account of Filipinization that Ralph Harrington Doane was the final American consulting architect to serve in the Philippines. When Doane departed in 1918, he was replaced by Juan Arellano and Tomás Bautista Mapúa, who served as the first Filipino co-supervisors of the Architectural Division of the Bureau of Public Works (BPW). As was the case with most Filipinos occupying civil service positions, both Arellano and Mapúa had already worked for the BPW under American predecessors, and both had received at least part of their education in the United States. Graduating from Cornell in 1911, Mapúa was one of the first products of the Pensionado program. On his return, he became the first registered architect in the Philippines. Arellano took a somewhat less direct path toward the BPW. Born into a cosmopolitan family, he was first exposed to the architectural profession by his father, Luis C. Arellano, an accomplished master builder, and an assistant to the Catalan architect Juan Josep Hervás i Arizmendi, who worked as Manila's municipal architect from 1887 to 1893. Following his father's sudden death, the younger Arellano quit school at the age of thirteen to support his family, taking a job as a draftsman at the Bureau of Lands. After work hours, he studied painting under one of the Philippines most acclaimed artists, Lorenzo Guerrero. In

1904, at the age of sixteen, he sent *Woman Descending a Stairway* to St. Louis, where the painting was exhibited alongside the work of other Filipino artists at the Louisiana Purchase Exposition. Only four years later, at the Jamestown Ter-Centennial Exposition, Arellano made another appearance: this time, not as an artist represented by his work, but as a human subject placed on display.[9]

Filipinos on Display

That Arellano came to the United States as a living object of fascination was not unusual. In fact, that was the experience of many (if not most) Filipinos traveling to the United States in the first years following the Spanish-American War.[10] The "Philippine Reservation" at the St. Louis World's Fair, in 1904, which placed over 1,200 Philippine natives on display, was by far the most notorious example; but the display of Filipinos—and especially of "Igorots," Negritos, and other "uncivilized" and "semicivilized tribes"[11]—was a practice with a history that dates back to the late seventeenth century.[12] The first major exposition of Filipino subjects, however, happened in 1887, at the Exposición de las Islas Filipinas in Madrid, during the waning years of the Spanish Empire. There, *Ilustrados* (members of the Filipino intelligentsia), including José Rizal and the painter Juan Luna, both living in Europe at the time, had either seen or heard of the display of Igorots, who were presented to the Spanish audience as "typical" native inhabitants of the Philippines. Though Rizal objected to the dehumanizing treatment of the men and women placed on display—to whom he referred, on occasion, as his "brothers"—he and his fellow *Ilustrados* made a point of distinguishing themselves from the displayed natives, presenting themselves as examples of Philippine society at large by demonstrating their "civilization" through their education, sartorial sophistication, artistic achievement, athleticism, eloquence in Spanish, and loyalty to Spain. This was, Paul Kramer argues, a "glancing rather than a frontal attack on Spanish imperial racism, which by predicating political rights on sociocultural features excluded Philippine peoples deemed 'uncivilized' from a Philippines 'assimilated' to Spanish culture." In Kramer's words, "the *Ilustrado* quest for Spanish recognition . . . delimited the boundaries of who would ultimately be recognized as 'Filipino.'"[13] Rizal's attempt to identify himself with his Igorot and Moro "brothers" notwithstanding, elite Filipinos generally rejected an association with the archipelago's unassimilated indigenous peoples, referred to by Americans as "wild tribes" or alternatively as "non-Christian tribes." That Filipino "savagery" was often used as an argument against granting the Philippines its independence stoked this tendency toward rejection. Indeed, creating as sharp a distinction as possible with "uncivilized" natives was a preoccupation of elite Filipinos for generations to come. As the prominent Philippine diplomat and statesman Carlos P. Romulo wrote in 1943, "one recurrent sense of annoyance," to Filipinos was that "stories were frequently sent to America concerning our wild tribes, the Igorots, in which they were represented as Filipinos. These primitive black people are no more Filipino than the American Indian is representative of the United States citizen. They hold exactly the same position—they are our aborigines."[14] This "annoying" conflation between Filipinos and the archipelago's indigenous population took hold even when there was an attempt made, as was the case in St. Louis in 1904, to make sense of the coexistence of the "wild" and "civilized" Filipino. In St. Louis elite Filipino spectators did not happen upon displays of their "uncivilized" brothers (as Rizal did in Madrid), but rather were integrated into the exhibition, displayed along a path that guided viewers past stages of a simulated evolutionary progress that located the archipelago's most "primitive" peoples on one end and Filipino elites on the other. In this way, *Ilustrados* were presented as the living results of a successful civilizing project, one that posited that first Spanish and now US colonization had accelerated what was depicted as a plastic evolutionary process. Though this "progressive" arrangement intended to suggest that the elite Filipinos occupying the far end of the evolutionary spectrum might eventually replace their colonial masters as rulers over their more primitive brethren, this particular point was lost on fairgoers. Coverage in the American press focused instead on staged performances of "savage" rituals. As many Filipinos had feared, the exhibit only served to advance the idea that the Philippines was an archipelago overrun by "savages."

As a concession to Filipinos angered by what they felt to be the overrepresentation of unassimilated natives at St. Louis, just three years later fair organizers at the Jamestown Ter-Centennial Exposition of 1907, held in Norfolk, Virginia, agreed to exclude from the Philippine exhibit Igorots and Negritos, considered the most primitive of the represented groups, but insisted on the inclusion of Muslim Moros (an exception that I will return to shortly). Presenting themselves as examples of the civilized majority, Arellano's cohort of Hispanized and Christianized Filipinos submitted their own "developed" bodies as proof of civilization. As an erudite cosmopolitan, Arellano's role at the Jamestown exposition was to draw a hard line between himself and the "savages" on display by literally embodying in physique, dress, and comportment both the benefits of American progress and the Filipinos' fitness for self-rule, including domination over their "less civilized" countrymen.

Whatever the case, Jamestown, for Arellano, was not his reason for coming to the United States, but merely his means of getting there. His true intention was to study architecture. Eventually making his way to Philadelphia, he took a job at the Philadelphia Commercial Museum as a photo colorist to support himself while he took courses at the Philadelphia Arts Institute, before enrolling full-time at the Drexel Institute.[15] Returning to the Philippines in 1916 (not even a full decade after he had placed his body on display at Jamestown), he took a job at the BPW, eventually taking over the Architectural Division. Clearly, by the time Arellano began his job at the BPW, he had experienced, on an extraordinary and intimate level, the burdens of serving as a model for the nation. It was a burden he must have felt acutely on July 16, 1926, the day he celebrated the inauguration of his largest and most important commission to date—the Philippine Legislative Building.

That Arellano's own body served as a model for the nation was a burden he transferred onto the Legislative Building—a structure not only designed and built to be occupied by Filipinos but also covered in representations of Filipino bodies. This decorative program underscored the idea that the building was not the achievement of any one individual but rather, as Thompson suggests, was the collective achievement of the Filipino race (as developed by US colonizers)[16]—a unity of which Arellano's "brain" was just one part. As such, Arellano's role as an architect was not limited to redesigning the Legislative Building (see figure 8.3), but also included his performance, in Frantz Fanon's words, as an "object among other objects."[17]

Being "designed by Filipino brains and built by Filipino hands" was, in this way, an argument for independence that simultaneously marked the thematization of the native body. Among the consequences of this thematization was that it rendered Arellano—and postcolonial artists and authors in general—as only capable of national accomplishments. The Legislative Building could never be seen as an architectural accomplishment in and of itself; rather, as Thompson points out, it was seen as an extension of Arellano's body. One of the direct effects of this is that neither Arellano nor any Filipino architect was ever described as an architect, but rather they were referred to only as *Filipino* architects, a designation that framed Filipino success as always already secondary—a cast copy of an American original.[18]

Shortly after the inauguration of the Legislative Building, Arellano traveled to Washington, DC, where the pro-Independence lobby arranged an exhibit of his drawings and sketches at the House Office Building. Members of the US Congress were invited to see for themselves the evidence that Filipinos were prepared for self-government. Catching wind of these events, the *New York Times* ran a short article about Arellano titled "Noted Architect Once Posed as 'Wild Man' at Jamestown." The piece detailed the seemingly miraculous transformation of Arellano, who, "twenty years after he first landed in the United States from steerage as a 'brown skinned . . . wild man,'" would return to the United States as a sort of valedictory homecoming.[19] In this biographical sketch, Arellano's accomplishments—his graduation from an American university, his first prize in an art competition in his second year of architecture school, his victory in a worldwide competition for his design of a bank,[20] and his general command of "ancient classic lines"—were offered to further dramatize the architect's fictionalized metamorphosis from a "wild man" into a highly cultured individual (figure 8.2). Far from presenting Arellano's accomplishments as his own, the article instead confirms the success and progressive nature of the American colonial project, at the precise moment that the United States wished to frame its withdrawal from the Philippines not as the admission of an historical error, but as evidence of a civilizing mission *accomplished*.

Though Arellano's reaction to the *Times* article is unknown, it is difficult to imagine that he would have been pleased with either posing as a wild man during the time of the exposition or being called a wild man—even if in the past tense. What is certain is that Arellano understood the peculiar constraints of his position. Though these narratives of the American development of the Filipino served Americans best, it also advanced the cause of an elite-driven independence movement, for which Arellano served as a highly symbolic advocate. That is to say, Arellano understood the strategic value of presenting his own success as the accomplishment of his colonizers, a condition of a politics of recognition.

Performing at Jamestown as if his own body was "developed" by his American colonizers, Arellano was made aware of his own existence "in triple." As Fanon described it, the racialized postcolonial subject is made aware of his body not in the first person, but in triple person: He is all at once responsible for himself, for his race, and for his ancestors. Within this "epidermal racial schema," Fanon recounts, he is forced to "cast an objective gaze over [him]self," by discovering his Blackness, his "ethnic features; deafened by cannibalism, backwardness, fetishism, racial stigmas, slave traders and above all, yes, above all the grinning *Y a bon Banania*."[21] The Black body is here objectified as "an object in the midst of other objects." At the Jamestown exposition, Arellano was not only depicted as an objectified body among others but required to thematize his own body as the condition placed on independence. To reject the success of the American colonial project of "racial uplift" would be to damage

FIGURE 8.2. Portrait of Juan Arellano. From *Philippine Republic*, January–February 1927, 3.

the cause of Philippine independence by serving as proof of a churlish rejection of the American "gift" of liberty. Within this schema, Arellano's individual accomplishments, as well as those of every Filipino architect that followed him, were inseparable from the nation as cause.

From Body to Building

Arellano did not design the Legislative Building from scratch; he reworked Doane's design for a national library (figure 8.3).[22] Modifying the building's entrance sequence, he placed a dais on the stair landing, enabling its use as a stage for public events, the first of which was the building's inauguration. The most conspicuous change, however, was to Doane's portico design, which he replaced with a more elaborate version that borrowed from the conventions of

FIGURE 8.3. (*left*) Ralph Harrington Doane's design for the entrance and portico of the proposed National Library in Manila. (*right*) Juan Arellano's revised design, used in the Legislative Building; from *Philippine Republic*, January–February 1926, 3.

the triumphal arch. A classical type wholly dedicated to communication, the triumphal arch incorporates redundant structural components to support a superimposed semantic structure. Though not technically an arch, the portico's communicative function is enabled by similar structural redundancies. The portico's columns, for example, bear both the actual and the symbolic weights of the lintel and the four figures positioned above the capitals. These figures represent what "Philippinologists" then considered the four sources of Philippine culture: Chinese, Hindu, Spanish, and Anglo-Saxon. Above the attic, two figures representing the arts and sciences flank a globe on which a Philippine eagle perches. Arellano nods to the triumphal arch by flanking the entry with two archlike exedrae, placing a sculpture group in each. In the right niche stood a group entitled "Home," while another group titled "Progress" stood in the left.

Indeed, dozens of bodies adorned the building—a decorative strategy that posed a problem. What should these bodies look like? On what model should they be built? The answer was far from straightforward. Starting around at least the late nineteenth century, the canon itself was increasingly challenged by the emerging fields of anthropology and ethnology, as could be seen, for example, in the racialized structural rationalism of Viollet-le-Duc.[23] For Viollet-le-Duc, the source of style and structure was not universal, but climatically particular, an ideal encapsulated by his concluding exhortation in *The Habitations of Man of All Ages* to "know thyself." To know oneself as a *national* subject was not an introspective task, but a project in which citizens were compelled to identify with a generalized ethnological object. However, as anyone with a basic knowledge of the Philippines knew, the national self was an unstable invention incommensurable with its varied population. Indeed, while still a history professor at Princeton, Wilson used the archipelago's heterogeneity to disqualify a Filipino claim to national sovereignty. In his words:

> No people can form a community or be wisely subjected to common forms of government who are as diverse and as heterogeneous as the people of the Philippine Islands. . . . They are of many races, of many stages of development, economically, socially, politically disintegrate, without community of *feeling* because without community of life, contrasted alike in experience and in habit, having nothing in common except that they have lived for hundreds of years together under a government which held them always where they were when it first arrested their development.[24]

Compelled to reconcile his early diagnosis of an arrested Philippine development with his campaign promise to grant the Philippines its national sovereignty, Wilson adopted development as a transitional colonial project. Though today we mostly associate development with the postwar era and understand it primarily in economic terms, race was the first object of development practice. The tools of this particular kind of development were education and environmental modification in the form of landscape, architecture, and public works projects.[25] Promoters of what was then referred to as "race development" argued that both education and environmental design could be marshaled directly toward racial improvement (figure 8.4). A second nature enriched by US industrial progress was intended to act as an accelerant to evolutionary time. More significantly, by substituting a definite temporal framework with the open-ended time of "development," it left the political question of national sovereignty in the hands of the colonizer.

The bodies that occupy Arellano's pediment, which is situated behind and above the colonnaded entrance (see figure 8.1), play a special role vis-à-vis "race development"—not as environmental agent, but as a symbolic projection of the ideal end—the conclusion of a program of race development that is frozen in the form of a racialized national body. Offering an answer to what Wilson identified as a problematic heterogeneity, Arellano presented the nation in the process of its unification (figure 8.5). Three figures, each representing one of the archipelago's three principal island groups—Luzon, Mindanao, and the Visayas—occupy the center of the pediment. The female figure in the middle represents Luzon, the archipelago's largest and most populous island. The male

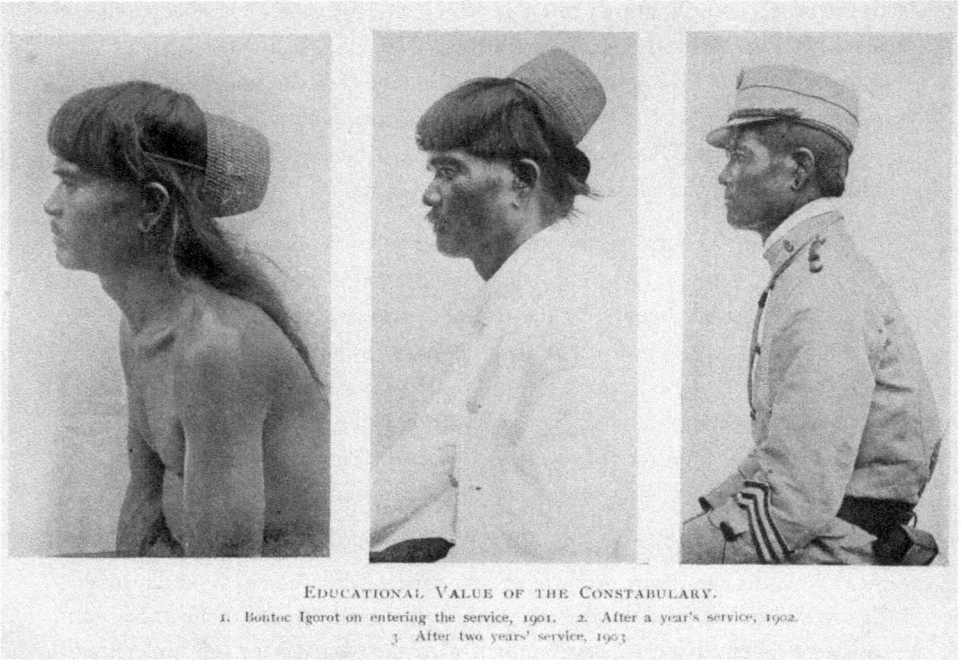

EDUCATIONAL VALUE OF THE CONSTABULARY.
1. Bontoc Igorot on entering the service, 1901. 2. After a year's service, 1902.
3. After two years' service, 1903.

FIGURE 8.4. An example of "race development." The original caption reads: "Educational Value of the Constabulary. 1. Bontoc Igorot on entering the service, 1901. 2. After a year's service, 1902. 3. After two years' service, 1903." From Frederick Chamberlin, *The Philippine Problem, 1898–1913* (Boston: Little Brown, 1913), 161.

FIGURE 8.5. Juan Arellano and Otto Fischer-Credo with Ramón Martínez and Atelier, pediment of the Legislative Building. Drone photo, 2016.

figure to her right represents Mindanao, the southernmost island group, and the only one with a majority Muslim population.[26] To her left sits a female figure who represents the centrally located island group of the Visayas. Luzon's elevated position, along with the scepter she holds in her right hand, identify her as the sovereign. Her regal stoicism is juxtaposed with Mindanao's defiant expression, on the one hand, and the downcast gaze and fully deferential posture of the Visayas, on the other. Mindanao and the Visayas face away from each other—illustrating the mythologized conflict between them. Historically, both the Spanish and American colonial regimes regarded the Visayans as the victims of centuries of Moro violence, a perception shaped by the successful Christianization of the Visayans and the largely unsuccessful attempts to colonize and Christianize the Moros. Here, Luzon is charged with protecting the effete and feminized Visayans, as well as exerting control over the masculinized and martial culture of Mindanao. By presenting Luzon as the only power fit to manage this internecine conflict, this hierarchical arrangement served the purposes of a native elite (dominated by Tagalogs from Luzon)—a group that was both protective of their own claims to power and reliably amenable to American political and economic goals.

Luzon, Mindanao, and the Visayas do not sit alone, but are flanked by personifications of Learning and Law on the left and Commerce and Agriculture on the right, who recline in casual repose, somewhat indifferent to the national trio. Indeed, it is the trio that must attend to these figures: the obstinate Mindanao, whose body is angled toward Law and Learning, must take heed of their lessons; the Visayas, draped in a fine cloth of native fiber for which the region was known, must take her cues from Commerce and Agriculture. The nation, in other words, must orient itself toward these universal values, depicted here as classical (i.e., white) figures, racially distinct from the national trio. Perhaps unique to national personifications is the fact that their attributes include not only signifying objects but also (and more importantly) costume and ethnographic features. Luzon wears a *baro't saya*, a nineteenth-century hispanized version of precolonial dress. Luzon's garment is noticeably less fine than that worn by the Visayas—a nod to the weaving skills of the islands' women. Mindanao wears a form-fitting shirt and holds a kris, the traditional weapon of the Moros. His sarong and headdress indicate both his geographical origins and his Muslim faith. The native dress of Arellano's national trio differs from both the politicized sartorial choices of the nineteenth-century *Ilustrados* and from the dress and tattooed skin of the so-called wild tribes—images of whom appear nowhere in the building.[27] The dress of the national trio splits the difference between these two poles, presenting distinctive, conspicuously "civilized," character-giving forms of national expression.

Figuring out which groups were fit to lead a nation was a self-consciously executed task within the context of Wilsonian internationalism—an order sorted out on a global map of nested hierarchies in which Anglo-Saxons assumed a position at the top, while other dominant ethnic groups they ordained as relatively more civilized assumed sovereignty over their own national subalterns.[28] Briefly stated, the building monumentalized a global systematization of techniques of racial management. Thus, though Wilson is celebrated— even today—as a hero of Philippine independence, his advocacy should not be viewed as a cause he championed on account of a deep-held belief in racial equality. It was, to the contrary, a means of instantiating race as the basis of a new world order. Within this system, claiming authorship over the idealized native body, or the "self," was a prerequisite for national self-determination. This can be seen in the representation of the trio's ethnographic features, which—unlike the native costumes which present the three figures as culturally distinct— serves to articulate a racial unity.

Arellano was not directly responsible for modeling this racial unity. Beyond sketches and a few directives, he left the execution of all of his sculptural groups to a set of collaborators. Lacking confidence in native talent, especially given the pediment's unprecedented scale, Arellano hired a German sculptor named Otto Fischer-Credo to both execute the sculptures and train native Filipino assistants. A recent graduate of the École des Beaux-Arts in Paris, Fischer-Credo had previously attended Berlin's Akademie der Künste. Though classically trained, when the German sculptor came to the Philippines, he was immediately charged with assimilating the anthropological challenge to the classical tradition.

To do this, Fischer-Credo turned to ethnological and anthropological descriptions of the "typical Filipino," likely mining the work of Henry Otley Beyer, the American anthropologist who is today still referred to as the "dean" of Philippine anthropology. Beyer described the typical Filipino as a "uniform Malay type," possessing a medium stature, "excellent muscular development," broad shoulders, slender waists, small hands and feet, brown complexion, straight black hair with virtually no beard or mustache, and black or brown eyes, "set rather slanting under an intelligent brow."[29] Like many of his contemporaries, Beyer viewed the Moros as being culturally distinct, but of the "same racial stock" as the Christianized Filipino—an inclusion that demonstrates that it was race, and not culture, that determined one's eventual eligibility for Philippine citizenship.[30] To be clear, this unity was to the exclusion of the Philippines'

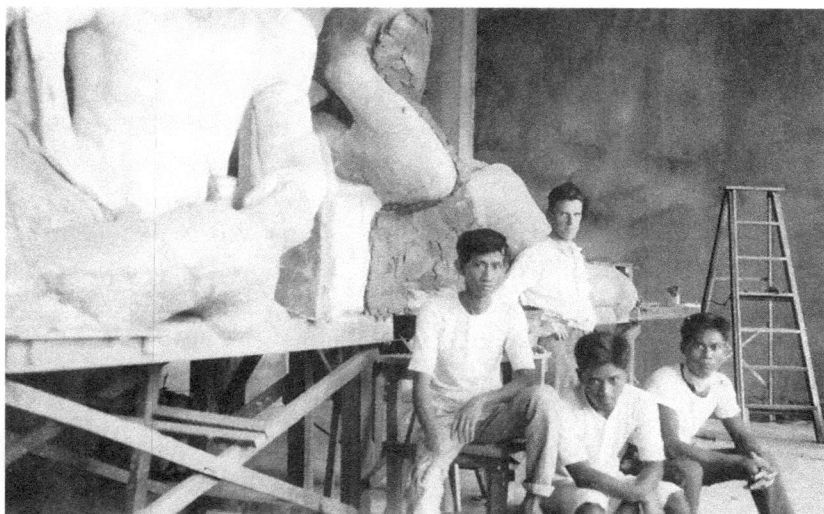

FIGURE 8.6. Otto Fischer-Credo (*at rear*) and three members of his atelier.

racially defined Negritos and Igorots who were left unrepresented at the Legislative Building.

The wealth of anthropological information available to Fischer-Credo did not seem to help him much. The national trio appears stiff and ungainly in parts. Luzon is more chair than body—a scaffold for native costume, a lack of refinement echoed by Mindanao's strange proportions and flattened, block-like head. The Visayas is the most elegant of the three, but even her subtle posture seems graceless when compared to those of her classical counterparts. Fisher-Credo and his native atelier (figure 8.6)—the prior experience of whose artisans consisted mostly of carving, in wood, the European likenesses of Jesus, Mary, and the saints—had little practice modeling the Filipino, and it showed. This clumsiness reveals the fabrication of the fictional "naturalism" that lay at the center of a new national culture.

An Iconological Study

To be clear, the context that Arellano operates within is not the nation as such, but is rather the nation as situated within the global setting of liberal internationalism: a political, social, and cultural system that both consciously and unconsciously produced its own sets of customs and conventions.[31] Certain elements of Arellano and Fischer-Credo's pediment point to this broader context. Most obvious is that the personification of the ethnos (in the form of the national trio) is enclosed within a neoclassical space, plainly legible as the undiminished structure of Western imperium. Subtler details tell us more about how Wilsonian internationalism actually worked. Take, for example, the awkward gaps that separate the native trio from the white allegorical figures. These spaces, occupied by a seemingly useless furniture, serve no allegorical function *except* to create distance between the figures—to, de facto, segregate them from one another. What might otherwise appear as a compositional weakness instead transmits one of liberal internationalism's clandestine imperatives. Among other things, this separation suggests that the reconciliation of the postcolonial nation's inner racial principle with a classical ideal would not materialize in the form of a mixed-race figure—even if merely symbolic. Francis Burton Harrison (just like Wilson, who appointed him to govern the Philippines) considered intermarriage both a problem in and of itself, and problematic on account of the threat it posed to the stability of the racial state.[32] In direct reference to interracial unions, Harrison warned that it was essential to consider this "delicate matter" because "the race question . . . is apt at any moment, and in the most unexpected manner, to crop up and baffle the plans and policies of all those who are in good faith wrestling with public issues."[33] That is to say, in order to be able to politically attend to "the race question," one must begin with clearly defined races. Wilson's well-known support of anti-miscegenation laws can be recast in this light not only as evidence of his racism, but also as central to his larger vision of a segregationist decolonization—a "stabilizing" vision for liberal internationalism that had at its center the idea of a racial purification within nations, and racial diversity without. According to this system, national borders provided *the* clearly demarcated color lines that would structure liberal internationalism.[34]

Though generally regarded as a reflection of his progressive outlook, Wilson's aims with the League of Nations, following World War I, were wholly consistent with his racism.[35] The world order as imagined by the architects of the league—Wilson, Robert Cecil of Great Britain, and fellow committed segregationist Jan Smuts of South Africa—was a peace structured by clearly defined racial hierarchies and on a process of unequal integration, especially of the world's Black and Brown peoples.[36] As W. E. B. Du Bois and others pointed out, the league included no provisions for Black representation, even though "the great majority of the peoples of the mandated areas are Negroes."[37] This structural inequality animated the proceedings of the Second Pan-African Congress, which Du Bois helped plan as a series of countermeetings to the Paris Peace Conference. Black exclusion from the League allows us to think, along with Du Bois, of the League's ordering of the world, and the ethnonational units that it helped to shape, as the same force that motivated Wilson's earlier and more overtly segregationist practices, including his exclusion of African American students from Princeton dorms and his resegregation of federal civil service workplaces. It is by design that this racist homology is severed. The success of the League of Nations depended on the assent of the colonized to the new structure of empire. It is for this reason that the League's formal covenant does not reveal its own contentious history—one must recover from the archives the various objections of the Pan-African League, or the exclusion of the "racial equality clause" proposed by the Japanese delegates. Though it appeared incidental, the silences built into the Legislative Building offer rare visual evidence of the racism that undergirds this new liberal world order.[38]

Like the segregating gap, the importance of Fischer-Credo's role is often overlooked, as much of his work in the Philippines is attributed to his apprentice Ramón Martínez (part of a critical compulsion to attribute Filipino art and architecture to "Filipino brains and hands"). His work in the Philippines should be understood, however, not only for the imprint it left on the Philippines but also for the influence it exerted on the direction of his career. Constructing racialized personifications of the nation became both a specialty and a lifelong pursuit for Fischer-Credo. Following eight years in the Philippines, the artist caught wind of new opportunities for artists in his homeland. Back in Germany, he joined legions of German artists whose practice would be defined by the consolidation of race with nation.[39] As a sculptor serving the Third Reich, both Heinrich Himmler and Adolf Hitler sat for him. Though striking, this detail should not be reduced to what may seem to some an astonishing coincidence. More importantly, it sheds light on liberal internationalism's management of the ethno-state, and on the global influence and currency of its identity-based aesthetic regimes.

Liberal Internationalism and Publicity

In December 1920, Woodrow Wilson accepted the Nobel Peace Prize for the role he played as the lead architect of the League of Nations. It was small consolation for the US Senate's rejection of the Treaty of Versailles, mostly due to the attached Covenant of the League of Nations, which both Republicans and a sizable number of Democrats had opposed on account of the threat they felt it posed to national sovereignty. Objectors were particularly concerned about the potential loss of jurisdiction over issues of "immigration, naturalization, elective franchise, land ownership, and intermarriage"—that is to say, about issues directly related to racial management.[40] Embedded within that web of concerns was control over what the United States would do with its own Far Eastern colony.

The rejection of the treaty was especially ironic as far as the Philippines was concerned, because the archipelago served Wilson as an important proving ground for the covenant of the League, particularly for Article 22, which established the mandate system for former territories of the Ottoman Empire. The details of the system closely mirrored Wilson's Philippine policy. In fact, Wilson's lame-duck request to grant the Philippines its independence was likely motivated by his desire to conclude a carefully planned out process of decolonization, which he likely had assumed would fall under the jurisdiction of the League of Nations.[41] As that possibility faded, his request was a last-ditch attempt to claim authorship over an exemplary model of decolonization.

Unsurprisingly, Wilson's plea fell on deaf ears—the Philippines remained a US colony for close to three more decades. True to expectations, Governor-General Wood vetoed sixteen of the fifty bills that the legislature sent up to his office in his first year alone. By comparison, in Harrison's six years as governor-general, he vetoed only five pieces of legislation. With increasingly limited legal recourse, *Nacionalistas* turned toward publicity.[42] In this capacity, the Legislative Building answered to multiple authorities and audiences: not only to the Jones Law's requirement to maintain "a stable government," or to the League of Nation's prerequisites for "self-determination," but also, and perhaps most importantly, to what Wilson called the "world court of public opinion."[43]

Arellano and the *Nacionalistas* stated their case before this presumed court in a Beaux Arts neoclassicism that legibly referenced the architecture of Western liberal democracies. By placing Filipino bodies within this "universal" scaffold, Arellano conveyed a *Nacionalista* desire for independence, presented as both derived from and bestowed by Western civilization. Neoclassicism was not strictly an ideological choice. At the time, nearly all architecture schools in the United States participated in a standardized architectural program laid out by the Society of Beaux-Arts Architects.[44] As such, neoclassicism was the dominant idiom in which the US-educated Filipino architects (including Arellano) were trained. Executing buildings in this style was thus also seen as an opportunity to demonstrate the success of US technical training in the form of a fully developed native virtuosity.

Though it is difficult to know just how effective Arellano's architectural performance was at publicizing US Philippine policy, the apparent popularity of the American approach had (according to Harrison) already taken hold of the imaginations of the world's colonized populations. By 1922, the year that

Harrison published *The Cornerstone of Philippine Independence*, the global "Effect of American Policy" (the title of the book's concluding chapter) could be heard in "Madras, where the Indian movement for home rule [was] . . . inspired by Philippine policy," and in the testimonies of "visiting delegations of Chinese . . . [whose] belief in the honor and unselfishness of America was firmly based upon our attitude toward the Filipinos." Echoes were also heard in "the harbors of Malaysia" in Java, Ceylon, Indo-China, and "even in the far-away mountain passes of Armenia."[45] Neither Harrison nor the *Nacionalistas* would leave the good news of native deliverance to rumor or faulty interpretation. The Legislative Building monumentalized the success of the Wilsonian approach as a postcolonial future first made manifest in the Philippines.

In January 1927, an image of the Legislative Building appeared on the cover of the *Philippine Republic*, a magazine intended to promote Philippine independence to an American audience (as it is they who ultimately determined the fate of the Philippine Republic). A quote from Ruskin, appearing underneath the heading "The Philosophy That Is Guiding the Filipinos," read:

> Therefore, when we build, let us think that we build (public edifices) forever. Let it not be for present delight, nor for present use alone, let it be such work as our descendents will thank us for, and let us think, as we lay stone on stone, that a time is to come when those stones will be held sacred because our hands have touched them, and that men will say as they look upon the labor and wrought substance of them, "See! This our fathers did for us."[46]

No stones, of course, were laid in the construction of the Legislative Building, which was then the largest concrete monument built in the Philippines. The quote was further misleading because Ruskin's criticism of neoclassicism and of industrially produced architecture was well known. On account of its symmetry and use of serial forms he considered neoclassicism perfectly consonant with systems of enslavement and industrial production.[47] The gothic, by contrast, revealed in each uniquely carved stone the "individual value of every soul."[48] The Legislative Building, covered in the cast "machine ornament," would have revolted Ruskin. Only a select few of the hands that worked on the Legislative Building were those of skilled craftsmen. Most of the laborers were drawn from the same masses of deskilled labor that built every concrete structure that preceded the Legislative Building.[49] That it was difficult to remember that, like nearly all of the objects addressed throughout this book, this building, too, was made of reinforced concrete was by design, as those who looked on it—even those who worked on it—were not tasked with identifying *what* material the building was made of, but rather were asked to identify *with* its distinctly Filipino form.

Arellano in Search of a Native Style

Nearly a decade of Republican rule followed the inauguration of the Legislative Building. During that time *Nacionalistas* continued to advocate for national sovereignty, appealing to an international audience against and over a Republican administration that continued to trim the political agency gained during the Wilson/Harrison administration. In this context Arellano continued his search for an appropriately pitched native architecture, decisively breaking with neoclassicism after the completion of the Legislative Building and the equally grandiose Bureau of Posts building. It helped that his next large commission was a decidedly modern program—a movie theater. This would not just be any theater, but would be, in the words of Senator Juan Bautista Alegre, a "people's theater"—one envisioned to play an important role in enrolling the masses into the project of the Philippine nation building.

Work on the theater began in earnest when, in 1928, Thomas Earnshaw, the mayor of Manila, secured a ninety-nine-year lease of the Mehan Garden to the newly formed Metropolitan Theater Company (packed with members of Manila's commercial elite) for the symbolic amount of ₱1. The company sent Arellano to the United States to consult with Thomas W. Lamb, a theater specialist and Art Deco pioneer, though Arellano had already become familiar with the style on a visit to Paris in 1925, where he visited the Exposition Internationale des Arts Décoratifs et Industriels Modernes.[50] Freed of any of the conventional constraints of neoclassicism, Art Deco allowed Arellano to combine a deep well of native imagery with a modern mode of construction.[51] At the Metropolitan Theater, inaugurated in 1931, every surface, trim, fitting, and fixture was given over to some decorative theme. The marquee was a backlit grid of stained glass with an abstracted composition of sun rays, waves, and Philippine flora. Wrought iron gates were arranged into dense compositions of Greek keys, zigzags, sun rays and scalloped clouds, and large columns sheathed with backlit capiz were set under the entrance's concrete awning. Throughout the building, stained glass lighting fixtures and brightly glazed ceramics were arranged in freely mixed patterns lifted from native themes including flora, tattoo work, and wood carving. One was led to the main theater by concrete banisters cast in the shape of bamboo shafts, and within the theater one sat beneath a spectacular vaulted ceiling of voluptuous mangoes and banana clusters set against arrangements of geometricized tropical foliage.[52] As a techno-tropical spectacle, Arellano's catalog of native imagery presented itself at the theater as thoroughly adaptable to modern development.

At around the same time, and at a distance from cosmopolitan Manila, Arellano experimented with adapting indigenous tectonics to modern programs,[53] though, as if to suggest the arrested evolutionary development of these othered Philippine groups, this work was confined to provinces mostly populated by unassimilated non-Christian tribes.[54] For an unbuilt subprovincial capitol building in Banaue (an Ifugao province), for example, and for his design for the Cotabato Municipal Hall in Moro Mindanao, Arellano enlarged barely modified indigenous building types—the Bontoc dwelling and the Tausug house—by simply replacing traditional materials with reinforced concrete and galvanized iron. In Cotabato he completed his design with the traditionally carved forked finial of the Tausug home. Though this could be understood as a reflection of a desire to protect or even celebrate indigenous culture, Arellano's modernization of indigenous cultural forms was part and parcel of an attempt to shore up a *Nacionalista* demonstration of self-governance, a key aspect of which was to present the willingness and ability of a native elite to manage racialized minorities.[55]

The Architecture of the Commonwealth:
Toledo's Deracinated Neoclassicism

It was not until the election of another Democratic president, this time, Franklin D. Roosevelt, that *Nacionalistas* secured a timeline to be granted national sovereignty. In 1934 the US Congress passed the Tydings-McDuffie Act, which specified that the Philippines would operate as a commonwealth for a transitional ten-year period, after which "the United States shall recognize the independence of the Philippine Islands as a separate and self-governing nation."[56] As Paul Kramer points out, passage of the act did not reflect the end of a process of a politics of recognition or the fulfillment of a "colonial compact"— one that outlined an American responsibility to socially, politically, and economically educate Filipinos, while Filipinos were charged with the task of demonstrating their capacity to self-govern. Rather, it had more to do with the popularization of the racist and racialized currents that subtended both the League of Nations and the aestheticized nativism of the Legislative Building. Also titled the "Philippine Independence Act, " the bill was propelled through Congress by violent anti-Filipino protests[57] and a powerful agricultural lobby, which paired Philippine "independence" with protectionist measures and a highly restrictive immigration quota (of fifty Filipinos per year).[58] The United

States, however, still desired to maintain the economic benefits of its colonial arrangements; this too had an architecture.

Arellano's "native" style represented only one side of Janus-faced internationalism. As if to divide the Legislative Building into two, his contemporary Antonio Toledo developed a neoclassicism nearly devoid of native references. If Arellano's architecture was guided by a desire to transform and reinterpret native forms, then the work of Toledo revealed the compatibility of the nation with the new international structure of empire. Toledo's twin buildings—the Bureau of Agriculture and the Bureau of Finance, planned just after the passage of the Tydings-McDuffie Act and completed in 1939—were the first built directly on the mall at the center of Daniel Burnham's plan (today named the Rizal Court). Composed in a highly disciplined Corinthian order and devoid of legible native references, the twin buildings were far more refined than the crude neoclassical structures Toledo had first worked on as a draftsman at the BPW under William E. Parsons. Their style was suitably appropriate, not only because the buildings occupied the most configured portion of Burnham's imperial plan, but also because the Bureau of Agriculture and the Bureau of Finance—which were founded to develop trade and industry—directly served the purposes of the "transitional" period, which was "to stabilize trade relations between the United States and the Philippines."[59] What this actually meant was that, despite the Philippine Constitution's inclusion of restrictions on property acquisition and the extraction of natural resources by American individuals and corporations, those laws were not in effect during the Commonwealth period. As will be discussed in chapter 9, this was an arrangement that a newly "independent" Philippine Republic was coerced into extending into the postwar period. Americans and US corporations could continue to exploit Philippine labor and natural resources as they had during the colonial regime, availing themselves of the technical aid offered by the bureaus and legal protections written into the Tydings-McDuffie Act. A monumental home for these bureaus assured US investors of a postcolonial commitment to the "commercial opportunity" that was the center of the US colonial program from the start.[60]

9

STRENGTH

DEFENSIVE ARCHITECTURES AND
MANILA'S DESTRUCTION

That concrete changed people's lives was not something that had to be explained. Technology's power was, as Leo Marx and Merrit Roe Smith put it, "gained by experience rather than through the transmission of ideas."[1] This was true of the role that concrete played in all arenas of society, but perhaps no historical field is more influenced if not determined by technology than warfare. Anyone who bothers to compare the US fleet of steel-sided ships and modern naval guns to the decrepit Spanish flotilla it defeated immediately understands how ridiculous it was to attribute the US's rout in 1898 in Manila Bay to Admiral George Dewey's heroism or tactical genius.

Unlike Dewey's steam-powered fleet, reinforced concrete anchored itself to the colony, changing not only warfare, but all the history that unfolded in its wake. This chapter addresses two episodes—the only apparent bookends of the history of *Concrete Colonialism*. The first episode opens in the aftermath of the Spanish-American War, with the earliest large-scale use of reinforced concrete in the Philippines: the construction of a series of island forts built to protect Manila Bay from possible naval invasion. The chapter closes with World War II and the transformation of the entire city of Manila into a concrete theater of war. Separated by a forty-year interim in which the archipelago itself was remade by concrete, these two episodes demonstrate the ways that the material binds the Philippines to the United States into a durable colonial entanglement.

The Concrete Battleship

In February 1910, on a sandbar off the coast of New Jersey, the US military set up a mock battle between state of the art offensive and defensive technologies, aiming their new 12" Mark 8 naval guns at a 20'-thick wall of concrete, reinforced with heavy steel beams. The wall was successfully pierced, thereby confirming the mathematical hypothesis of the guns' power. Just nine months earlier, nine thousand miles away at the entrance to Manila Bay, construction began on Fort Drum—one of the "state of the art" island forts the United States was building to guard the entrance to the Manila Harbor.[2] More commonly referred to as the "Concrete Battleship," Fort Drum was unique in the history of the US coastal fortifications. Fort Drum—along with Fort Hughes (Caballo Island) and Fort Mills (Corregidor), the largest of the island forts built to guard Manila Bay[3]—were part of Theodore Roosevelt's expansion of the fort modernization program, which added new fortifications to Panama, Hawai'i, Los Angeles, and the Philippines in 1905. Construction of Fort Drum began in 1909, when the tiny island of El Fraile was razed to the low-water mark (figure 9.1). Over the next five years, a multideck concrete island was built to resemble a battleship—poured in the shape of a dreadnought and completed with steel-plated sides and a caged mast. Its main artillery feature was a set of fourteen-inch guns housed in superimposed armored turrets. The interior of the fort held a large engine room, powder and shell rooms, storerooms and tankage, plotting rooms, and accommodations for three hundred personnel. Its design and construction, which included what appeared to be the overzealous use of reinforced concrete, were a response to the rapid technological advance of heavy ordnance that had developed during and in the wake of the American Civil War, when masonry walls had failed under the assault of smoothbore cannons.[4]

Despite its impressive appearance, the concrete battleship was obsolete long before its completion. As the ballistics test had already proven, "state of the art" was an increasingly unstable condition. Either unsure of how to change course, or unwilling to scrap the tremendous efforts already invested in the fort,

FIGURE 9.1. (*top*) El Fraile Island, Manila Bay; (*center*) Fort Drum, aka the "Concrete Battleship," during construction; (*bottom*) the Concrete Battleship as completed, 1910. Archives of the Coast Defense Study Group.

the government continued with its plan to fortify the island, ultimately (and rather arbitrarily) settling on a wall thickness of twenty-eight feet. But as the engineers who redesigned Fort Drum understood fully well, it was a desperate and futile attempt to outpace the rapid advance of ballistic power.

Concrete's defeat at the hand of ballistic power was only half of the problem. The Concrete Battleship began construction a year after the United States signed its first contract with the Wright Brothers to build its first military aircraft—an event that would, within the next decade, render the massive investment in Manila's Harbor defense system almost worthless. What, at the time, was a mere theoretical threat became a source of real anxiety in the years following World War I, when Japan purchased large numbers of surplus military aircraft from France and Britain. By 1920, Japan had moved on to production, manufacturing close to a dozen military aircraft under various licenses. In that same year, Japan deployed military aircraft in combat roles during the Soviet intervention in Siberia. By 1928, it had produced its own designs with the aid of hired German engineers. Though Japan's invasion of Manchuria in 1931 was not conducted by air, it offered sufficient evidence of Japan's accelerating imperial ambition. In that year, Manila—an American capital that lay just 1,800 miles southwest of Japan—was without an air raid shelter of any class or kind. Paschal N. Strong, then a young lieutenant in the Army Corps of Engineers stationed on the island of Corregidor, gave this ominous description of the situation in 1932: "I suspect that the Department Commander had sleepless nights as he considered the bird's eye view of a fortress designed when the Wright brothers first flapped their wings. I remember especially our only two really long-range guns . . . sited in the middle of a circular concrete blanket, they resembled from the air two inviting bull's eyes . . . And nowhere in the three square miles of the 'Rock' [as Corregidor was called] was there an air-raid shelter where even a rabbit could hide."[5]

What Strong fails to mention in his fear-soaked chronicle of life on Corregidor is that, just as Manila Harbor's military installments took on the appearance of targets (from an aerial perspective), so too did the city of Manila itself, which lay less than twenty nautical miles from Corregidor. In that same year, some 6,600 miles away, Stanley Baldwin—at the time the United Kingdom's de facto Prime Minister—delivered a well-known speech portending the grim realities of aerial warfare.[6] Purposefully inducing terror, Baldwin wanted the "man on the street" to fully "realize that there is no power on earth that can protect him from being bombed, whatever people may tell him. The bomber," Baldwin warned, "will always get through."[7] Baldwin's speech spiraled into macabre detail about how the advent of aerial warfare threatened the existence of entire cities—their physical structures, cultural institutions, ancient monuments, and civilian inhabitants.[8] Even before a single bomb was dropped, the deadly promise of the technology itself forced the world's leaders, engineers, and architects to consider the city in terms of its bare material condition.

Aerial bombardment rendered the millennia-old architectural discipline of fortress design obsolete. For the first time in history, technologies of defense would be unable to repel technologies of attack. At this historical juncture, when the capacity to destroy large swaths of humanity was first realized, Baldwin "wondered at the conscience of the world." At the same time, he insisted that disarmament treaties like those that resulted from the Washington Naval Conference in 1921–22 would not work. Indeed, though a commission of jurists appointed in the aftermath of that conference had drafted rules governing aerial warfare, those rules were never adopted in a legally binding form because all the major powers involved deemed them "unrealistic."

Well-laid plans to defend Manila were wasted, and Strong was left nearly alone to imagine how he might address the threat of a heavily armed Japanese air force. The defense strategy abruptly transformed from calculations of material strength to a strategy of invisibility. Strong was caught between the Philippine Commander's fear of annihilation and the US's attempt to feign a commitment to diplomacy: executing this order would have violated one of the conditions of the Washington Treaty, which specifically forbade the additional fortification of the mandated islands of the Pacific. With no official budget, Strong proceeded by scraping together whatever supplies he could, procuring drills and old compressors from Filipino gold miners and locating thousands of tons of condemned TNT that the US military was about to destroy for being "unfit for human destruction." Strong enlisted army wives living on Corregidor to save their old magazines, which was then used to wrap the TNT—which arrived as loose powder instead of solid blocks—into useable cartridges. Labor was not hard to come by. It had become customary to use prison inmates, or "bilibids,"[9] as they were called, on cash-strapped American public works projects, and the Malinta Tunnel, begun in 1932, was no different— one thousand inmates serving life sentences were placed at Strong's disposal. Meanwhile, a company of engineers from the Philippine Scouts (an American-trained paramilitary force) "provided an excellent gang of foremen, clerks, et cetera." As was common for Bureau of Public Works projects, a white foreman was used—in this case a "frequently sober" Irish sergeant who "drove the workmen [so] hard" that the workers eventually retaliated against him. Nevertheless, to Strong he "was precious beyond rubies."[10]

FIGURE 9.2. Plan of
the Malinta Tunnel on
the island of Corregi-
dor, ca. 1932. National
Archives and Records
Administration, Col-
lege Park, Maryland.

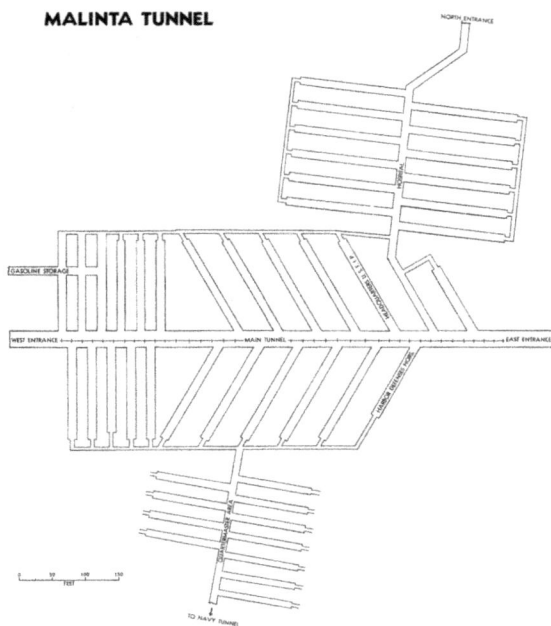

MALINTA TUNNEL

Designed to be completely undetectable from the air, the extensive tunnel system was described by Ralph Harrington Doane as resembling the "backbone of a fish with twelve smaller bones slanting from each side" (figure 9.2). The large central tunnel (the backbone) was fifteen feet high and twenty-four feet wide, while the smaller tunnels were each ten by twelve feet in height and width and about one hundred feet long, ample enough to accommodate Corregidor's sizable military population. Shortly following the completion of digging, the tunnel's volcanic rock walls began to peel off in large chunks, forcing Strong to line the walls in concrete—an expense he had initially hoped to avoid. Ironically, the cement (like much of the cement in the Philippines at the time) was purchased from a Japanese supplier, and Strong suspected that the Japanese knew what the cement was for and envisioned a time when they would themselves be able to benefit from the shelter once they had successfully invaded the Philippines.

Once complete, the Malinta Tunnel was not only a means to evade aerial bombardment; it was also a secure position from which the United States could remotely engage in warfare radically transformed by telecommunications, cryptographic, and information technologies. In fact, much of World War II would

FIGURE 9.3. Malinta Tunnel interior, 1942. National Archives and Records Administration, College Park, Maryland.

be played out in an invisible network thickly populated with file clerks, typists, cryptographers, engineers, and logistics specialists (figure 9.3). Battles were won not only on the open field, but from within Corregidor's tunnels, as was the case when Station CAST—the United States Navy's main signals monitoring and cryptographic intelligence fleet radio unit—broke into the highest security Japanese diplomatic cypher (codenamed PURPLE by US analysts). Thus, the US's new fleet of crypto-warriors "fought" a war from deep within a mountain, while nearby Manila and its citizens remained exposed to the sky.

If the Malinta Tunnel was an early example of a general transformation in territorial military defense strategy—one in which a nation's defensive capabilities would henceforth be calculated not as a function of the strength of its defensive structures, but as a function of distance, time, distribution, intelligence, visibility, and speed—it was also an architecture conditioned by international laws of war. In legal terms, what changed was that the old rules governing land and naval warfare specified the places that *may not* be bombarded (e.g., undefended areas), while the new international laws of war specified the only places that *may* be bombarded—areas defined by the still-murky standards of international law as "military objectives," now classified as "legitimate" targets.

As such, aerial warfare divided the globe into a field of civilian life, on the one hand, and militarized targets of "fair game," on the other. Cities, however—especially industrial ones—could not be so easily divided. Legitimate military objectives included not only purpose-built military programs like Manila Bay's harbor defenses, but also programs and areas with "military possibilities" like privately owned plants and factories, railroads, wireless stations, and harbor installations—all of which were tightly woven into Manila's urban fabric. Rendering the city even more vulnerable was that most new construction in the city was built out of concrete, the strength of which was enough to classify a building as a "military possibility."

Despite Manila's vulnerability, nothing was done to protect it. Very little, in fact, could be done beyond clinging to the slim hope that the leaders of industrialized nations would abide by the new international laws of war.[11] With Japan's formal withdrawal from the Washington Naval Treaty and from the League of Nations in 1933, the situation darkened for Manila. Almost predictably, the city was completely destroyed during World War II. However, unlike London, Berlin, Tokyo, or Dresden, it was not destroyed by aerial bombardment. Rather, Manila was destroyed in a torrent of earth-bound artillery and machine gun fire, grenades, and flame throwers. It was a city torn apart "building by building, floor by floor, and room by room"—a fate predetermined by what Americans had built, and by the material with which they had built it.[12]

A Concrete Theater of War: Material Knowledge
and the Expendable City

Japan launched an attack on the Philippines on December 8, 1941, just ten hours after the attack on Pearl Harbor. In the interest of saving Manila from destruction, General Douglas MacArthur declared Manila an "open city" on Christmas Day, 1941.[13] His strategy was effective. With the exception of limited damage wrought by a first round of air raids aimed at the still poorly defined category of military objectives Manila suffered relatively minor damage as the result of aerial bombardment following the US retreat in March 1942, when MacArthur made his famous declaration, "I shall return." MacArthur, in fact, returned two years later on October 20, 1944, at Leyte. A massive affair, the Leyte landing was the largest amphibious operation undertaken in either hemisphere during the entire course of the war. With a full complement of cameras trained on him, MacArthur waded toward the shore, in the general direction of Ralph Harrington Doane's provincial capitol building—a damaged though still august reminder of all that the United States had promised to the

FIGURE 9.4. US soldiers form an honor guard in front of the Leyte provincial capitol building, in Tacloban, for the handover ceremony restoring the Philippines to sovereign rule following the Japanese occupation, October 24, 1944. National World War II Museum, New Orleans.

Philippines. Eager to memorialize the moment, just three days following his landing, MacArthur raised the American and Philippine flags in front of the capitol building, signaling the formal restoration of civil power within that area to the president of the Commonwealth, Sergio Osmeña, declaring, "On behalf of my government, I restore to you a constitutional administration by countrymen of your confidence and choice" (figure 9.4). Taking a characteristically mawkish turn, MacArthur continued, "as our forces advance, I shall in like manner restore the other Philippine cities and provinces until throughout the entire land you may walk down life's years erect and unafraid, each free to toil and to worship according to his own conscience, with your children's laughter again brightening homes long darkened by the grim tragedy of conquest."[14] As if to repackage the entire US colonial project as a gift of freedom personally handed by MacArthur to his "little brown brothers," the event concluded with ceremonial rounds of artillery fire, followed by a simple parting statement directed at Osmeña: "Now, Mr. President, my officers and I shall withdraw to leave you to the discharge of your responsibilities."

The ceremony at Leyte was a mere dress rehearsal for the production that MacArthur was planning for Manila. Taking control of the archipelago, however, proved a far more difficult task than he had anticipated. Fighting in Leyte continued for months. When he finally reached Manila, MacArthur expected that Japanese forces would spare the capital by declaring it an open city, just as he had done almost three years earlier. Eager to march victoriously into the city MacArthur instead received conflicting intelligence reports—some of which detailed a Japanese retreat from Manila, while others relayed observations of a last-stand defense of the city. Communication was poor, and Japanese forces were divided—both reports were accurate. Whatever the case, MacArthur could not be swayed from his grand vision of victory in Manila. Long before US forces reached the city, MacArthur began organizing a victory parade. Capitalizing on the drama of Daniel Burnham's city plan, the procession began along Rizal Avenue, looped around Taft Avenue, and proceeded to Dewey Boulevard (passing MacArthur's old home atop the Manila Hotel) before ending at precisely 11 a.m. in front of Juan Arellano's Legislature Building. As he had done at Leyte, MacArthur would deliver a speech, followed by Osmeña. Afterward, a band would play "The Star Spangled Banner," followed by "The Philippine Hymn" (the Philippine Commonwealth's English language anthem).

As several military historians have argued, MacArthur's visions of victory, fed by a heady blend of ideological righteousness and thirst for glory, blinded him to the particular dynamics of urban warfare, and of specific problems posed by the design and material condition of the city itself. Fighting in an urban environment offered distinct advantages to a weaker defending force—attacking forces must enter through open streets, while defending forces have the advantage of taking cover in the shelter of buildings, positions that benefit from superior visibility (figure 9.5). This material condition was especially relevant to Manila, the core of which was constructed almost entirely of reinforced concrete. Tall buildings of strong manufacture, paired with open Haussmannian

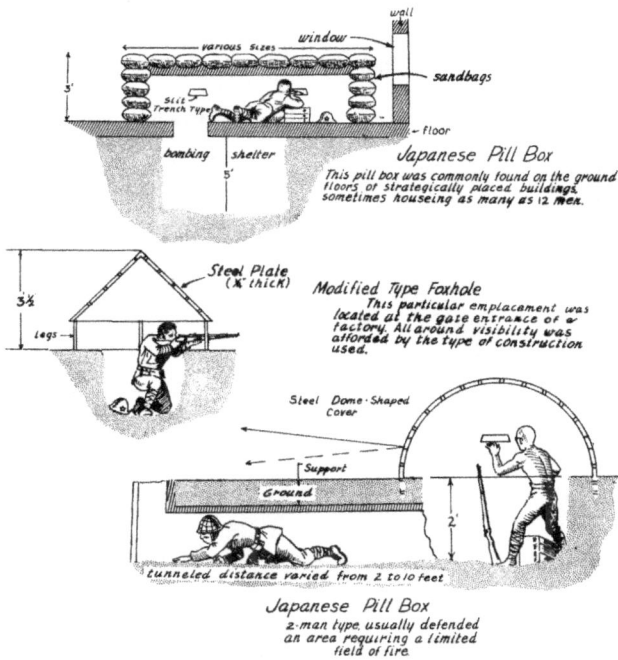

FIGURE 9.5. Examples of defensive emplacements established by the Japanese in Manila's buildings during World War II. From *Japanese Defense of Cities as Exemplified by the Battle of Manila* (Headquarters Sixth Army: A.C. of S., G-2, 1945), annex 30.

boulevards, made for a perfectly defensible city—and not by happenstance. As an urban planning strategy conceived at the height of class and labor conflict in his native Chicago, Burnham's wide boulevards were in part developed to control large urban populations.[15] In keeping with Burnham's plan, all of Manila's major thoroughfares radiated outward from the centermost citadel of Intramuros—an inner core surrounded by forty-foot-thick walls. Encircling Intramuros was Burnham's park (Intramuros's filled-in moat)—a large, clear field that stood several stories below the medieval wall, precluding anything but a direct attack at close range. This ring of lawn was surrounded by the recently completed concrete buildings of the capitol group, adding another formidable perimeter of defense (figure 9.6).

Japanese forces strengthened their position with minimal interventions, erecting barricades across wide avenues, and scattering them with mines and pillboxes. Dewey Boulevard was converted into a landing strip (which required

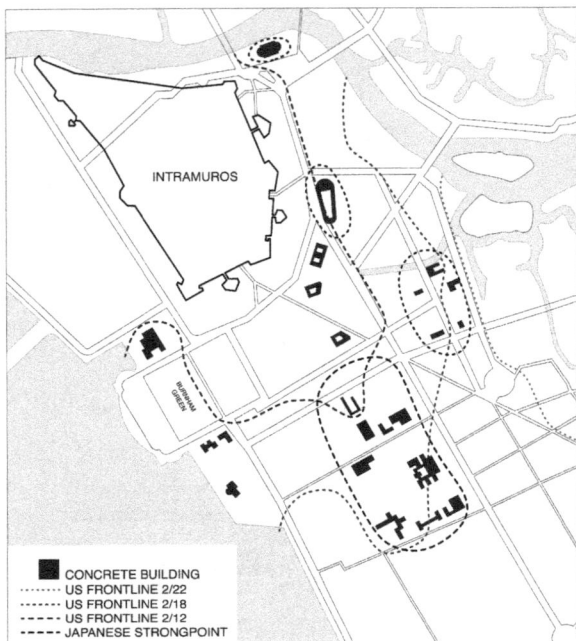

FIGURE 9.6. "Capture of Manila." Map by the author, based on a map in *Japanese Defense of Cities as Exemplified by the Battle of Manila* (Headquarters Sixth Army: A.C. of S., G-2, 1945).

INTRAMUROS

CONCRETE BUILDING
.... US FRONTLINE 2/22
········· US FRONTLINE 2/18
----- US FRONTLINE 2/12
----- JAPANESE STRONGPOINT

little more than the removal of some palm trees). Every reinforced concrete building was occupied—including churches, private homes, factories, department stores, and schools. Each housed between a handful and a few dozen troops; all were provisioned with arms and rations that would last at least two months. Sandbagged emplacements were built at all of the buildings' windows and doors. If US forces were able to penetrate the building, they found themselves drawn into a tangled maze of booby-trapped corridors and rooms. These techniques, deployed in every defended structure, were most sophisticated in the buildings of the capitol group, in the city's center. By the end of Japanese preparations, Manila had been transformed in its entirety into a well-defended and giant military objective. Without a Japanese retreat, there could be no liberation of Manila that did not also imply the total destruction of the city.

Though there is evidence that Japanese forces intended to fully withdraw, the US military failed to open up a line of retreat, completely surrounding Manila on February 11. This is an important point because the ultimate decision to "exterminate [Japanese forces] in place"[16] was justified in once-classified reports as a response to the supposedly unique psychological profile of Japanese soldiers, who would choose death before retirement or withdrawal. This racialized characterization of the Japanese soldier as a "fanatical enemy" was countered by the actual behavior of Japanese prisoners of war, who revealed themselves to be both mild and cooperative, expressing gratitude at receiving good treatment.[17] Though this behavior should have forced Allied leaders to rethink their stereotypes of the enemy, an entrenched race prejudice was used to validate the use of extreme military force.

Whatever the case, the stated objective was to capture Manila as intact as possible, while protecting its civilian population. To do so, MacArthur banned both aerial strikes and large artillery preparations; but this order was abandoned by Major General Robert Beightler, who argued that the use of heavier artillery was a necessary response to "alarming casualty rates" in the early stages of the battle. In fact, the early stages of battle—which focused on securing the water supply system and the city's northern neighborhoods—were successfully achieved with minimal casualties, suggesting that the city might have escaped with only superficial damage. Many of those areas, however, were less densely populated with concrete buildings. Reports coming back to Beightler from civilians and guerillas painted a picture of the center of the city as a "veritable fortress . . . far stronger than the defenses already encountered." Those descriptions compelled Beightler and other commanders to "abandon all pretense" of saving Manila's buildings. As Beightler put it, "to me, the loss of a single American life to save a building was unthinkable."[18] Thus, the next stage of the Battle of Manila began only once both sides had been virtually sealed within strong carapaces of American manufacture—the Japanese military in American-built concrete buildings and the American military in mobile steel tanks. The Battle of Manila was not just a battle between human forces, then—if war is ever just that—but a battle between modern war machines and buildings of strong industrial manufacture. In many ways it was a battle that simply repeated the face-off between naval guns and the concrete wall at Sandy Hook except now trapped between the tanks and the buildings were thousands of Filipino civilians and a small and increasingly desperate force of Japanese soldiers.

The city that the Americans had built—designed to withstand the region's powerful earthquakes—had, under urban warfare conditions, been transformed into an impressive instrument of defense, a transformation that also rendered the city a target. The civic, municipal, and other institutional buildings, were, after all, built out of the very same stuff as Manila's formidable harbor defenses. Under these conditions, the objective of "capturing the city" became an elusive abstraction. Beightler had already discarded the idea of saving the physical city. According to his plan, artillery fire would not be directed against structures such as churches and hospitals that were known to contain civilians. This restriction, according to the 37th Division's report, "would not prove effective, as often it could not be learned until too late that a specific building held civilians."[19] What Beightler presented as a choice between buildings and American lives was in fact a choice between American troops and Manila's civilian population. Civilian lives and the destruction of the city itself were treated as the collateral damage of industrialized and mechanized warfare.

By February 12, 1945, about two weeks into the battle, Japanese resources were seriously depleted, with a small force of about six thousand soldiers reduced to fighting principally with light machine guns, rifles, hand grenades, and even bamboo spears. Both sides found themselves engaged in a battle fought "street-to-street, building-to-building, and room-to-room."[20] The US forces began their attack on the Japanese "strongpoints"—each of them tall reinforced concrete buildings. Between February 13 and 16, Americans cleared La Salle University and Santa Escolastica College; starting on February 15, they cleared the Rizal (baseball) Stadium; between February 18 and 22, they invaded the Philippine General Hospital, the nearby medical school, the new buildings of the University of the Philippines, Manila City Hall, Arellano's Post Office, and the Manila Hotel. The final standoff would take place within Antonio Toledo's twin Finance and Agriculture buildings and Arellano and Doane's Legislative Building.

The most heavily manned Japanese strong point, the Legislative Building's Beaux Arts parti, was scrambled by a scattered network of booby-trapped corridors, pillboxes, and entrances to underground tunnels that led to Intramuros (figure 9.7). In order to seize control of the building, the Army had no choice but to employ a "method of assault" designed to "tear the building asunder."[21]

The assault began with 155mm howitzers aimed at the building from ranges of less than six hundred yards. For two full days, dozens of tank guns fired at the lower floors of Doane and Arellano's building, until enough damage was done for infantrymen to move in (figure 9.8). As the lower portions of the outer walls disintegrated, the walls and roof settled; but the concrete was so strongly reinforced that the structures bent rather than collapsed.[22] After three days of point-blank fire, "the north wing had been demolished and the south wing had been damaged beyond repair." Smaller arms were then aimed at the upper stories to drive Japanese soldiers into the ruins of the first floor and basement. Immediately on the cessation of fire, infantry assault teams entered the building through breaches in the walls, clearing the enemy garrison in a number of hours.

At the same time as the assault on the Legislative Building, US forces moved to clear Intramuros. Once again, the generals assembled a massive artillery

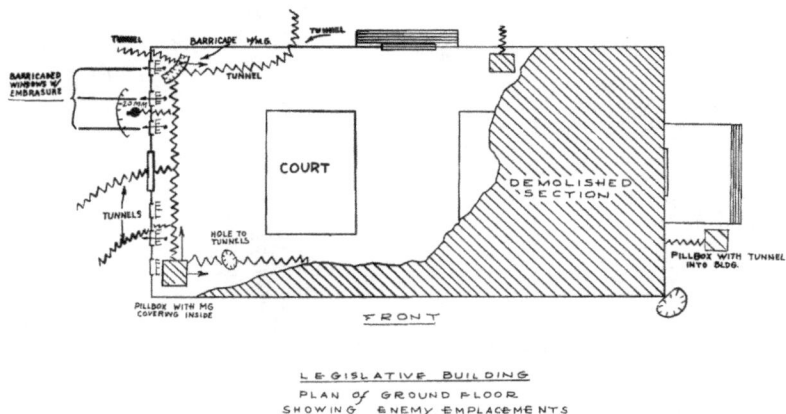

FIGURE 9.7. "Legislative Building: Plan of Ground Floor Showing Enemy Emplacements." From *Japanese Defense of Cities as Exemplified by the Battle of Manila* (Headquarters Sixth Army: A.C. of S., G-2, 1945), annex 22.

FIGURE 9.8. Portico of Juan Arellano's Bureau of Posts partially destroyed by artillery fire. Photo by Carl Mydans for *Life* magazine, April 2, 1945.

FIGURE 9.9. Aerial view of Manila destroyed, 1945.

preparation. Unlike the reduction of the reinforced concrete buildings of American manufacture, which required days of direct fire, Intramuros's thick though brittle volcanic stone walls required only one hour to breach. Describing the conflict as a narcissistic battle between two American technologies, the military historian Robert Ross Smith wrote, "the reduction of government buildings represented the triumph [of American artillery, tanks, and tank destroyers] over modern, American-built, reinforced concrete structures." Throwing in a dig at Spanish technological inferiority, Smith added that "the subsequent reduction of the Spanish walls and stone buildings must have been in some ways anticlimactical to the troops involved."[23] By the end of the monthlong battle, Manila was unrecognizable (figure 9.9). An estimated twenty-thousand Filipino fighters had died in combat while an estimated two hundred thousand more civilians died from starvation and disease.[24] The artillery attacks were of such destructive force that it made little difference whether or not the city was subject to aerial bombardment; the result, Smith noted, "would be the same: Manila would be practically razed." Of all the Allied capitals, only Warsaw, aerially bombed by the Luftwaffe, saw as much damage.[25] Not only were the completed buildings of the capital group destroyed; so were large sections of Intramuros, dozens of centuries-old churches, the infrastructure responsible for 70 percent of the utilities, 75 percent of the factories, 80 percent of the southern residential district, and virtually all of Manila's business district.[26]

Another "New Birth of Freedom"

Manuel Quezon did not live to witness the end of the war, and he could not have foreseen the complete destruction of Manila, or the decimation of its population. It is impossible to know how the destruction of Manila would have affected his views regarding the further militarization of the Philippines. While in exile, Quezon spent his time working to maintain American interest in the Philippines, overseeing the publication of the *Philippine Republic* magazine,[27] and delivering as many speeches as his health allowed (he suffered from tuberculosis, which he died of in August 1944). To stay in touch with the population he had left behind, he issued shortwave radio missives to the Philippines, which the Japanese were unable to block. He also prepared his memoirs for publication, a task he was unable to finish. The manuscript would, however, be rushed to publication, under the title *The Good Fight*, shortly after Quezon's death.

Quezon's preface describes the seemingly unlikely path of someone who once fought in arms against the United States but had, in the course of his lifetime, converted to fight on his conqueror's behalf. The goal of his book, he argued, was "to throw into bold relief the fruit of America's colonial policy in the Philippines, namely, the voluntary sacrifice made by the Filipino people of their lives and fortunes, fighting side by side with the United States against a common foe [and] . . . to offer, inferentially a pattern which may be followed if the redemption of the [world's] teeming millions of subjugated peoples is ever to be attempted."[28] As could be seen by Quezon's own attestations, American investment in a Filipino political elite paid extraordinary dividends. Indeed, the book intended to legitimize not only the American military presence in the Philippines, but expanding US military empire. Eager to amplify Quezon's voice, MacArthur wrote an introduction to *The Good Fight*, emphasizing that Quezon, deceased by the time of the publication, spoke not only as "official representative of his country [but as] . . . the acknowledged leader of a race." This voice, MacArthur emphasized, was the deadliest of weapons against the enemy because it told, in the voice of the native, the "story of a nation that was given by the United States a new birth of freedom achieved in a manner unparalleled in the history of colonization."[29]

MacArthur's reference to "a new birth of freedom" was, of course, an invocation of Lincoln's conclusion to the Gettysburg Address. For Lincoln, abolition marked a transformational moment for the nation, one in which "freedom" was reborn as a freedom for all—a universal freedom. For MacArthur, "a new birth of freedom" extended beyond the outlines of the union as preserved by Lincoln, to embrace the entire globe as an empire of American liberty. As

MacArthur and other US leaders surely understood, the idea that the United States had given freedom to the Philippines was a message best delivered not by the victor, but by a subject who viewed himself as a leader grateful to be conquered by an imperial power committed to "freedom."[30]

On February 27, instead of the elaborate victory parade he had planned, MacArthur passed through Manila's streets amid "burned-out piles of rubble," the shells of "once famous buildings," and "air still filled with the stench of decaying unburied dead." With little fanfare, he officially handed over "full constitutional government" to Sergio Osmeña.[31] His melancholic address, delivered in Malacañang's eerily preserved and near empty state reception room, failed to acknowledge either American or personal responsibility for what had transpired. Despite Manila's destruction and the death of an estimated one million Filipinos over the course of the war, MacArthur insisted that the ultimate result was "a redemption of your soil and the liberation of your people." The liberation that MacArthur referred to as "long sought" was not from fifty years of US colonialism, but from the "bitterness, struggle, and sacrifice" of three years of Japanese occupation. Though it was presented as an unforeseen dramatic chapter that interrupted the US's unbroken record of benevolence, in fact it was a chapter anticipated from the very start and one inscribed in the very construction of the "Concrete Battleship"—a monument to a militarization whose charred ruins still, to this day, mark the entrance to Manila Bay.

The Bases Agreement: "A Question of Sovereignty"

In May 1943, in accordance with conditions laid out in the Tydings-McDuffie Act, Manuel Quezon formally called for the completion of a tentative bases agreement—which before the war was the most contentious issue between the Philippines and its soon-to-be-former colonizer. Quezon acknowledged that the finalization of the agreement was against the multilateral spirit of the UN (the assumed future arbiter of all disputes between sovereign nations). In a bizarre rhetorical maneuver, he argued that the Philippines was not yet independent, and thus there was no reason why the United States and the Philippines could not agree on their future relationship. This agreement was reached when Quezon, in his role as President of the Government in Exile, assumed extraordinary unilateral powers. Filipinos, Quezon boldly conjectured, would be glad to offer bases to the United States at no cost for fifty years. In Quezon's mind, compromised sovereignty was worth the promise of security. In June of 1944, the US Congress passed Joint Resolution 93, authorizing the US president to negotiate with Philippine authorities and then, at his discretion, to retain naval, air, and army bases in the Philippines. In 1945, Sergio Osmeña (acting president following Quezon's death in August 1944) resecured the provisional bases agreement in a secret deal with then-president Truman. Though Osmeña was defeated in the presidential election of 1946, the victor, Manuel Roxas, promptly assured US officials that they could write their own ticket as to the size and location of US bases.

The 1947 Military Bases Agreement allowed for the maintenance and development of twenty-three military installations, including the two largest American military bases on foreign soil: Clark Air Force Base and Subic Naval Base. The agreement also allowed the United States to recruit Filipino volunteers into the US Armed Forces, while simultaneously prohibiting the Philippines from granting base rights to any other country. Furthermore, it placed no restrictions on the uses to which the United States could put the bases, nor the types of weapons that it could deploy or store there. Clark alone covered 130,000 acres, larger than the entire island of Granada, while Subic was roughly four times the size of Washington, DC (or about the size of Singapore). The chapter that supposedly marks the close of "formal" US empire is thus characterized by the commencement of a huge construction project—not only Clark's concrete blankets of runway and Subic's concrete fingers of reclaimed land, but dozens of schools, a zoo, theaters, a parade ground, the world's largest commissary or BX (base exchange), and housing for over fifteen thousand people. At its height, Clark Airbase was the most urbanized military facility in history and by far the largest American military base overseas.[32]

In 1962, the *Military Engineer* published an article describing building conditions at Subic. With an almost audible tone of paternalistic surprise, the author of the article wrote that "Philippine contractors have been quick to learn and adopt American methods," under the "close supervision and inspection by the Navy contracting officer [who has] . . . helped to train the labor forces in time and labor saving methods." The "Philippine construction industry and the knowledge acquired by the Philippine contractors" was, the author concludes, "remarkable, particularly when it is considered that the Philippine Republic is just 15 years old." Astonishingly, the author fails to acknowledge the fifty years of concrete building that, as I have argued, in many ways defined the US colonization of the Philippines.

After World War II, Subic and Clark proved highly valuable to the US military during the Korean War, in the 1954 Taiwan Strait Crisis, and for covert operations directed against mainland China and Sukarno's Indonesia during the 1950s and '60s. It was especially crucial in a logistical and transshipment capacity during the Vietnam conflict, and it provided critical logistical support to the Philippine government in its campaign during the 1950s to suppress the Hukbalahap, the NPA (Communist New People's Army), the Moro Islamic Liberation Front, and the Wahhabi Filipino Grupong Abu Sayyaf.[33] Even after Clark and Subic were closed in 1992, when the Philippine Senate refused to extend the conditions of the Military Bases Agreement, the Philippines remains the US's most important strategic ally in the region, providing a military bulwark against China's expansionist activities. Though US military colonialism would be an especially ambitious project in the Philippines, it was only part of a global strategy that eventually bloomed into a massive, networked, extraterritorial military empire that today encircles the entire planet. Though this empire of "points" is elusive to some, it only seems that way from the perspective of the cartographer—as an almost invisible abstraction.[34] An experience of concrete cannot be reduced to a graphic. Its sheer weight binds it stubbornly to the earth, transforming the daily lives of those who live on, against, and underneath it. Those who were promised the benefits of its physical protection placed their faith in the strength that rendered their bodies the collateral damage of concrete colonialism.

10

RECONSTRUCTION

FROM COLONIAL PROJECT

TO "FOREIGN AID"

World War II resulted in a scale of loss and damage previously unimaginable. Across the globe, aerial bombing laid waste to homes, schools, factories, civic buildings, and entire city centers. In the aftermath, large zones of historical urban fabric built of wood, stone, and brick were replaced with modern reinforced concrete structures—Tokyo's *danchi*, council housing in London, and the *Unité* in Marseilles among them—with many of these projects benefiting from US postwar reconstruction aid. Manila's reconstruction was markedly different from those of European and Japanese cities in that much of what was rebuilt with US aid were structures built by the United States to begin with. Manila's rapid reconstruction, and that of several other US-built Philippine cities and towns, offered a new opportunity for the United States to reconstruct the terms and limits of a new era of neocolonial practice.

In the aftermath of the Battle of Manila, one could not help but notice the peculiarity of one particular ruin—that of the Legislative Building (figure 10.1).

FIGURE 10.1. Ruins of the Legislative Building, February 1945. National World War II Museum, New Orleans, Digital Collections.

The central portion of the building, as noted by the military historian Robert Ross Smith, "still stood above its wings like a ghost arising from between toppled tombstones."[1] That this "ghost" remained was not an accident. Unlike most of the cities that lay in ruin after World War II, the damage it suffered came from the ground and not from the air. Otto Fischer-Credo's pediment would have been largely out of reach, and of little use to destroy. Though the rifles, flamethrowers, tank guns, and bazookas directed at the Legislative Building could hardly be described as instruments of precision, it did seem that US troops purposefully avoided defacing their target. Whatever the case, it was hard to miss the symbolism. The mostly intact pediment standing above the ruins performed not as a symbol of destruction, but as an emblem of endurance and renewal. It is images like these that enabled historians like Smith to characterize the destruction of the Philippines as a "triumph." Though battered it remained recognizable. A semblance of what MacArthur called the East's "citadel of democracy" remained, if only for rhetorical purposes. Given that this chapter begins in 1946, it might seem appropriate to shift our attention to the end of a colonial era. This closing chapter of the US colonial period in the Philippines, however, is not marked by the destruction of colonial structures, but is rather marked by its reconstruction.[2] Reconstruction, then, in this context, should not only be thought of as a physical restoration of the archipelago's war-torn environment, but as part of a reconstruction of US empire.

FIGURE 10.2. (*left*) Ceremony in Rizal Stadium celebrating July 4, 1946, Philippine Independence Day. (*right*) A photo of the scene outside the stadium, showing rusting war machinery in the foreground and the reconstruction of the Legislative Building in the background. *Life* magazine, July 22, 1946.

Manila's postwar destruction marked a disorienting conclusion to US colonial rule. As scheduled and specified in the Tydings-McDuffie Act, on July 4, 1946, ten years after the establishment of the Commonwealth government, and only ten months after Japan's formal surrender, the United States formally withdrew from the Philippines. The two images in figure 10.2 were taken at around the same time. Amid the wreckage of war, arrangements were made for a lavish celebration. The Luneta was cleared of debris, white tablecloths were set for a state dinner at Malacañang, and fireworks were shot from the base of Intramuros's ruins. In the largest, most public gathering, held in a Rizal stadium pockmarked with bullet holes, ceremony organizers built a towering plywood propylaeum, festively decking it with flags and festoons. In the middle of the stadium, on a rostrum shaped to represent the new ship of state, US Ambassador Paul McNutt gently lowered the American flag as Philippine President Manual Roxas raised the flag of the Philippine Republic.

By the time the United States granted political independence to the Philippines, there was little left to be grateful for. Much of the concrete capital that the United States had built—conceived of as symbols of US colonial generosity and of its "unique" and progressive colonial policy—had been spectacularly obliterated by its own destructive hand. Never before had the Philippines looked more like a wretched and expensive liability.

If the images that documented the event seemed jubilant enough, it was only because photographers cropped out the charred remains of a city in total ruin. In the aftermath of war, hundreds of thousands of Filipino survivors were left jobless, orphaned, and homeless, and were forced to improvise shelters in the ruins of the US's liberation effort.

On December 16, 1946, provincial governors, treasurers, district engineers, and superintendents of schools convened at a ceremony to witness Frank A. Waring, chairman of the Philippine War Damage Commission, present Philippine President Manuel Roxas an advance payment of $1 million on the first claim filed by the government of the Philippines under the provisions of the Philippine Rehabilitation Act of 1946. The initially promised $100 million (with a yet to be determined amount to be "given" through loans) was an arbitrary number unconnected to an actual assessment of material damage. Despite arguments to more strictly limit funds, the Rehabilitation Act ultimately provided $620 million in economic aid to the Philippines.

Soon hundreds of contractors, many of them American, began to bid for projects.[3] To aid the reconstruction efforts, the United States government purchased materials and machinery, and reopened the CEPOC factory in Naga, Cebu.[4] As work rapidly proceeded, thousands of US soldiers were stationed in the Philippines to maintain order, provide food, and render other social and emergency services. Soothing their own trauma in the aftermath of a brutal war, many young men took solace in indulging Filipino children with chocolate and candy, tossing shiny, cellophane-wrapped scraps of humanity from the back of their trucks. (When I was a child, these were the stories my mother, father, uncles, and aunts told me of Americans. It is still the explanation they offer for their own passionate and extraordinary American patriotism, the result of a lasting impression of benevolence that aligns sharply with Philippine popular sentiment, even today.)

Funds for the rehabilitation of public buildings were at the sole discretion of the commission, though decisions were made "in consultation with proper officials of the Philippine Government." Realizing, even before work began, that the $57 million allocated for public claims was "inadequate," the commission determined to "allocate money for reconstruction which would be of maximum benefit to all the people of the Philippine Republic."[5] The stated order of priorities was (beginning with the most important) hospitals, dispensaries, waterworks, education, national government buildings, provincial and municipal buildings, and government corporations. As far as the construction of government buildings was concerned, the goal was "for the nation to be fully operational in the shortest possible time." Thus, the commission decided that each award should be sufficient for the construction of reconstruction of "a useful, usable unit."[6] Amid the smoking ruins of total devastation, Ralph Harrington Doane's assertion of beauty's necessity to democracy seemed irrelevant and even frivolous.[7] The haste with which public and private buildings were rebuilt resulted in the substandard reconstruction of much of the capital city. Even the buildings that were supposed to be the crowning achievement of American democratic tutelage were largely stripped of the architectural detail initially sponsored by the United States in demonstration of their largesse.

In photos of Arellano's Legislative Building taken before the Japanese bombing of Manila (see figure 8.1) and after its postwar reconstruction, the structure looks almost identical, and distinctions are even more difficult to detect in person since the referent no longer exists. The elaborate cartouche that crowned the balcony is today gone, as are the sentry figures that disguised the balcony's awkward corners. The open-air gallery of Corinthian columns was replaced by a shallow façade of pilasters. The carefully modeled cornices were, despite the relative ease of reproduction, also omitted. The idea behind the reconstruction efforts was to capture general impressions and global effects while ignoring finer details and fussy art. Arellano, who at first worked with the Rehabilitation Committee, became so frustrated with imposed budget constraints and with a lack of commitment to his original design that he quit. Yet, despite the significant shortfalls of the reconstructions, few noticed a difference; what mattered more was that, amid the massive destruction and sense of devastation, a piece of the city that citizens had thought permanently lost suddenly reappeared—phoenixlike—from the ashes.

It was essential that the War Damage Commission presented its work as a wholly disinterested and benevolent act—not as compensation for the exploitations of colonization, but as a gift of "good will from the United States to another liberty-loving and independent nation."[8] "Reconstruction" was seized on not only as an opportunity to rebuild a war-torn Philippines, but also as one in which the United States could reposition its relationship with its soon to be former colony. The opportunity could not have come at a more convenient moment. As Rupert Evans, former director of the Department of the Interior's Division of Territories and Island Possessions, put it, the "time has passed when the peoples of the Indies, Indo-China, Burma, and India would permit white men to dictate the tenor of their lives."[9] In the aftermath of war, the management of a distant colony seemed less tenable than ever. The recognition of Philippine national sovereignty, however, would not come without conditions.

The funds promised by the Rehabilitation Act—those eventually used in the reconstruction of Manila—were contingent on the Philippines' acceptance of the Bell Trade Act of 1946, which laid out the economic conditions under which the United States would grant the Philippines its "independence." In effect, the Bell Trade Act engineered the Philippines' lasting economic dependence on the United States. Authored by Missouri Congressman C. Jasper Bell, it created a system of preferential tariffs, undermining the Philippine government's control over imports and exports; pegged the Philippine peso at the overvalued rate of ₱2 to one dollar; obligated the Philippine government to not place restrictions on currency transfers to the United States (i.e., corporations who earned profits made in the Philippines were under no obligation to reinvest any amount of those profits); required the perpetuation of prewar free trade relations until 1954; and required that the Philippines not export products that might "come into substantial competition" with US-made goods.[10] Perhaps most significantly, though, it granted US citizens and US corporations equal rights or "parity" with Philippine citizens in any future "exploitation" of natural resources and in the operation of public utilities—a clause that required an amendment to the 1935 Philippine Constitution, which had limited the right to exploit resources in the public domain to Philippine citizens or to corporations in which they controlled 60 percent of the capital. Revealing the one-sidedness of this so-called parity, no similar rights were given to Philippine citizens in the United States. As the former Philippine ambassador to the United States, Eduardo Romualdez, pointed out, the various pacts "negotiated" during this period

> had been concluded in a context in which the Philippines did not have full freedom of action and had been compelled by circumstances to accept provisions which in later years seemed intolerable. . . . The Trade Agreement was not negotiated. Its provisions were dictated by one part, (and) accepted with great reluctance by the other. To be precise, the provisions of the Agreement were determined by the United States Congress in the Philippine Trade Act (Public Law 371, 79th Congress) which had been approved on 30 April 1946, less than ten weeks before the Philippines was to be declared independent. . . . The message was clear. No just compensation for war damage would be made until the Philippine Congress and the Filipino people had accepted the Trade Agreement, including the constitutional amendment concerning "parity" rights.[11]

The Bell Trade Act was passed on July 2 (a decidedly unsymbolic date), just two days before the United States granted independence to the Philippines on July 4. The act outraged Filipino nationalists like Claro M. Recto and Jose P. Laurel—even Sergio Osmeña. The reliably pro-American president commented, at the time, that the act was "a curtailment of Philippine sovereignty, (a) virtual nullification of Philippine Independence."[12] The ailing nation, however, was in no position to refuse aid, and the United States exploited the public's disorientation. In a plebiscite with a 30 percent turnout, Filipinos voted to accept the conditions. Thus, though the physical reconstruction of Manila was the most visible change in the aftermath of the Battle of Manila, it may also have been the least significant. The twin Finance and Agricultural Buildings, the Legislative Building, the reconstructed buildings of the University of the Philippines, the post office, and others, were like a small army of Trojan horses carrying a hidden load of economic reforms and structural adjustments that heralded the Philippines' conversion into a US neo-colony. Despite being poor imitations of the originals, the reconstructed buildings of the capitol group were intended to stand the test of time as monuments to American "benevolence."[13] A bronze plaque was prominently placed on every reconstructed government edifice, which read "Rebuilt with the aid of the people of the United States of America under the Philippine Rehabilitation Act of 1946" (figure 10.3).

After 1945, architecture in the Philippines—once used to symbolize what the United States owed to the colony (i.e., its national sovereignty)—became instead a symbol of what the Philippines owed to the United States for its magnanimity (figure 10.4). Philippine national identity would be forever bound to this concrete affirmation of indebtedness to the United States. The rehabilitation program allowed the United States government to monumentalize its status as the liberator of the Philippines while offering cheap cover for the construction of more elusive forms of US empire. What appeared to be a peace offering was in fact a new imperial strategy. If the standing spectacle of reconstruction was an exercise in "soft power," the Military Bases Agreement and the Bell Trade Act demonstrated how the United States was unwilling to completely relinquish benefits rendered by the colony. This hybrid strategy arguably left the United States in a better position—diplomatically, economically, and militarily—than when it held the archipelago as a colony.

The US's stronger military position became increasingly important as political conditions rapidly changed in East Asia in the aftermath of World War II. Of particular concern to the United States was the creation of the Democratic People's Republic of Korea on September 9, 1948, followed just a year later by the establishment of the People's Republic of China. The eighth and penultimate semiannual report of the War Damage Commission (covering the period ending in June of 1950) pointed out that the Philippines "may serve as an important link in the chain designed to block communist encroachment"—not only as a

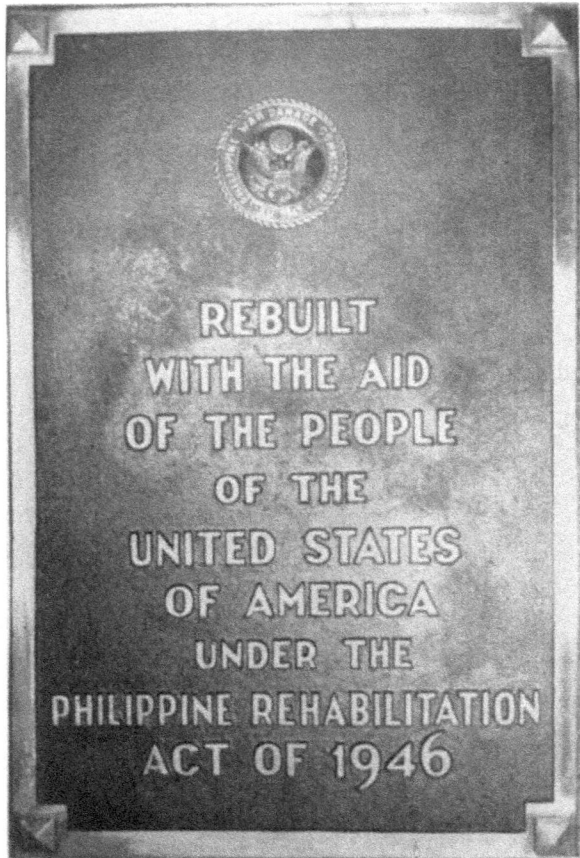

FIGURE 10.3. Bronze plaque placed on all government buildings reconstructed with US aid. From Philippine War Damage Commission, *Semiannual Report of the United States Philippine War Damage Commission* (Washington, DC: Government Printing Office, 1947–51).

military buffer, but as a means of building a lasting loyalty by subduing "those elements in the Philippines which are sympathetic to the communist cause (who) will find it more difficult to spread their doctrines only if the general economic condition of the people is improved."[14]

As a nominally sovereign nation, the Philippines would continue to be exploited, though without any formal rights to economic or political redress to which it could make a moral claim under colonial conditions. The War Damage Commission also covered a fraction of the costs of rebuilding. As the final report pointed out, regarding private claims, "replacement costs in the Philippines are approximately three times more than before the war," which meant that "claimants probably received no more than 20% of today's cost of reproducing their homes, farms, and businesses."[15] Thus, while the legal frameworks and social conditions were set in place for the extraction of the archipelago's

FIGURE 10.4. The Legislative Building during its reconstruction. The sign posted in front of the building reads: "Rehabilitation project aided by the United States of America through the United States-Philippine War Damage Commission." From Philippine War Damage Commission, *Semiannual Report of the United States Philippine War Damage Commission* (Washington, DC: Government Printing Office, 1947–51).

natural resources, skilled labor, and most accomplished professionals, the nation/neo-colony bore responsibility for rebuilding their economies in the devastating aftermath of a war brought to the Philippines by the United States.

Even before the war, the United States was beginning to reorder its foreign policy. It was, for example, not lost on the United States that colonial sovereignty over the archipelago was not worth the money invested. For various reasons, US capital shied away from the Philippines. Glaringly, just two years before the Japanese invasion of the Philippines US foreign investments in the Philippines totaled only a third of what was invested in Japan.[16] After World War II, economic aid was distributed not only according to the damage suffered during the war, but was more strongly determined by the perceived economic importance of the nation receiving aid. This was revolutionary. In the past it was the "losers" of war who paid indemnity to the victors. This changed completely after World War II, when the United States paid not only for the reconstruction of the cities and countrysides of its allies (through the Philippine War Damage Commission and the Marshall Plan), but also funded the reconstruction of Japan and Germany through GARIOA (Government Aid and Relief in Occupied Areas Program). The perceived economic importance of the Philippines is reflected in the fact that the United States granted only $473 million in reconstruction funds to the Philippines (roughly 40 percent of the claimed value of the damage),[17] while aid to Japan totaled $2.2 billion dollars. Thus, even as the United States made an elaborate show of condemning Japanese brutality, avarice, and imperial ambition, far larger amounts of money would be invested into stimulating its economy than would be spent on behalf of the Philippines.[18] Even that aid, however, was dwarfed by the Marshall Plan, which poured $13.3 billion into the economies of Western Europe—with France and the United Kingdom alone receiving $4.6 and $6.6 billion, respectively.[19]

In 1951, the Damage Commission closed shop as planned. Believing the United States had absolved itself of its responsibility toward the Philippines, the US Congress rejected several bills to pay off a standing balance on verified claims (figure 10.5). When, in July of 1957, for example, George P. Miller of California—a former member of the Insular Affairs committee and one of the authors of the original Philippine Rehabilitation act of 1946—introduced a bill to pay the balance on the claims, Congress failed to pass the bill. Reminding the US Congress of its moral obligation to the Philippines, Miller spoke of the "special and peculiar relations between our two countries during the last half century"—carefully avoiding the use of the word "colony."[20] In May 1962, when the US Congress rejected yet another bill to pay off the balance on the claims, it enraged the newly elected Philippine President Diosdado Macapagal, who retaliated by canceling an official visit to Washington and officially changing Philippine Independence Day, at the time celebrated on July 4, to June 12—to commemorate Emilio Aguinaldo's proclamation of independence from Spain. Macapagal's political brinkmanship worked. Three months later, Congress passed a similar bill by an overwhelming margin of 159 votes.

Issuing a statement in which he hailed the action of Congress as the fulfillment of "a long-standing moral commitment," the newly elected President John F. Kennedy remarked that the bill's passage "corrects the record of last May when, partly through a misunderstanding of the issues involved, an earlier

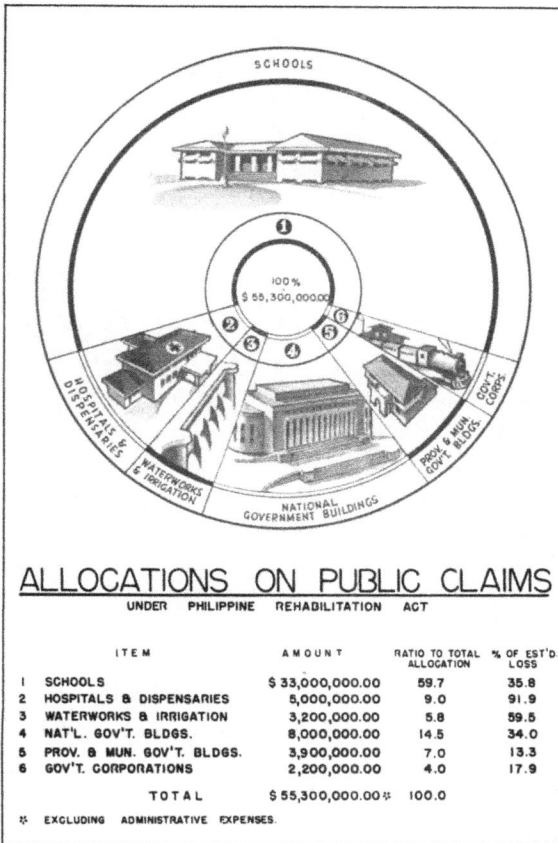

FIGURE 10.5. Pie chart showing allocation on public claims under the Philippine Rehabilitation Act. From Philippine War Damage Commission, *Semiannual Report* 9 (1951), 28.

ALLOCATIONS ON PUBLIC CLAIMS
UNDER PHILIPPINE REHABILITATION ACT

	ITEM	AMOUNT	RATIO TO TOTAL ALLOCATION	% OF EST'D. LOSS
1	SCHOOLS	$ 33,000,000.00	59.7	35.8
2	HOSPITALS & DISPENSARIES	5,000,000.00	9.0	91.9
3	WATERWORKS & IRRIGATION	3,200,000.00	5.8	59.5
4	NAT'L. GOV'T. BLDGS.	8,000,000.00	14.5	34.0
5	PROV. & MUN. GOV'T. BLDGS.	3,900,000.00	7.0	13.3
6	GOV'T. CORPORATIONS	2,200,000.00	4.0	17.9
	TOTAL	$ 55,300,000.00 ✻	100.0	

✻ EXCLUDING ADMINISTRATIVE EXPENSES.

PUBLIC CLAIMS DIVISION   PWDC

version of this bill was defeated."[21] There was, however, more on Kennedy's mind than fulfilling a moral obligation. In May 1961 Kennedy began sending more troops and military advisors to South Vietnam, responding to President Eisenhower's foundering effort to contain Communism in that region. By the time Congress approved the payment of the war damage balance there were already 3,400 troops and military advisors in South Vietnam, a number that rose to eleven thousand by the year's end.

The key advantage of the Philippines' reconstruction program over territorial colonial sovereignty was that it was a finite arrangement with a foreseeable end and a controllable budget. It was also a global reconstruction of US empire—one that seized on widespread disaster of World War II to redraw the map as a complex territory of strategic allies and areas of interest.[22] It was the mo-

FIGURE 10.6. The Legislative Building (*left*), the Finance Building (*center*), and Palma Hall of the University of the Phililppines (*right*), shown in the immediate aftermath of World War II and following "rehabilitation." From Philippine War Damage Commission, *Semiannual Report* 9 (1951), 31–37.

ment when the United States turned away from the territorial colony to the standard lexicon of US development strategy. This included international development aid, technical assistance, and securing rights to build and maintain military infrastructure. This "aid" enabled the United States to renegotiate the terms of its engagement with the Philippines to its direct advantage. Though reconstruction may have obscured the irresolvable contradictions of the US's imperial "misadventure"—the relics of concrete colonialism may still clarify a different story (figure 10.6).

AFTERWORD

As a sophomore in college, I was waiting for a friend to meet me in San Francisco's Union Square, at the foot of the monument that marks its center. Though I had sat at the base of this column before, I had never bothered to read its inscription. The side facing the St. Francis hotel reads: "ERECTED BY THE CITIZENS OF SAN FRANCISCO TO COMMEMORATE THE VICTORY OF THE AMERICAN NAVY UNDER COMMODORE GEORGE DEWEY AT MANILA BAY MAY FIRST MDCCCXCVIII." I had never thought to ponder what direction the wingless victory faced. Though her toe aligns with San Francisco's city grid, her body opens to the southwest, and her laurel wreath points southeast, centering Manila as its distant target (figure 11.1). As with most war monuments, its commemorative role had long since been eclipsed by its present function as urban ornament. Nevertheless, it was surprising to see "Manila Bay" occupy such a prominent spot in the center of the city. This was especially

FIGURE 11.1. The dedication of the Dewey Monument in Union Square, San Francisco, with President Theodore Roosevelt presiding, May 14, 1903.

the case because most people—including myself at the time—know little, if anything, about the US colonial occupation of the Philippines.

The persistent historical amnesia surrounding the US colonial project in the Philippines is, as Cedric Robinson has argued, rooted in a demand for historical coherence that has proven more insistent than a demand for other truths.[1] Historical narratives are, as Hayden White emphasized, "verbal fictions, the contents of which are as much invented as found and the forms of which have more in common with their counterparts in literature than they have with those in the sciences."[2] The root cause of this amnesia is that the history of the US colonization of the Philippines does not conform to the dominant historical narratives of either country. This historical amnesia afflicts the Philippines as much as it does the United States, despite the omnipresence of the concrete relics of US empire that I discuss throughout this book—which rarely, if ever, are seen as evidence of US empire. To the contrary, Manila's Legislative Building (for example) presents the United States as a sponsor of national sovereignty, rather than a colonial oppressor, while the bombed-out ruins of the island forts stand as reminders not of the US's military suppression of Philippine resistance to its rule, but of the US's "liberation" of the archipelago from Japanese occupation.[3] In short, the preponderance of concrete proof of US empire does not render its history self-evident. Understanding these monuments, ruins, and infrastructures has required that they be reunited with the documents that detailed their conception, construction, and reception—the most complete versions of which are found not in the Philippines but in the United States. Research for this project has therefore always felt somehow out of place. Despite these dislocations, US empire is everywhere. That is because the outlines of a concrete colonialism do not only unfold in the distant colony, or in the rarefied space of the archive, but in front of me, in daily interactions with people and things. Archival research has become entangled with memories and relationships—both personal and professional—in ways I could never have anticipated.

I was born on March Air Force Base, near Riverside, California. My father, an internist (then working as a flight surgeon), and my mother, a registered nurse, raised me and my brother in a red-tiled mission-style house. For a time, my grandmother, a retired math teacher, and my grandfather, formerly a school principal, lived with us, teaching us how to read and write. Both born in 1909, they were trained in the American system and taught exclusively in English. Some of my first memories are of my grandmother singing nursery school rhymes to me in an English heavily seasoned by a sharp Batangueña accent: "I have two hands, my left and my right / Hold them up high so clean and bright / Clap them soft-ly, one two three / Clean lit-tle hands are good to see." My grandparents' vocations, my parents' professions, their love of Spanish mission-style architecture, and even *I Have Two Hands* (part of a strictly standardized colonial curriculum emphasizing personal hygiene) were in one way or another bound to colonial history.[4]

Other details of my family history are, for related reasons, unretrievable. Many years ago, as a teenager, I asked my mother about her grandparents.

Though she knew her grandmothers—whom she described as kind, beautiful, and devout—she told me she never knew her grandfathers, whose names she could not even recall. None of her siblings can recall their names either. My best guess is that they died in the Philippine-American War. This would explain why no one spoke of them, and why no one seems to remember them. My mother's family is from Batangas, one of the last provinces in the archipelago to be "pacified" during the "Philippine Insurrection" (later the Philippine-American War).[5] One of the legacies of this hard-fought rejection of colonial rule is the lasting stereotype of the Batangueño as a fierce and defiant people. The history of resistance, in other words, was not forgotten so much as it was neutered and naturalized into an inherited character trait. It was to being half Batangueña, for instance, that my parents attributed my seemingly congenital stubbornness.

Though omnipresent, the ghosts of US colonial history in the Philippines float by most people unnoticed, sensed only by those attuned to their presence. And even then their significance is rarely understood. When I met my partner in graduate school, he knew little about the Philippine-American War. And yet, when I first visited his family home in Vermont, his uncle—an amateur family historian—pointed out that a portrait hanging on the wall of their family home was of my partner's great-great grandfather, Charles S. Wallace, who served in the Philippines during the Philippine-American War as a first lieutenant in the Signal Corps (figure 11.2).

I kept an eye out for Charles S. Wallace in the archives. One day, I stumbled across him. In delivering the report on the progress of his construction of a telegraph line from San Jose to San Joaquin on the island of Iloilo, Wallace wrote:

> The people are mostly in sympathy with the insurgents and unwilling to work. It was found necessary to impress all labor employed outside of San Jose (Antique province). The roads are wretched, bridges rotten or entirely gone, and transportation crude and scarce. . . . The people through this province showed a disinclination to work that was pathetic. On entering a pueblo where it was desired to change workmen, I would immediately notify the presidente of the number of laborers I would require the following morning, and he would invariably assure me that they would be there at the hour named, but in no instance did the men appear. In every case I found it necessary to send the guard through the town taking every able-bodied man found until the number required was secured. . . . The occupation of these people is raising rice and fishing. As this is not the planting season, and fishing is done by traps, visited once or twice daily, the men pass their time in almost complete idleness.[6]

FIGURE 11.2. Wall of portraits in a Vermont family home, 2014.

Each word of Wallace's report was wholly predictable. Though, for what are perhaps obvious reasons, it landed differently. I wondered then, and still do, what he would think of our children, his descendants.

More than a decade later, in 2017—on a playground in Cambridge, Massachusetts, where I had just moved to start my new job at Tufts University—a woman looking after her granddaughter approached my mother, who was looking after hers. Recognizing my mother as Filipina, she initiated conversation with her, explaining that she had once taught English in the Philippines, shortly after college, and mentioning along the way that she was also a professor at Tufts. I would soon meet the professor myself, and during the course of our first conversation, she revealed that William Cameron Forbes was her great uncle. After learning that Forbes was an important figure in this book, she kindly invited me over to her house for brunch—an old, grand house designed by the prominent nineteenth-century architect, William Ralph Emerson (W. C. Forbes's first cousin, twice removed). On our arrival, she told us that she had inherited Forbes's home (he was a lifelong bachelor). She made us a Spanish tortilla and a salad served out of a heavy kamagong bowl—which Forbes had brought over from the Philippines. I could not help but recall the chapter from *The Romance of Business* where Forbes describes empire "as we encounter it at the breakfast table."[7] It seemed almost unbelievable to me that I was sitting at the very table he was quite likely imagining.

When the professor moved out of her home in Milton she kindly gave me a small archive of Forbes's documents and personal effects—baby photos, photos of him playing polo, a photocopy of a sketched portrait by Henry Singer Sargent, huge scrapbooks (on which his book *The Philippine Islands* was based), atlases, maps (some of which now hang in my office), and an old copy of the 1910 *Manila Times* guide for "Settlers and Investors."[8] Each time I rummage through this material, I marvel at its presence. About a year after that brunch, I asked the professor if she knew of a Native American stone bowl that Forbes wrote about in *The Romance of Business*. She forwarded my email to an extensive family network and, three years later, sent me a response. Her cousin had found the bowl in the attic of Ralph Waldo Emerson's home, carefully identified with a handwritten label. She sent me a photo of it (figure 11.3).

The bowl, one of Forbes's "family treasures," was retrieved one day when his grandfather, Ralph Waldo Emerson, was supervising workmen digging a hole to plant an elm tree. In the chapter "The Story of Steel," Forbes used the bowl to illustrate a progressive theory of American time—one in which the arrival

FIGURE 11.3. Native American stone bowl displayed at the Ralph Waldo Emerson house, Concord, Massachusetts. The note inside reads "This dish was found by John Dove in digging a hole for the Elm planted by R. W. Emerson on the 15th May, 1874." Courtesy of Beatrice Manz.

of an Anglo-Saxon civilization to the Americas enabled a historical leap from the Stone Age to the Age of Steel. For, whereas "*our* ancestors in Britain were hammering tools out of stone when . . . the wooly haired rhinoceros . . . gigantic Irish elk . . . and cave lion were roaming about the country,"[9] on the land now known as the United States those same tools were still being fashioned just a few centuries ago; and "even now one can pick up arrowheads, spearheads, stone bowls and dishes and other evidences of a Stone Age among the Native Americans." The bowl, Forbes pointed out, was not an ancient artifact, but rested close to the surface of the present day. Its "discovery" allowed Forbes to confect a romantic narrative of an epoch-making material transformation, the benefits of which he found so indisputable that he assumed as a personal mission its acceleration and global expansion. Forging an alliance with modern materials allowed him, or so he thought, to draw a straight line between his own intentions and the world as we know it.

As in much of the world, the use of concrete is today pervasive in the Philippines, in infrastructural, commercial, civic, and even in domestic architecture, where it is a material of aspirational desire.[10] Today, overseas Filipino workers (OFWs) dream in concrete. The last time I was in the Philippines, I visited "Little Italy," a dense neighborhood nestled on a hillside in my mother's hometown of Mabini. Since the late 1970s residents from this area, including relatives of mine, have through word of mouth found domestic work, much of it in Rome (a migrant pattern particular to this area). Large concrete homes, painted in shades of travertine, some of them sheathed in stone tile, are topped with sheet metal painted in flat approximations of terracotta or patinated copper. For most of the year these houses are eerily empty while those who built them work to ensure they can be maintained for rare occasions when family is able to gather. This, too, is a story of concrete colonialism. Countless *others* haunt the space between the stone bowl and the concrete world that I address throughout this book. Some I have mentioned, and others I have not. Though this book is haunted by them, it cannot speak for them, nor does it aim to represent them. Rather, it describes a material world that may help orient us toward their presence.

Notes

INTRODUCTION

1. It is interesting to note that Amos Miller writes this passage not in praise of the Anglo-Saxon, but as a criticism. In describing Manila as a "dream city," he engages in a sort of Orientalist fantasy outside of capitalist time. To this effect, Miller wrote:

> Here is a land where men are not measured by results, where life is not contained in the abundance of things that a man possesses, where something besides balance sheets and bedrock chances are the final goal, if indeed, it has any destination. And the old east is rich in that one commodity in which the new West is utterly and hopelessly bankrupt. We [the author here occupies the voice of the Filipino] are millionaires in *time*. We may not be long on houses and lands and every new day does not lay at our feet the opportunity of a lifetime to get in on the ground floor, but we have time and to spare; and with all their progress and power and pomp, the kings of commerce are miserable paupers pitiably begging, as they rush along, for a morsel of time in which to stop and live. (Miller, *Interesting Manila*, 51)

2. Fitch, *Critic in the Orient*, 49.

3. Forbes, *Philippine Islands*, vol. 1, 395.

4. The nipa hut is a vernacular building type made of bamboo and nipa fronds.

5. Roman concrete was called *opus caementicium*. In its noun form, concrete is a more literal usage of the Latin root word *concretus*—the perfect passive participle of the verb *concrescere*, which means "to grow together." It is therefore a precise description for a material that is the outcome of a series of physical and chemical processes in which an admixture of water, stone, sand, and gravel are mixed into a slurry activated by cement, the ingredient that enables the mixture to grow together as a monolith. The scholarship on the history of Roman concrete is vast and spans a number of disciplines. See, for example, Malacrino, *Constructing the Ancient World*, and Oleson, *Building for Eternity*

6. Ingold, *Making*, 74.

7. There are, of course, notable exceptions. The effacement of concrete's characterless smoothness becomes a preoccupation of Brutalist architects who begin to experiment

with board-formed and bush-hammered concrete. See, for example, Kubo, Grimley, and Pasnik, *Heroic*, and Banham, *New Brutalism*.

8. I refer here, of course, to the oft-quoted speech delivered by Daniel Burnham, in which he famously said "Make no little plans, they have no magic to stir men's blood." Burnham, quoted in "Stirred by Burnham," *Chicago Record-Herald*, October 15, 1910.

9. Michel Foucault argues that, beginning in the early seventeenth century, the sovereign must know not only laws, but more crucially those elements that constitute the state—specifically, a reality or knowledge of the state that was called "statistics," which is a set of technical knowledges that describes the reality of the state itself. Foucault, *Security*, 273–74.

10. The "Three-age System" was formalized in 1836 by the Danish antiquarian, Christian Jürgensen Thomsen. Heizer, "Background of Thomsen's Three-age System."

11. Adas, *Machines as the Measure of Men*, 12.

12. Faulty concrete is difficult to perceive with the human eye. Contractors can reduce costs by drastically reducing the amount of reinforcement and/or the amount of Portland cement in a concrete admixture, rendering the material dangerously weaker. The catastrophic destruction seen following the 2010 earthquake in Haiti and the 2023 earthquake in Giazantep, Turkey, was, in this way, not just willfully negligent, but intentional. On the connection between faulty concrete engineering and "natural disaster," see Muir-Wood, *Cure for Catastrophe*, ch. 5, "Risk Made Concrete."

13. Allais and Meggers, "Concrete Is One Hundred Years Old," 75–89.

14. Cox, "Use of Concrete in India" 24–35; Tappin, "Early Use of Reinforced Concrete."

15. On Hennebique's expansion into the Maghreb, see Frapier and Vaillant, "Organization of the Hennebique Firm," and Lambert, "Bridges as Ambassadors," 66–73. Hennebique's "official" recognition by colonial authorities in Algeria, Lambert argues, was more important than the relationship it forged with railway companies and industrialists working in protectorates (like Tunisia and Egypt, where it opened offices in 1898) where it was relatively easy to win over engineers working with railway companies and industrialists who were unencumbered by the "narrow and puerile administrative formalism" typical of both cosmopolitan France and its directly ruled colonies, then governed by the conservative Département des Ponts et Chaussées. In the Philippines no such conflict existed as the government directly supported the use of reinforced concrete from the beginning—in direct support of railway companies and other industrialists. Indeed, though Egypt was not a formal colony of Britain, William Cameron Forbes saw Britain's indirect rule over Egypt as a strong model for the US colonial project in the Philippines, where he was governor-general from 1909 to 1913. See the correspondence between Forbes and Charles W. Eliot, then president of Harvard University, and President William Howard Taft in "W. Cameron Forbes Letters Comparing Egypt and the Philippine Islands, 1909-1910," MS Am 2765, Houghton Library, Harvard University.

16. Stierli and Pieris, *Project of Independence*, 10. For early reinforced concrete construction in China, see Han and Wang, "Transplantation and Adaptation," and Zheng and Campbell, "Reinforced Concrete in Modern Shanghai."

17. Between 2012 and 2014, China emplaced more than ~4.7 billion tons, a greater amount than the US did cumulatively throughout the entire twentieth century (approx. 4.6 billion tons). Smil, *Numbers Don't Lie*, 285.

18. Jennings, *Imperial Heights*. See also Wright, *Politics of Design*. For more on the planning of Baguio see McKenna, *American Imperial Pastoral*.

19. As detailed, for example, in Sklar, *Corporate Reconstruction*, 84 n58.

20. On the relationship between "reconstruction" and US empire, see Ekbladh, *Great American Mission*.

21. Shoemaker, "Typology of Colonialism." See also, Shibusawa, "'U.S. Empire' and Racial Capitalist Modernity."

22. The general outlines of this argument are laid out in Latour, *Reassembling the Social*.

23. Giedion, *Building in France*.

24. On the necessity of "narrating connection" in the construction of US imperial histories, see Kramer, "Power and Connection."

25. Moro and indigenous resistance have been constant from Spanish colonial times until today. As Enseng Ho argues, Moro resistance has long been shaped by far-reaching cosmopolitan Islamic Hadrami networks. See Ho, "Empire Through Diasporic Eyes."

26. Though transformed, this is a struggle that continues to this day—for example, in the secessionist movements of the historically Muslim south, and in the highlands where indigenous groups continue to struggle against large-scale dam building. On the Muslim struggle, see, for example, Ho, "Empire Through Diasporic Eyes." And on the latter see Davis, "Palm Politics."

27. Williams, *Tragedy of American Diplomacy*, 46.

28. For Andrew Carnegie's "anti-imperial" position, see Carnegie, "Distant Possessions."

29. Turner, "Significance of the Frontier," 31.

30. Turner, "Middle West," 795.

31. Immerwahr, *How to Hide an Empire*.

32. My use of "clusters of historical details" is largely inspired by the work of Rafael, *White Love*, 4.

33. Shibusawa, "'U.S. Empire' and Racial Capitalist Modernity," 858.

34. Shibusawa, "'U.S. Empire' and Racial Capitalist Modernity," 876.

35. Forbes, *Inauguration Address*, 19.

36. Forbes, *Inauguration Address*, 10.

37. Forbes, *Inauguration Address*, 11.

38. On eliminating the scandal of slavery in the Philippines, see Salman, *Embarrassment of Slavery*.

39. Robinson. *Black Marxism*, 164.

40. Robinson, *Black Marxism*, xlix.

41. See Edison Portland Cement Co., *Romance of Cement*, and Lesley, *History of the Portland Cement Industry in the United States*.

42. Edison Portland Cement Co., *Romance of Cement*.

43. The *Quarterly Bulletin, Bureau of Public Works* became an annual publication between 1921 and 1931, when it was published under the title *Bulletin, Bureau of Public Works*.

44. Niemeyer, "American Historical Collection of Filipiniana."

45. An example, addressed briefly in chapter 5, is when farmers sued the *Tabacalera* (tobacco company) during the construction of the Tarlac Canal. Today an indigenous-led anti-dam movement represents the most forceful opposition to concrete colonialism as such. See Delina, "Indigenous Environmental Defenders."

46. Benjamin, "On the Concept of History," 389–401.

47. Cronon, *Changes in the Land.*

48. Megan Black offers a compelling and thorough account of the reassessment of US territory as material through the imperial institutional history of the Bureau of the Interior in her book *The Global Interior.*

49. I refer here not only to what William Rankin describes as a major shift in geographical representation, but to a *material* reordering of space that encompasses not only the kind of military engagements that went hand in hand with wartime map-making, but also encompassing economic changes that elude geopolitical representation. See Rankin, *After the Map.*

50. Wright, "Daniel Hudson Burnham," 184.

51. Louis Sullivan intended this characterization of Burnham as a harsh indictment of Burnham's debased architectural practice. See Sullivan, *Autobiography of an Idea*, 285–7.

52. Michael Osman offers a particularly clear illustration of this fusion of managerialism and architecture in "Managerial Aesthetics of Concrete."

53. Mumford, *Sticks and Stones*, 124.

54. Sullivan, *Autobiography of an Idea*, 325.

55. Smil, *How the World Really Works.*

56. Elinoff and Kali, *Social Properties of Concrete.*

57. Chow, "Politics and Pedagogy."

58. Rafael, "Cultures of Area Studies," 91–111.

59. Scholarship on the architecture of the Philippines, such as Winand W. Klassen's *Architecture in the Philippines*, Gerard Lico's more recently published heroic textbook, *Arkitekturang Filipino*, and Ian Morley's multiple volumes on urban planning in the Philippines, including *American Colonisation and the City Beautiful, Cities and Nationhood,* and *Remodelling to Prepare for Independence,* are rarely considered relevant outside of the Philippines or at most Southeast Asia. The limited reception of this work is in part a symptom of a nationalist and regionalist discourse that in significant part took shape in the period and under the conditions examined in this book. The work of Abidin Kusno (on Indonesia), Lawrence Chua (on Thailand), and Gwendolyn Wright (on French Indochina) has reached a wider readership, as have edited volumes collected under the regionalist heading of "Southeast Asia," including Jiat-Hwee Chang and Imran bin Tajudeen's *Southeast Asia's Modern Architecture.* Lai Chee-Kien addresses this issue in his article "Beyond Colonial and National Frameworks." This book attempts to historicize the "national frame" such that it can be understood within a broader history in which it took shape.

60. Barad, *Meeting the Universe Halfway.*

61. Summerson "What Is the History of Construction?"

62. Summerson "What Is the History of Construction?"

63. As Adrian Forty points out, François Coignet realized this as one of concrete's potentials, writing in 1861 that "whatever can be done in Paris . . . can be done in every land." Quoted in Forty, *Concrete and Culture,* 97.

64. The term *decolonization* introduced in the 1930s and popularized in the 1960s was, Raymond Betts argues, "seldom restricted in application to a particular political activity or a neatly defined era . . . and was interpreted to be both a calculated process of military engagement and diplomatic negotiation between the two contending parties: colonial and anticolonial." Betts, "Decolonization," 23–38.

CHAPTER 1. THE "MASTER MATERIAL" AND THE "MASTER RACE"

1. Witt, "Why Concrete Is the Master Building Material," 159–61. After returning to the United States from the Philippines, Witt became an industry expert on Portland cement, holding academic positions at the University of Pittsburgh and a variety of research positions, including the directorship of the Portland Cement Association in Chicago. He wrote *Portland Cement Technology* in 1947, and an updated edition in 1966, perhaps the most comprehensive book on the subject. Both editions were widely used academic and industry references.

2. The recommendation in full on "Masonry Constructure" reads:

In a tropical climate costly structures put up with granite, marble, or other building stones, in the manner of public buildings in Europe and America, would be out of place. Flat walls, simply built of concrete (with steel reinforcing rods to resist earthquakes), and depending for their effect upon beautiful proportions rather than upon costly materials, are from all points of view most desirable for Manila. The old Spanish buildings with their relatively small openings, their wide-arched arcades, and large wall spaces of flate whitewash, possess endless charm, and as types of good architecture for tropical service, could hardly be improved upon. (Burnham and Anderson, "Report on Improvement of Manila," 635)

3. United States Geological Survey, *San Francisco Earthquake and Fire.*

4. Estes, *Earthquake Proof Construction,* 32–34.

5. Estes, *Earthquake Proof Construction,* 34.

6. Mabry, "Regulation, Industry Structure, and Competitiveness."

7. "Cement Tariff in the Philippines," 338.

8. Stocking, cited in Vitalis, *White World Order,* 46. See Stocking, *Race, Culture, and Evolution,* 112, 121. For other historical perspectives on development, see, for example, Engerman, *Staging Growth.* On the endurance of the Darwinian connection see Mazrui, "From Darwin to Current Theories."

9. Hall, "Point of View Towards Primitive Races."

10. The word *altruism* was used liberally, especially by US colonial officials. See, for example, Shuster, "Our Philippine Policies."

11. Black, *Global Interior.*

12. Blakeslee, "Introduction," 3.

13. Blakeslee, "Introduction," 3.

14. Odum, "Standards of Measurement."

15. Boas, "Changes in the Bodily Form."

16. Huntington, "A Neglected Factor." See also Huntington, *World Power and Evolution*. Just as soon as Odum and Huntington attempted to systematize race development practice, the journal began to shift its approach to race. This was especially the case in the aftermath of three closely related events—the end of World War I, the 1919 passage of the Jones Law, and Wilson's League of Nations proposal—after which the journal aligned itself with Wilson's internationalist project. The *JRD* turned away from the colonial retention of the Philippines and toward supporting the cause of Philippine nationalism. Accordingly, the *JRD* platformed the contributions of Filipino *Nacionalistas* Manuel Quezon and Maximo Kalaw. Though the shift from benevolent colonialism to the promotion of an "indigenous"-led national sovereignty was both complex and gradual, the transition was inaugurated by the Jones Law (the first formal promise to grant the Philippines its independence). This coincided with the journal's publication under its new title, *Foreign Affairs*. See Vitalis, *White World Order*.

17. Kramer, *Blood of Government*.

18. Beardsley, "Progress of Public Works in the Philippine Islands," 174.

19. Koch, "Methods and Practice," 239.

20. Koch, "Methods and Practice," 239.

21. Davis, *Building Character*; Merwood-Salisbury, *Chicago 1890*.

22. Worcester, *Philippines Past and Present*.

23. William Cameron Forbes, Journal, William Cameron Forbes Papers, Library of Congress, Manuscript Division, MSS20982, volume 1, 366n.

24. The "Lake Mohonk Conference of Friends of the Indians" was a conference founded by Quaker brothers Albert and Alfred Smiley in 1883. There, wealthy white "philanthropists" and others invested in the "Indian problem," while gathered on stolen Mohican and Munsee native lands in upstate New York to discuss methods aimed at assimilating Native Americans into mainstream society, which included breaking up the reservation system, and various approaches to "education." When it was realized that many of their conversations were also applicable to formerly enslaved populations, and (after 1898) to the "primitive" populations of Cuba, the Philippines, and Puerto Rico, the group appended the catchall phrase "and other dependent peoples" to the conference title.

25. Forbes, "What Had Best Be Done," 117–23.

26. Forbes, "What Had Best Be Done," 117–23.

27. Rafael, *White Love*, 22.

28. William Cameron Forbes, "The Address of the Governor General at Zamboanga," Forbes Papers, Houghton Library, Harvard University, fMS Am 1192.4, volume 7, 2295.

29. Jones, *Misgovernment in the Philippines*, 9–11, 24–27; see also Forbes, *Reply to Jones*.

30. On Georg Simmel's concept of the character of calculability, especially as it relates to empire, see Mitchell, *Rule of Experts*. See also Simmel, "Metropolis and Mental Life."

31. Forbes, *Inauguration Address*, 14.

32. Forbes, *Inauguration Address*, 14.

33. Forbes, *Romance of Business*, 15.

34. Demolins, *Anglo-Saxon Superiority*, 128; the book appeared in English two years after its first edition, in 1897, in French. For the estimation of its "striking success," see Fetter, "Review."

35. White, *American Century.*

36. Burnham and Anderson, "Report on Proposed Improvements."

37. Fetter, "Review," 117.

38. Robinson, *Black Marxism*, xii.

39. Timothy Mitchell points out the book's popularity in Egypt, and its importance especially relative to a project of developing Egyptian character; see *Colonizing Egypt*, 111.

40. Demolins was the editor of *La Science Sociale.* Though Robert Vitalis does not address Demolins or his work directly, he lays out the common origins of a now defunct discipline of "race development" and American social science, on which Demolins was deeply influential. Vitalis, *White World Order.*

41. Hall, "White Man's Burden," 83.

42. The idea of preserving race was typical of the Boasian generation of anthropologists and ethnologists, who practiced what came to be known as "salvage anthropology." This was especially the case with Native Americans. Alfred Kroeber at UC Berkeley, for example, is best known for his attempt to record the languages and lore of "disappearing" California Indians. See Clifford, "The Others."

43. Beardsley, "Progress of Public Works," 174.

44. Beardsley, "Progress of Public Works," 174.

45. Beardsley, "Progress of Public Works," 174.

46. Clark, "Labor Conditions in the Philippines," 845.

47. According to union records there were more than 100,000 participants. Guevarra, *History of the Philippine Labor Movement.*

48. Politically cautious, Taft staged an openness toward unionization by inviting leaders from the American Federation of Labor to organize unions along more conservative, decentralized, and "apolitical" lines. Eliding a direct affront to the burgeoning labor movement, the adoption of race as a master narrative enabled US colonists to discuss labor issues using a set of terms that both excluded native voices and preempted the formation of international worker solidarity. Membership in the UOD reached twenty thousand in its first year, a year in which a number of strikes were organized. De los Reyes was eventually arrested on charges that he conspired to organize workmen to force up the price of labor. He was released after serving half of his four-month sentence, on the condition that he cease his labor organization activities. Dimonador Gomez, a Spanish Filipino physician, added "Filipina" (UODF) to the organization's name to suggest a nationalist orientation. He too was arrested, sentenced to hard labor, and released on conditions similar to those of de los Reyes. For more on labor conditions in the Philippines in the early years of US colonialism, see Guevarra, *Philippine Labor Movement*, 845; Kerkvliet, *Manila Workers' Unions*; and Wurfel, "Trade Union Development." For more on de los Reyes's role in the organization of the union movement, see Anderson, *Under Three Flags*; and Scott, "Minority Reaction."

49. The development of bamboo construction as a modern trade would not have been out of the question. Architect William le Baron Jenney (1832–1907), in fact, attributed the skeleton frame (one of the technologies that enabled the construction of skyscrapers) to the Filipino bamboo house. The skeleton frame, Jenney argued, was not the product of "invention," but was rather "nature's child," that is, the outcome of a process of evolution that Jenney claimed he first observed among the "primitive" people of the Philippines. In

an often repeated tale, at just seventeen years old, Jenney visited the archipelago in 1849 aboard one of his father's whaling ships (of the Jenney and Gibbs line). According to Jenney, he watched Philippine natives building bamboo and nipa houses, a process that began with the selection of a bamboo grove where they left "large deep-rooted trees as columns for isolated piers . . . and [used] lighter cuts for lateral or diagonal braces, floor supports, and partitions, all banded together with thongs at the intersections." These buildings, Jenney wrote, were barely disturbed "during the prevalence of typhoons and earthquakes . . . while larger [stone] buildings are destroyed." In this way, his partner William Mundie recalled, Philippine natives "unconsciously developed a system which gave to [Jenney], the alert young engineer and architect, the principles which had their part in the most extraordinary revolution in the construction of buildings ever recorded in history." See Turak, *William Le Baron Jenney*, 20. As Joanna Merwood-Salisbury argues, there is reason to question the sincerity or truth of Jenney's story, especially on account of its similarity to arguments put forth by Gottfried Semper in his famous work *Der Stil in technischen und tektonishen Künsten* (Style in the Technical and Tectonic Arts), and also because he instrumentalizes the story to argue for the inevitability of the skyscraper form. Merwood-Salisbury, *Chicago 1890*. See also Davis, "Seeds That Float."

50. Forty, *Concrete and Culture*, 226. On "deskilling," see also Ferro, "Concrete as Weapon."

51. Forty, *Concrete and Culture*, 226.

52. Forty, *Concrete and Culture*, 226.

53. Here I refer to Césaire's famous equation, "colonization = thingification," in Césaire, *Discourse on Colonialism*, 42. I also refer obliquely to Ferro's "Concrete as Weapon."

CHAPTER 2. STABILITY: THE FOUNDATIONS OF US EMPIRE

1. Kipling's observations of Chicago, especially those contained in this chapter's epigraph (*American Notes*, 90), closely reflect Kipling's sketch of Calcutta, "A Real Live City," the first chapter of his *The City of Dreadful Night*.

2. Vitruvius, *Ten Books on Architecture*.

3. Kipling, "A Real Live City," 8.

4. Lucia Allais and Forrest Meggers point out that an equation arrived at in 1969, which takes into account modern concrete's reaction to atmospheric carbon dioxide (which is steadily increasing), predicts concrete's lifespan to be about a century. Allais and Meggers, "Concrete Is One Hundred Years Old," 75–88.

5. On the Treaty of Chicago in the context of Indian Removal see, for example, Bowes, "American Indian Removal."

6. Frederick Jackson Turner argued that the development of the "West" was both dependent on and culturally and politically distinct from that of the "East" because the West "needed capital; it was a debtor region, while the East had the capital and was a creditor section." See Turner "Significance of the Section."

7. Peter Chardon Brooks became the wealthiest man in New England by insuring New England's merchant ships. The Presidential Committee on the Legacy of Slavery, *Legacy of Slavery at Harvard*, 22.

8. Peter Brooks to Owen Aldis, quoted in Condit, *Chicago School*, 52.

9. Tallmadge, *Architecture in Old Chicago*, 143.

10. Root, "Great Architectural Problem."

11. Root took special interest in professional codes and standards; see Root, "Code for Guidance."

12. The article was motivated, at least in part, by an intense competition between the two cities for economic primacy. The most recent blow to New York was Chicago's winning bid to host the Columbian Exposition. See "Crust at Chicago."

13. Baumann, *Art of Preparing Foundations*.

14. See, for example, Hines, *Burnham of Chicago*, 49.

15. The use of rails in architecture was not new. The abundance of iron rails in Paris was, as Walter Benjamin argued, one of the two "conditions of emergence" for the Parisian arcades (the other being the boom in the global textile trade). However, unlike the arcades—a *superstructure* that hovered above the heads of Paris's consuming classes—the raft foundation was a *base*: buried several feet below ground level, it was visible only in the form of the new heights it made possible. Benjamin, *Arcades Project*, 4.

16. Monroe and VanBrunt, *John Wellborn Root*, 231.

17. Monroe and VanBrunt, *John Wellborn Root*, 231–32.

18. Shankland, "Construction of the World's Fair."

19. Trachtenberg, *Incorporation of America*, 211. This contrast would set the Chicago exposition apart from the Paris Exposition of 1867, in which the vitreous galleries of the fair were virtually indistinguishable from the glassed-in arcades of the city that was the fair's setting. Thus, the Paris Exposition presented a commodified world without escape, while the World's Columbian Exposition presented at least the semblance of escape. Mitchell, "World as Exhibition."

20. It is important to emphasize that though these spheres or zones were exempt from many if not most forms of regulation, they were areas created *by the state* as "special economic zones" (to use contemporary terminology). For the long history of these zones see Orenstein, *Out of Stock*, and Slobodian, *Crack-Up Capitalism*.

21. Relentless protests and criticism plagued the Columbian Exposition, including the growing unrest that would eventually result in the Pullman Strike of 1894, one of the most consequential labor actions (and government responses) in US history. Labor practices within the exposition were also criticized, especially by an under- and unfairly represented cohort of Black exhibitors and by organized labor. See, for example, Wells, *Reason Why*. For a broad overview of the various social and political crises plaguing the exposition, see Brands, *Bound to Empire*, and Silkenat, "Workers in the White City."

22. Aristotle's division of the world into five climatic zones can be found in his *Meteorologica*. For more on acclimatization theory in the context of the US colonization of the Philippines, see Anderson, *Colonial Pathologies*. See also Osborne, "Acclimatizing the World."

23. Ripley, "Acclimatization." A voluminous literature on acclimatization was summarized in 1923 by Andrew Balfour who published two articles in *The Lancet* with extensive bibliographies, "Sojourners in the Tropics" and the two-part "Problems of Acclimatization."

24. Considered a luxury commodity during the Spanish colonial era, the production of "artificial" ice was a relatively new technology, only displacing a lucrative global trade in natural ice in the late 1880s. See Smith, *Crystal Blocks*, 3. The first artificial ice factory in East Asia was built in Hong Kong. See Yanne and Heller, *Signs of a Colonial Era*.

25. Toward similar ends, in September of 1901, only months before construction was completed on the Insular Cold Storage and Ice Plant, President Taft made a trip on horseback to the mountain province of Benguet, searching for a site for a new summer capital that would be more hospitable to the Anglo-Saxon constitution. McKenna, *American Imperial Pastoral*.

26. The criticism came from James LeRoy, member of the Second Philippine Commission (the Taft Commission). He argued that the money spent on the ice plant and other projects that supplied and comforted American soldiers only indirectly benefitted the Filipino people "in so far as its use . . . contributed to bring peace." See LeRoy, *Americans in the Philippines*, 292.

27. For a parallel story of acclimatization, ice, and US empire see Kawehipuaakahaopulani Hobart, *Cooling the Tropics*. See also Ludovice, "Ice Plant Cometh."

28. Forbes, *Philippine Islands*, 388.

29. Sawali are woven split-bamboo mats, usually used to construct walls.

30. The port area was a constant site of focus for the colonial government. Pier 7, the largest of the port projects addressed in the chapter "Scalability," did not occur until after Forbes's departure. Forbes, *Philippine Islands*, 203.

31. Conant, "Economic Basis."

32. On the instabilities of a country in a state of development, see Sklar, *United States as a Developing Country*.

33. Roosevelt, "First Annual Message to Congress."

34. Despite the rising abundance of US Portland cement, the unreliable quality of US-produced cement led many architects and contractors at the turn of the century to purchase British and German cement. See, for example, Lesley, *History of the Portland Cement*. In this book and in many other US industry–funded books and magazines there is a constant focus on the comparable strength and quality of particular brands of US cement, which pride themselves on internal production standards; in the case of Lesley's book, the brand is Giant Cement, sold by the American Cement Company (the book's publisher).

35. The first regulatory agency in the United States, the Interstate Commerce Commission, was formed in 1887 to regulate railroads to ensure fair rates and eliminate rate discrimination. This was the US's first independent agency, or so-called Fourth Branch of government. On the history of the US regulatory state see DeCanio, *Democracy*.

36. Forbes, *Inauguration Address*, 12.

37. Forbes, quoted in Spector, "William Cameron Forbes in the Philippines," 76.

CHAPTER 3. SALUBRITY: CHOLERA AND THE
"HOUSING QUESTION" IN THE TROPICAL COLONY

1. Anderson, *Colonial Pathologies, 104*.

2. Worcester, *History of Asiatic Cholera in the Philippines*.

3. Reynaldo Ileto argues that the numbers did not significantly subside until a combination of heavy rains and the increasing immunity of the populace took hold two years into the epidemic. Ileto, "Cholera and the Origins," 51–83.

4. Ileto, "Cholera and the Origins," 51–83; and Anderson, *Colonial Pathologies*.

5. Ileto, "Cholera and the Origins," 51–83.

6. The 1908 epidemic occurred just as the Insular Government was preparing Manila for the arrival of Roosevelt's "Great White Fleet." Filipino merchants waited anxiously for the arrival of US sailors to spend their spare cash on American goods. From docks bedecked in stars and stripes, Filipinos assembled to watch Admiral Charles Stillman Sperry put his ships through their paces with range-calibration exercises and battle practice. Fearful of bringing cholera on board, Sperry prohibited his crews from disembarking. Fearful of the backlash of the Manila merchants, Governor-General Smith cabled William Howard Taft (then Roosevelt's secretary of war) to urge Sperry to reconsider, to no avail. The attention this event attracted abroad motivated Dean C. Worcester to write *History of Asiatic Cholera in the Philippines*, a document presented mostly in a defensive mode that nevertheless called for the "radical improvement" of existing conditions.

7. To accommodate Manila's flatness, Owen L. Ingalls, the system's engineer, adopted a pumping system, in which the sewer vault would be placed at a minimum depth of five feet below the surface, set at a descending pitch until "the economy of construction required the sewage be pumped up into the pumping station." This system created a new invisible topography below Manila's flat surface. Heiser, *Annual Report of the Bureau of Health* (1909), 21. See also "Manila Waterworks."

8. For reasons unstated in the report of Municipal Board of Manila, the sewer system excluded the districts of Pandacan and Santa Ana. Municipal Board quoted in Pante, "Politics of Flood Control," 559–60. For more on the comprehensive sanitary treatment of Manila see Lico, "'Manila Beautiful.'"

9. Moses, *Unofficial Letters*, 75.

10. Perry entertained various theories and rumors, including cabbages smuggled in via lockers and coal bunkers due to the sky-high price of vegetables after their shipment from Hong Kong was prohibited. Another rumor was that a cargo of cabbages not certified to enter Manila Bay was thrown overboard into the China Sea and floated ashore to hungry natives living in Tondo. Though unable to prove any of these theories, the Surgeon General was "convinced that some smuggling was done from the ships by the natives." See United States Philippine Commission, *Annual Report*, 420.

11. "Report of the Philippine Commission."

12. The total population of Tondo in 1903 was 39,043, according to Bureau of the Census, *Census of the Philippine Islands*, vol. 2, 232.

13. Ingalls, "Report upon the Sewerage System," 169.

14. Ingalls, "Report upon the Sewerage System," 169.

15. See, for example, Frantz Fanon's distinction between "native" towns and European towns in *The Wretched of the Earth,* 39. See also Michael Vann's history of the segregated sewer systems of Hanoi: Vann, *Great Hanoi Rat Hunt*, and Vann, "Of Rats, Rice, and Race."

16. See, for example, Mumford, *City in History*, 401; and Garb, "Race, Housing, and Burnham's Plan."

17. Garb, "Race, Housing, and Burnham's Plan."

18. Burnham and Bennett, *Plan of Chicago*, 32.

19. Engels, "The Housing Question," 324.

20. Engels, "The Housing Question," 324.

21. Guerdrum, "Novel House," 356.

22. Heiser, *Annual Report of the Bureau of Health* (1909), 7 (emphasis added).

23. Guerdrum, "Novel House," 356.

24. Heiser, *Annual Report of the Bureau of Health* (1909), 74.

25. The terminology of *strong* versus *light* seems to have first appeared in 1912, when buildings of "light materials" in "strong materials" districts was first legally defined in order to impose a required distance between buildings of light materials in strong materials districts. Ordinance No. 158 specified the building materials that may be used in strong and light materials districts, respectively. It also gives the boundaries of the fire wall district and cites the regulations and restrictions under which fire walls must be erected. Heiser, *Annual Report of the Bureau of Health* (1913), 58.

26. The other pieces of legislation included (1) Ordinance 153—Section 247, which relate to the numbering of all buildings, including which were to be numbered, the plan and method of placing numbers, and the penalty for taking down, altering, or defacing numbers; (2) Ordinance 157, which appropriated sums of money for a sanitary improvement fund, specified the removal and rebuilding of nipa houses, the removal of midden sheds on Mariquina reservation and in the city of Manila, street work in sanitary barrios, Paco Market, extensions of water mains, sewers, and storm-water drains; (3) Ordinance 164, of which Section 195 relates to method of installing soil and drainage pipes and specifies materials to be used and method of construction; and (4) Ordinance No. 172, of which Section 124 specifies the kinds of light building materials that may be used in light material districts, and cites certain restrictions for the use of these materials. It also specifies height of light material fences. Heiser, *Annual Report of the Bureau of Health* (1913), 57–59.

27. Guerdrum, "A Novel House," 356.

28. Fox, *Annual Report of the Bureau of Health* (1911), 38.

29. Heiser, *Annual Report of the Bureau of Health* (1910), 9–12.

30. Heiser, *Annual Report of the Bureau of Health* (1910), 9–12.

31. Heiser, *Annual Report of the Bureau of Health* (1910), 12 (emphasis added).

32. In volume 1 of *Capital*, Marx interchangeably uses "relative surplus-population" and "reserve army of labor" to refer to a population that can be drawn on if needed. Marx, *Capital*, 650–55.

33. Of these "light" sites, Tondo was considered especially problematic: the Bureau of Health argued that it was ". . . a menace to the entire city of Manila, and that until this work is done, even the sanitary barrios will be useless." Fox, *Annual Report of the Bureau of Health* (1911), 20.

34. The question of who was responsible for housing workers attended the massive transformations and movements of population associated with the Industrial Revolution. Housing needs for cotton mill workers in Manchester, England, for example, were insufficiently met by the private market through the construction of workshop dwellings

and a variety of improvised urban-infill types. Early examples of capitalist-built workers' housing include those built by Merrimack Mills in Lowell, Massachusetts, or those by George Pullman of the Pullman Palace Car Company in Pullman, Illinois. Examples of publicly built housing estates include Neues Frankfurt, spearheaded by Frankfurt, Germany, mayor Ludwig Landmann, who in 1925 hired Ernst May to build over twelve thousand units of public housing. May and his entire Frankfurt team, known as the May Brigade, eventually decamped to the Soviet Union to oversee ambitious state-funded city building projects. On improvised workers' housing in Manchester, see, for example, Crinson, *Shock City*. On early US company towns, see Crawford, *Building the Workingman's Paradise*. On Neues Frankfurt, see, for example, Henderson, *Building Culture*. On May's work in the Soviet Union, see, for example, Crawford, *Spatial Revolution*. Self-help housing schemes became popular in the 1950s in developing economies like Peru's, where modernist architects sought to combine the benefits of "formal" design expertise with "informal" native building know-how. For an in-depth analysis of the Peruvian example, see Gyger, *Improvised Cities*.

35. If cholera was detected, sanitary officials implemented an aggressive and systematic cholera eradication strategy within the sanitary barrios. For example, in September 1908, following a small rise in cholera cases in the hospitals, which the Bureau of Health identified as signaling the "probability of an epidemic," the bureau deployed a six-hundred-man disinfection squad, which included lime squads, fire engines (with pressurized hoses filled with disinfectants), and street-spraying wagons (also armed with disinfectants). For this particular campaign, "daily output of disinfectants was enormous" and included "about 75 tons of lime, and about 700 gallons of carbolic acid or its equivalent." When they ran out of chemicals, they resorted to an experimental use of electrolyzed salt water then being tested in the Bureau of Science's laboratories. When lime squads ran out of lime, the frenzied action did not stop, as they were asked to take up shovels, hoes, rakes, and brooms to dig ditches to cover errant excreta. Fox, *Annual Report of the Bureau of Health* (1911), 19.

36. Fox, *Annual Report of the Bureau of Health* (1911), 19.

CHAPTER 4. REPRODUCIBILITY: THE BURNHAM PLAN AND THE ARCHITECTURE OF AN "EFFICIENT MACHINE"

1. Foucault, "What Is an Author?"

2. John Ruskin is the earliest and most influential critic of an industrially produced architecture. See, for example, his critique of London's Crystal Palace in *Opening of the Crystal Palace*. On copies, duplication, and revivals see Reeser Lawrence, *Architecture of Influence*.

3. Mumford, *Culture of Cities*, 438.

4. This was especially the case in the aftermath of World War II, when the monumental bombast of fascists prompted artists, architects, and historians to thoroughly question the usefulness of the monument. See Giedion, "Need for a New Monumentality."

5. On standardized plans of provincial capitol buildings see Lico, *Arkitekturang Filipino*, 345.

6. The "consulting architect" was the lead position within the architectural division of the Bureau of Public Works. Only three Americans held this position before the Filipinization of the Bureau, when, as a part of a transition to Philippine national sovereignty, all American personnel were replaced by American-trained Filipino architects. The first person to fill the consulting architect position was William E. Parsons; Burnham's hand-picked executor for his Manila plan, he was succeeded by George Corner Fenhagen, who served less than one year, and was followed by Ralph Harrington Doane. Chapter 7 addresses the significance of both Filipinization and of the work of Fenhagen and Doane during this transitional period.

7. Doane, "Story of American Architecture in the Philippines, Part II," 121.

8. Doane, "Story of American Architecture in the Philippines, Part II," 117.

9. On the BPW's use of corvée labor, see, for example, Jackson, "A Military Necessity."

10. According to the *Annual Report of the Director of Forestry of the Philippine Islands, 1906–1907*, 85 million of the 100 million feet of lumber used annually in the archipelago consisted of Oregon pine (aka Douglas Fir). Ahern, *Annual Report of the Director of Forestry*. See also Ahern, *Opportunities for Lumber*.

11. On returning to the US, Bourne was employed either as an architect or draftsman for the Public Services Commission and its successor, the Transit Commission, the state agencies charged with building the New York subways. Landmarks Preservation Commission (New York), "Bedford Park Congregational Church," http://s-media.nyc.gov/agencies/lpc/lp/2062.pdf.

12. Hines, *Burnham of Chicago*, 197.

13. Orquiza, *Taste of Control*, 42.

14. Hines, *Burnham of Chicago*, 211. See also Hines, "American Modernism in the Philippines."

15. Emphasis is mine. Anderson to Forbes, 1905 (month and day unknown), Forbes Papers, Houghton Library, Harvard University.

16. Burnham and Anderson, "Report on Proposed Improvements at Manila," 633.

17. Burnham and Anderson, "Report on Proposed Improvements at Manila," 633.

18. Hines, "American Modernism in the Philippines," 316.

19. "Stirred by Burnham," 1.

20. Tafuri, *Architecture and Utopia*, 35.

21. Forbes, *Inauguration Address*, 11.

22. The first reinforced concrete building in the Philippines, the Hamilton Fashion Building (today the Olsen Building), was completed just a year earlier in 1907. Lico, *Arkitekturang Filipino*, 305.

23. See Day, *Manila Hotel*. Jamaica Kincaid discusses the prestige associated with Antigua's Hotel Training School, a popularity that is intertwined with the twin legacies of slavery and imperialism. Kincaid, *A Small Place*.

24. Wooley, "New Hotel Building in Manila."

25. From the Manila Hotel menu, March 18, 1936, quoted in Orquiza, *Taste of Control*, 42.

26. Burnham, "Report on Potential Improvements at Manila," 633.

27. Burnham, "Report on Potential Improvements at Manila," 633, note b.

28. The business of leisure was of special interest to Forbes, who expanded the amount of prime urban real estate dedicated to upper-class leisure, transforming the park that was to replace the moat around Intramuros with a golf course, and personally purchasing a prime piece of real estate for the Manila Polo Club, which he sold to members of the club in 1921. Manila Polo Club, "Club History and Milestones," accessed, June 18, 2024, https://manilapolo.com.ph/about-us/club-history-milestones/.

29. Parsons, "Report of the Consulting Architect," 147.

30. Hines, "Imperial Façade," and Hines, "American Modernism in the Philippines."

31. Rebori, "Work of William E. Parsons, Part I."

32. William Cameron Forbes was especially committed to the use of prison labor for public works projects. Kramer, *Blood of Government*, 315–17. Industrial education, especially in prisons, was patterned after the education system developed in Indian boarding schools. See, for example, Paulet, "To Change the World."

33. Rebori, "Work of William E. Parsons, Part II," 433.

34. On Spanish colonial education in the Philippines, see Schwarz, "Filipino Education." On "social engineering" see May, *Social Engineering in the Philippines*. On American colonial education in the Philippines see Steinbock-Pratt, *Educating the Empire*; and Schueller, *Campaigns of Knowledge*. Other "tailored" colonial purposes included, for example, the production of cart wheels that conformed to new archipelago-wide standards for roads, a workshop for which was developed in Bilibid Prison. See Lewis, "Bilibid," 80–84.

35. When the United States acquired the Philippines from Spain, provinces were classified as either *corregimientos* (unpacified military zones) or *alcaldías* (pacified provinces). Following the signing of the Treaty of Paris in 1898, the American administration placed the entire archipelago under a military government, incorporating each province at the cessation of armed conflict, when the military deemed it pacified. Between the First Philippine Republic's declaration of war and the enactment of the Philippine Organic Act in 1902, the Insular Government organized the civil governments of most of the forty-six provinces according to provisions set forth in the Provincial Government Act. Areas where guerilla fighting continued were annexed to adjacent "pacified" provinces after full pacification. The exception to this general pattern was the newly formed Moro province, which included present day Zamboanga, Cotabato, Davao, and Lanao. There, military occupation of the entire region lasted long after the organization of the civil government. Certain provinces, after having been declared "pacified," were, on account of continued insurrection, later re-placed under the control of military governors due to continued insurrection (these included Cebu, Batangas, and Bohol). See "Act No. 173, July 17, 1901: An Act Restoring the Provinces of Batangas, Cebu and Bohol to the Executive Control of the Military Governor," Supreme Court E-Library, https://elibrary.judiciary.gov.ph/thebookshelf/showdocs/28/35639.

36. Rebori, "Work of William E. Parsons, Part II," 433.

37. As Parsons's successor, Ralph Harrington Doane pointed out that Filipinos often took pride in the grandeur of their local churches during the Spanish colonial period. This pride, however, he suggests, only takes hold as resentment over forced labor fades into the historical distance. The inducement of competition to beautify each town

was a strategy drawn into Pierre Charles L'Enfant's plan for Washington, DC, which included thirteen squares to be developed by the individual states in a sort of representative competition. See Doane, "Architecture in the Philippines," and Jackson, "L'Enfant's Washington."

38. Rebori, "Work of William E. Parsons, Part II," 423.

39. The Pensionado Act, passed in August 1903, established a scholarship program for Filipinos to attend college and receive advanced professional training in the United States. In exchange for their education, *pensionados* were required to dedicate at least three years to public service. Philippine Commission, "Act No. 854."

40. While Burnham's Union Station was itself monumental, it also enabled the clarification of L'Enfant's monumental Washington by, as John W. Reps points out, clearing the Washington Mall of the three railroads that crossed it and the privately run train stations that were built along its edges, and uniting them under one roof, under the oversight of the government, at a site removed from the center of the city's great symbol of state power. Reps, *Monumental Washington*, 117.

41. Parsons quoted in Rebori, "Work of William E. Parsons, Part II," 423.

42. Parsons quoted in Rebori, "Work of William E. Parsons, Part II," 423.

43. Getting the steel on time required an extra payment to the steel contractor—the Atlantic, Gulf, and Pacific company—in the amount of exactly ₱1500. McGregor, "Administrative Construction of the University Hall," 28.

44. McGregor, "Administrative Construction of the University Hall," 29.

45. Alatas, *Myth of the Lazy Native*.

46. McKenna, following David Harvey et al., presents these "extra-economic" measures as successful strategies of securing labor. Though this is true to a certain extent, it is reasonable to assume that it also produced resentment. McKenna, *American Imperial Pastoral*, 51.

47. Following the first colony-wide elections, *Nacionalistas* (who advocated for immediate and complete independence from the United States) led by Sergio Osmeña captured the majority of the eighty-seat assembly. In the celebratory aftermath, symbols of the revolution, especially the Philippine flag, were visibly displayed, with the notable exclusion of American flags. The Philippine Commission responded by passing the 1907 Flag Law Act (Act 1696), which prohibited the display of the Philippine national flag. Cullinane, "Bringing in the Brigands," 50–52.

48. Cullinane, "Bringing in the Brigands," 51. On "the period of suppressed nationalism," see Constantino, *Philippines: A Past Revisited,* and Agoncillo and Guerrero, *History of the Filipino People.*

49. Wurfel, "Trade Union Development."

50. Rebori, "Work of William E. Parsons, Part I," 309.

51. Doane, "Story of American Architecture, Part I," 29.

52. Doane, "Story of American Architecture, Part I," 29.

53. Doane, "Story of American Architecture, Part I," 29.

54. Ruskin, *Stones of Venice*, 164.

55. Benjamin, "Work of Art," 2.

56. Wood, *Forgery, Replica, Fiction*, 19.

CHAPTER 5. SCALABILITY: ALTERING
THE ARCHIPELAGIC INTERIOR

1. Anonymous, "Business Is Business." This poem is attributed to "Anonymous in Trumbull Cheer" in the *Quarterly Bulletin*. It appeared under several authors' names in other publications (e.g., Edgar Allen Guest, Everett W. Lord), sometimes with variations in the text. The poem's original author was Berton Braley (1882–1966), a poet whose work was syndicated in newspapers.

2. Roosevelt, *Winning of the West*, vol. 4, 26.

3. Cronon, *Nature's Metropolis*, 87.

4. López also established the Compañia Transatlántica Española international shipping line in 1881. He had started by founding the Compañia de Vapores Correso A. López in Cuba in 1850, then expanding into banking and other ventures. Beyond growing and trading tobacco, rice, and sugar, the Tabacalera was involved in commercial forest products and the production and sale of sugar, alcohol, copra, and abaca. On López's many business ventures, see Alharilla, *Un hombre, mil negocios*.

5. That the Cojuanco family, the most well-known member of which is Corazon Aquino née Cojuanco (who famously replaced the deposed President Ferdinand Marcos), is the current owner of the Hacienda Luisita is symbolic of the Philippines' failed attempts at land reform. Del Mundo, *Promised Land*.

6. Putzel, *Captive Land*, 54. On the industrialization of the sugar industry in the Philippines, see also Ventura, "From Small Farms."

7. The term *reclamation* here refers to the idea that irrigation would "reclaim" arid lands for human use. As early as 1888 funds were appropriated for the purpose of investigating the extent to which the US's arid regions could be redeemed by irrigation. The Act of August 30, 1890, provided that patents issued for lands west of the one-hundredth meridian would contain right-of-way reservations for ditches or canals constructed by authority of the United States. Fuhriman, "Federal Aid."

8. McNutt, "Irrigation in the Philippines," 49–53.

9. Forbes, *Philippine Islands*, 399.

10. Forbes, *Romance of Business*, 15.

11. Rail was also pursued in the Philippines, though it was privately developed by the Manila Railway Company, incorporated in Manila and London in 1892. During the Wilson administration, when the Manila Railroad was under significant financial duress during World War I, it became a state-owned enterprise. Forbes, *Philippine Islands*, 391–95.

12. Beardsley, "Progress of Public Works," 182.

13. *Roads in the Philippine Islands*.

14. Cameron, "Manila-South Road System," 26.

15. Gordon, "Experiment in Macadam."

16. Forbes, *Philippine Islands*, 384.

17. The Benguet Road led to the new summer capital in Baguio. For an extensive analysis and examination of labor vis-à-vis the road's construction, see McKenna, *American Imperial Pastoral*. Benjamin Weber places the use of prison labor in public works projects into a broader history of "prison imperialism" in Weber, *American Purgatory*.

18. Forbes was persistent in his desire to make use of a massive incarcerated population, sending two hundred convicts to work on Benguet Road, one thousand prisoners to build roads in Mindanao, another five hundred to work the Tabaco-Ligao Road, and so on. Criminal transportation and forced labor "were seen as the keys to preventing uprisings in [Bilibid] . . . as well as across the archipelago." Weber, *American Purgatory*, 38.

19. Though this law failed, in the next year, 1906, Governor-General Smith, "whose knowledge of psychology," Forbes noted, "was very subtle," authorized a double cedula or poll tax, with the "option" of five-days' labor, a measure ultimately approved. See Philippine Commission, "Act No. 1511." The approval of this measure was partially "induced" by the promise that each provincial board would receive part of a more than US $600,000 appropriation for roads and bridges. Forbes, *Philippine Islands*, 371–72. For an imperial perspective which also takes into account similar militarized road-building initiatives in Cuba and Peru, see Jackson, "Roads to American Empire."

20. Forbes, *Philippine Islands*, 377.

21. Spanish colonial administrators instituted a similar custodial system in Puerto Rico in the nineteenth century, in which caretakers were each assigned 6 kilometers of road, with a house built for each *caminero*. "Importancia de las Casillas."

22. Bureau of Public Works, *Road Book*, 1.

23. Forbes, *Philippine Islands*, 376.

24. Bureau of Public Works, *Road Book*, 1.

25. Emerson, quoted in Marx, *Machine in the Garden*, 792.

26. Larson, *Bonds of Enterprise*.

27. Forbes, quoted in "All Nationalities."

28. "Port Works."

29. Nye, *American Technological Sublime*, 33.

30. Though Forbes left the Philippines abruptly in 1913 (following Woodrow Wilson's inauguration), he returned in 1921, appointed by the newly inaugurated President Warren G. Harding as part of the Wood-Forbes mission, a "special mission" formed to investigate whether the Philippines should be granted independence or not. See Forbes, *Report of the Special Mission*.

31. It is worth noting that this observation was made in the book's penultimate chapter "Capital and Labor." Forbes, *Romance of Business*, 231.

32. De los Reyes, "Nueva Ciudad." For a history of portworks in Manila that references Reyes's vision, see Hawkins, "Episodic History."

33. The Eixample was the urban vision of Idelfons Cerdà, a progressive social thinker and parliamentary deputy of Spain's ephemeral First Republic. Cerdà's utopian plan for rational urban development became the blueprint for Barcelona's rapid expansion in the late nineteenth century. See Ealham, *Anarchism and the City*.

34. I am thinking here not only of Henri Lefebvre's "Right to the City," but also of the city as richly imagined and described by Nick Joaquin in, for example, *Almanac for Manileños* and *Manila, My Manila*.

CHAPTER 6. LIQUIDITY: AN INTERLUDE
ON PORTLAND CEMENT

1. The Philippine Bureau of Science, *The Philippine Islands*.

2. Today Vietnam is the third largest producer of cement in the world, after China and India—astonishing considering its relative size. In 1926 the Haiphong plant replaced its upright kilns with modern rotary kilns, an improvement that increased total capacity to 300,000 tons annually. By 1937 French Indochina exported 53 percent of the cement that it produced, its major clients being Java, South China, and Singapore. Miller, "Industrial Resources of Indochina."

3. In 1878, the Association of German Cement Manufacturers (later known as the Verein Deutscher Zementwerke, or VDZ) established the first-ever standard for Portland cement. See "History," VDZ, https://web.archive.org/web/20150116110736/http://www.vdz-online.de/en/vdz/history/.

4. In 1913, of the 425,000 barrels of cement imported nearly 50 percent was from Germany; Hong Kong supplied 26 percent; East India 11 percent; and Japan and China 6 percent each. Philippine Bureau of Science, *Mineral Resources* (1913), 37. Heidelberg cement—the first and dominant manufacturer of Portland cement in Germany—also, as Adrian Forty has pointed out, ensures its global presence by operating over 900 ships to move cement around the world to take advantage of local spikes in price. Forty, *Concrete and Culture*, 96.

5. West and Cox, "Burning Tests," 81.

6. Though I have not myself compiled or found statistics to corroborate this claim, virtually all references to proprietary systems made in the *Quarterly Bulletin, Bureau of Public Works* refer to the Kahn system (TrusCon). In general, the Hennebique system enjoyed a larger market share in francophone countries. See Simonnet, *Le Béton*. The first factory in the Philippines to produce steel reinforcing bars was a government-sponsored plant built in 1952 in Iligan, Mindanao. It is typical of both the colony and the postcolony to produce raw materials for metropolitan industries, while at the same time providing a market for its industrial manufactures. See "Our History," Philippine Iron and Steel Institute, http://philippineironsteel.org/our-history.

7. The Bureau of Science exhaustively tested the relative strength and performance of local aggregates. See, for example, the 115-page article on the topic published by the bureau: King, "Physical Properties of Philippine Concrete." Regarding the testing of important Porland cement, although there were already US standards for cement production (the US Army, American Society for Testing and Materials [ASTM], and the American Society of Civil Engineers [ASCE], for example, all issued standards in 1902), they varied widely, in terms of evaluative criteria. Though Reibling was generally in support of standards (he adopted ASTM and ASCE standards as baselines), he also worried that standards could discourage innovation in the industry. Reibling and Salinger, "Portland Cement Testing." See also Cochrane, *Measures for Progress*.

8. Established in July of 1901, the Bureau of Government Laboratories (reorganized in 1905 as the Bureau of Science) was developed as a "central institution in which laboratory work shall be done for all the bureaus which may need scientific assistance." Freer, "Bureau of Government Laboratories," 579.

9. Reibling, "A Bonus System."

10. A study of field relations for the production of Portland cement takes into account all factors relevant to cement production and distribution including transport lines and the availability of raw materials, such as complimentary siliceous and calcareous materials, argillaceous materials, fuel (coal), and at times gypsum (a retardant that accounts for a fractional amount of the final admixture). Bureau of Science, *The Mineral Resources* (1913), 36.

11. Philippine Bureau of Science, *Mineral Resources* (1913), 36.

12. As the Bureau of Science noted, there was sufficient domestic demand "to absorb the entire output of a single small manufacturing plant" and as such is "sufficient to leave a 'handsome margin of profit to the manufacturer.'" Bureau of Science, *The Mineral Resources* (1913), 36.

13. Faustino, "Nonmetallic Minerals," 42.

14. Notz, "The World's Coal Situation During the War."

15. Harrison, *Cornerstone of Philippine Independence*, 259.

16. Harrison, *Cornerstone of Philippine Independence*, 259.

17. Kalaw, *Self-Government*, 69.

18. Harrison, *Cornerstone of Philippine Independence*, 259.

19. Harrison, *Cornerstone of Philippine Independence*, 259.

20. Harrison, *Cornerstone of Philippine Independence*, 261.

21. The first rebar factory established in the Philippines, SteelAsia did not open until 1965.

22. Robb, "Philippine Cement," 23, 30.

23. Gozum, *Historical Survey*, 8.

24. The suggestion for the government to "get out and keep out of business" came after an unrelenting criticism of the Philippine National Bank. Wilson's Republican successor Warren G. Harding won the presidential election of 1920 in a major landslide, taking every state outside of the South, and winning the popular vote by the largest margin (by percentage) in US presidential election history. At the time of his election Harding, a staunch retentionist, was the chairman of the Senate Commission on the Philippines. Almost as soon as he took office, Harding sent a special mission to the Philippines to investigate whether it was, as Wilson argued in his final message to Congress, ready for independence. Led by former Governor-General William Cameron Forbes, and former military governor of the Moro Province (and just appointed governor-general) Leonard Wood, the two men predictably concluded that the Philippines was not prepared for independence. Though the reversal of Filipinization (on which much of the "mismanagement" of the colony was blamed), was politically impossible, when in office Wood flexed the power of the governor-general (by, for example vetoing one out of three bills that the legislature sent to his office in the first year of his tenure). Onorato, "Philippine Independence Mission," and Onorato, "Leonard Wood as Governor."

25. Gozum, *Historical Survey*, 8.

26. Gillis, "Role of State Enterprises."

CHAPTER 7. ARTIFICE: THE "BASTARD" MATERIAL
AND A LEGITIMATION CRISIS

1. For the epigraph source, see Doane "Architecture in the Philippines," 2. Doane's characterization of concrete as a "bastard" material is only slightly more crass than Frank Lloyd Wright's description (published nine years later) of the concrete as "mongrel" in *Architectural Record*. Wright, "Meaning of Materials" 102.

2. Wilson, "First Annual Message."

3. In Doane's words: "The annual appropriation for Insular Government buildings is made by the Legislature in one lump sum . . . the subdivision of the general appropriation to specific jobs is left to the Director of Public Works and the Consulting Architect, who with such latitude can apply funds saved on one building to another that has exceeded the estimated cost." Doane, "Story of American Architecture, Part I," 25.

4. "Jones Law of 1916."

5. Manela, *Wilsonian Moment*, 31.

6. Since 1907, the bicameral Philippine Legislature had consisted of a Philippine Lower House (previously called the Assembly) made up of an elected body of colonial subjects, and an Upper House (previously called the Commission), at first made up of exclusively American appointees. After the passage of the Jones Law, the Upper House was renamed the Philippine Senate, while the Lower House was renamed the House of Representatives.

7. Wilson to Allen Wickham Corwin, September 10, 1900, in Link, *Papers of Woodrow Wilson*, 573, quoted in Manela, *Wilsonian Moment*, 30. Erez Manela's contention that Wilson did not seriously take up the matter following this correspondence with Corwin is mistaken. The conclusion to Wilson's five-volume *History of the American People* (1902), in addition to two articles published in *The Atlantic*, considered the Philippine Question in the context of the US's ascendance as a "moral" global power.

8. Wilson, "Democracy and Efficiency," 298.

9. Wilson, "Ideals of America," 730.

10. Wilson, "Ideals of America," 722.

11. According to the trustee model of representation, the moral uprightness of a leader is proven by their ability to act in favor of their constituents. Burke's passionate support of Indians in the impeachment of Warren Hastings (the first de facto governor general of India), in which Burke famously took two days to read charges of indictment against Hastings, was a performance intended to uphold the legitimacy of the British Empire against the impeachable behavior of its worst practitioners. On Burke and trusteeship, see Mukherjee, "Justice, War, and the Imperium."

12. Wilson, "Democracy and Efficiency," 298.

13. Wilson, "Ideals of America," 731.

14. On Viollet-le-Duc and racialization of architectural character, see Davis, *Building Character*.

15. Wilson had himself thought about the question of character through the specific lens of architecture. As the president of Princeton he sponsored the spatial reorganization of the university as a series of colleges built around Oxbridge style quadrangles—an

attempt to tie the university's architecture to Anglo cultural roots. Ziolkowski, *Juggler of Notre Dame*, 195–283.

16. Doane, "Story of American Architecture, Part I," 28–29.

17. Doane, "Story of American Architecture, Part I," 29.

18. Coined by Joseph S. Nye Jr., "soft power" refers to US foreign policy in the waning years of the Cold War, when rock music and McDonald's were seen as forces equally if not more powerful than military arsenals. For a history that addresses architectural techniques of soft power, see Castillo, *Cold War on the Home Front*. It is worth noting that the strategy of "attracting" loyalty was not confined to the Cold War era. As explicitly laid out by the Spanish crown in the *Leyes de las Indias* (Laws of the Indies, 1573), both art and architecture were colonial techniques designed to induce loyalty to colonial power through both fear and attraction. On the Laws of the Indies see Mundigo and Crouch, "City Planning Ordinances."

19. Though some of the sculptors returned to their original trades after working in Doane's ateliers, others went into the business of precast architectural decoration, including Vidal Tampinco, who founded The House of Precast, still today the leading supplier of precast architectural ornamentation in the Philippines.

20. See, for example, Montgomery Schuyler's anonymously published satire "Architecture Made Easy."

21. In chapter 4, I discuss "building by administration" relative to the construction of Parsons's University Hall.

22. "Project Notes from District Engineers: Pangasinan," 17.

23. Quoted in Cameron, "Provincial Centers," 3–4.

24. Carnegie was in this instance referring to the industrially produced neoclassical buildings that were the direct predecessor of the Philippines' concrete neoclassicism. Carnegie, "Value of the World's Fair."

25. In a famously drawn-out metaphor Louis Sullivan compared Burnham's neoclassicism to a virus. Sullivan, *Autobiography*, 324.

26. Doane's statement closely mimics that of A. N. Rebori, who wrote: "Some time in the future, when the Filipino finally settles down seriously to the development of things artistic, we may look for the creation of an indigenous architecture expressive of the country and its people. Until then very little can reasonably be expected from a race without deep artistic tradition or scientific knowledge. In the meantime, the buildings erected and the city plan improvements executed by our Government, will stand as worthy examples, setting a high standard from which in the coming years native architects can derive abundant inspiration." Rebori, "Work of William E. Parsons, Part II," 434.

27. Historicist architecture refers broadly to revivals of various kinds and to the use of historical styles and motifs. Architectural organicism, which in the United States is mostly associated with Frank Lloyd Wright, was, as Charles Davis points out, a "transatlantic philosophy of design . . . disseminated through the architectural writings and experimental buildings of European and North American innovators including Eugène Emmanuel Viollet-le-Duc in France; Gottfied Semper in Germany; and H. H. Richardson, Frank Furness . . . [and] Louis Sullivan in the United States." Davis, *Building Character*, 3. On the conflict between organicism and historicism, see, for example, Hvattum, *Gottfried Semper*.

28. Quatremère de Quincy, quoted in di Palma, "Architecture, Environment, and Emotion," 49.

29. Martin, "Local Stone."

30. Martin, "Local Stone."

31. Much of the aggregate used in the construction of the roads and other infrastructure in or around Manila came from Talim and Malahi Islands (islands situated within the Laguna de Bay, the archipelago's largest lake, located approximately 30 kilometers east of Manila), where prisoners were sent to fulfill sentences of hard labor. Prison labor was likely used in Alaminos, as the use prison labor for low-skill jobs was common practice for the BPW. Weber, *American Purgatory*.

32. Doane, "Story of American Architecture, Part II."

33. For the story of mineral exploration and extraction in the Philippines, especially as related to the ultimately imperial nature of the US Bureau of the Interior, see Black, *Global Interior*.

34. Doane, "Story of American Architecture, Part I," 26.

35. Harrison, *Cornerstone of Philippine Independence*, 378.

36. Doane, "Story of American Architecture, Part II," 25, emphasis added.

37. Doane, "Story of American Architecture, Part II," 25.

38. Here I am alluding to Karl Marx's theory of the fetish. See Marx, *Capital*, 163–67.

CHAPTER 8. PLASTICITY: CONSTRUCTING RACE,
REPRESENTING THE NATION

1. Following the sneak attack on over one thousand Tausug villagers, only six survived. More people (and a higher percentage of them) were killed during the Moro Massacre than in other incidents in US history considered massacres, including the Battle of Wounded Knee and the My Lai massacre. Notably, the Moro Massacre took place in 1906—four years after the supposed end of the Philippine-American War. For a contemporaneous rebuke of the Moro Massacre see Twain, "Comments on the Moro Massacre."

2. For more on the internationalist dimensions of the Legislative Building, with an examination of its interior, see Martinez, "Nation Building."

3. Thompson, "Designed by Filipino Brains," 5.

4. As defined in chapter 7, *Filipinization* was the aggressive recruitment of Filipinos into all levels of government, a Wilson-era transitional policy intended to prepare Filipinos for self-rule.

5. Wright, "The Meaning of Materials," 102.

6. The plasticity of concrete forces a reconsideration of an ancient problem—that of the statue and its material (bronze), first recorded in Aristotle's *Metaphysics*. By examining this problem, Aristotle develops his hylomorphic theory, which posits that every natural body consists of both *hyle*, or matter (potential being), and *morphe*, or form (actual being). Simpson, *Hylomorphism*, 4

7. In December 1920, Wilson concluded his final annual message to Congress by arguing that the Philippines had, as required by the Jones Law, "succeeded in maintaining a stable government," and it was now "our liberty and our duty to keep our promise to

the people of those islands by granting them the independence which they so honorably covet." Up until this moment, Wilson had held off granting Philippine independence, justifying his arguments with diagnoses of "unpreparedness"—the same line of reasoning he used to argue against postbellum Black enfranchisement in the South. Wilson, "Eighth Annual Message."

8. In 1913 there had been 2,623 American and 6,363 Filipino officials; in 1921 there were 13,240 Filipino and 614 American administrators. Dolan, *Philippines: A Country Study*, 32.

9. Following the exposition, Arellano moved to Philadelphia. There, an American couple took interest in him, paying for classes at the Philadelphia Academy of the Fine Arts. He later transferred to Drexel to finish his bachelor's degree in architecture (1911). After graduating he traveled to Europe. Arellano was also a *pensionado*, but he did not participate in the program until 1926, when he received funds for advanced studies in the United States *after* the opening of the Legislative Building. "Juan Arellano."

10. Filipino American (Fil-Am) scholarship on the exhibition of Filipinos and other ethnological and anthropological subjects is vast. For a full description of the evolutionary arrangement of the St. Louis "Philippine Reservation," see Kramer, *Blood of Government*, 229–85.

11. The term *Negrito* was used to refer to more than thirty officially recognized ethnic groups who inhabit the Philippines, including the Aeta of Luzon, the Ati and Tumandok of Panay, the Agta of the Sierra Madre, and the Mamanwa of Mindanao. The exonym *Igorot* is Tagalog for "mountain people." It is not an ethnic or tribal designation and is viewed by some as pejorative. The terms *Ifugao* and *Ipugao* (also meaning "mountain people") are used more frequently by members of this aggregate group, which is now officially referred to as the Cordilleran peoples. The recognized Cordilleran ethnolinguistic groups are the Bontoc, Ibaloi, Ifugao, Kalanguya/Ikalahan, Isneg, Tinguian, Kalinga, and Kankanaey. On anthropological theories of settlement of the archipelago and how they interacted with colonial policy and the rise of Filipino nationalism, see Aguilar, "Tracing Origins."

12. In 1691 the buccaneer turned "natural scientist" William Dampier purchased a man known as Prince Jeoly on the island of Mindanao as a slave, placing him on display in London amid a collection of zoological and botanical artifacts. Originally from the island of Miangas, he was given the nickname "The Painted Prince." Following his death from smallpox a year after his arrival, his skin was preserved and placed on display at the Anatomy School in Oxford. See Barnes, "Curiosity, Wonder."

13. Kramer, *Blood of Government*, 37.

14. Romulo, *Mother America*, 58. In 1968, at a talk at the University of the Philippines, Romulo recanted. Reflecting changing political attitudes toward Philippine indigenous groups, he claimed that what he *meant* was that the Igorots were the *real* Filipinos.

15. Arellano's arrival in Philadelphia was not arbitrary. It likely had something to do with William P. Wilson, a biology professor at the University of Pennsylvania and founder of the Philadelphia Commercial Museum, where Arellano worked. Wilson had served as chair of the Philippine Exhibit in St. Louis (which became the basis of the museum's Philippine collection). Most of the exhibit at Jamestown was on loan from the Philadelphia Commercial Museum.

16. As Carmi S. Thompson puts it: "America may take pride in this building, as well as Filipinos. . . . We have encouraged the display of Filipino capabilities in every line of human endeavor . . . it was not until the Stars and Stripes flew in the Philippines that the Filipino people ever had anything like a fair chance to show that they possess the same virtues and abilities and genius as other races possessing independence and occupying a more prominent position in world affairs. The results of America's policy speak for themselves. The building shown above is but one of many similar evidences that could be cited in justification." Thompson, "Designed by Filipino Brains," 5.

17. Fanon, *Black Skin, White Masks*, 89.

18. This identification by nation holds true for most non-Western architects.

19. "Noted Architect Once Posed," 13.

20. Though the competition was held in New York, the design was for the Bank of the Philippine Islands. Lico, *Arkitekturang Filipino*, 309.

21. Here, Fanon points to how the racist and colonial cliché of the friendly Black African was used to sell a consumer product (a chocolate drink called Banania). Fanon, *Black Skin, White Masks*, 92.

22. The new Legislative Building broke with Daniel Burnham's plan for Manila (see figure 4.2), rising on a site intended for the national museum and library, situated at the hinge between the Rizal court and an arm of the municipal and cultural building programs that wrapped around the eastern (city-facing) side of Intramuros. Two possible reasons explain this change. By reserving the site originally intended for the capitol, the design acknowledged that national sovereignty had not yet been achieved. Another purely pragmatic consideration was that Ralph Harrington Doane, the last American consulting architect to serve in the Philippines, had, before his departure in 1918, already developed, along with his Filipino assistant, Antonio Toledo, a design for the site—albeit for a library. With only two years between the passage of the Jones Act and the 1920 presidential elections, there was not enough time to develop plans for the original site, let alone to begin construction. A quicker and more convenient solution was to reconfigure Doane's library. For a more detailed account of the history of the Legislative Building, see Martinez, "Nation Building."

23. For more on Viollet-le-Duc and the connections between race and architectural organicism, see Davis, *Building Character*.

24. Wilson, "Ideals of America," 732.

25. In the context of what came to be known as International Relations (IR), the earliest applications of the word *development* was as a reformulation of evolution as an active project (as opposed to passive process). This is perhaps most clearly demonstrated in writings in the *Journal of Race Development*, published by Clark University between 1910 and 1922, after which it merged with *Foreign Affairs*. For a detailed history of the *Journal of Race Development*, especially relative to a history of IR, see Vitalis, *White World Order*.

26. US efforts to encourage Christian immigration to Muslim Mindanao are recorded as early as 1913 with the US sponsorship of Christian agricultural colonies. For more on the peripheralization of rural Muslims by Christian immigrants, see McKenna, *Muslim Rulers and Rebels*.

27. On the symbolism of Philippine sartorial cultures see Coo, *Clothing the Colony*, and Clutario, *Beauty Regimes*.

28. See Kalaw, "Recent Policy."

29. Henry Otley Beyer, quoted in Harrison, *Cornerstone of Philippine Independence*, 16.

30. In the words of the American Dominican friar and church historian Ambrose Coleman, "Christianity has effected a wonderful transformation in the character of the people, softening and refining it, as we may judge by contrast presented by their cruel and bloodthirsty neighbors in Mindanao and the Sulu group, who, nevertheless, belong to the same race, and whose characteristics they must originally have shared." Coleman, *Friars in the Philippines*, 10.

31. I use *liberal* here to distinguish it from other forms of internationalism, including communist internationalism, the context in which the term was first used. Fred Halliday identified three types of internationalism, liberal, hegemonic, and revolutionary, and separated them somewhat from their ideological histories by providing functional definitions. Halliday, "Three Concepts."

32. On the "one-drop rule" of race, see, for example, Davis, *Who Is Black*, and Guterl, *Color of Race*.

33. Harrison justifies his anti-miscegenation stance by arguing that "both races, Americans and Filipinos, disapprove of intermarriage, and interracial unions are not likely to be happy ones, with the pressure of both communities in opposition." Harrison, *Cornerstone of Philippine Independence*, 59.

34. This can be read as Wilson's answer to W. E. B. Du Bois's observation that "the problem of the Twentieth Century is the problem of the color line." Du Bois, "Forethought."

35. See for example, Mazower, *No Enchanted Palace*, and Getachew, *Worldmaking After Empire*.

36. On "unequal integration" and the standard narrative of decolonization as driven by the imperatives of liberal internationalism, see Getachew, *Worldmaking After Empire*.

37. W. E. B. Du Bois, "The Negro and the League of Nations," ca. November 1921, W. E. B. Du Bois Papers, UMass Amherst, series 3, articles, https://credo.library.umass .edu/view/full/mums312-b210-i073. For contemporary scholarship on the significance of Du Bois's internationalism see, for example, Lake, *Drawing the Global Colour Line*, and Getachew and Pitts, *W. E. B. Du Bois*.

38. Though Joseph R. Nye Jr. coined the term "liberal international order" mainly in reference to the Marshall Plan, it was a fully worked out strategy in the Philippines long before the outbreak of World War II. See, for example, Nye, *Soft Power*.

39. Though Fischer-Credo never again worked in an official capacity for any nation after World War II, the representation of race remained an artistic preoccupation. His large sculpture *Asiatic Head* (1958) was once prominently displayed on the campus of the University of British Columbia before it was deaccessioned in 2022. See the record of the Morris and Helen Belkin Art Gallery, https://belkin.ubc.ca/collection_outdoor /otto-fischer-credo-asiatic-head-deaccessioned/.

40. Democratic Senator James D. Phelan (California) clarified that "Western Senators and others will oppose any loophole by which oriental people will possess such equality

with [the] white race in the United States. It is [a] vital question of self-preservation." This was Phelan's response to the proposed "racial equality clause" introduced by Japan and nearly included in the covenant. Congressional Record—Senate, March 20, 1919, pg. 3182. On the racial equality clause see, for example, Kawamura, "Wilsonian Idealism."

41. In Wilson's words, "The people of the Philippine Islands have succeeded in maintaining a stable government," and it was now "our liberty and our duty to keep our promise to the people of those islands by granting them the independence which they so honorably covet." Wilson, "Eighth Annual Message."

42. For example, in an appeal to an American audience, following Wood's first year in office, Manuel Quezon, president of the Philippine Senate, and Camilo Osias, president of the National University (later University of the Philippines), published a politically cautious but pointed criticism of Wood, dedicating their book to "All Lovers of Free-dom." Quezon and Osias, *Governor General Wood and the Filipino Cause.*

43. On architecture and its relation to "the world court of public opinion," see Allais, *Designs of Destruction.*

44. Drexler, *Architecture of the École,* 9.

45. Harrison, *Cornerstone of Philippine Independence,* 326.

46. Ruskin, quoted on cover of the *Philippine Republic,* January–February, 1927.

47. Ruskin identifies three types of ornament: "1. Servile ornament, in which the execution or power of the inferior workman is entirely subjected to the intellect of the higher; 2. Constitutional ornament, in which the executive inferior power is, to a certain point, emancipated and independent, having a will of its own, yet confessing its inferiority and rendering obedience to higher powers; and 3. Revolutionary ornament, in which no executive inferiority is admitted to all." Ruskin, *Nature of the Gothic,* 8.

48. Ruskin, *Nature of the Gothic,* 9.

49. On deskilling, see Forty, *Concrete and Culture,* 226, 240–42; Ferro, "*Concrete as Weapon.*"

50. Martinez, "Crystals in the Colony," 3.

51. On his trip to the United States in 1926, Arellano studied Art Deco under the direct tutelage of Thomas Lamb, the foremost designer of Art Deco theaters, cinemas, and skyscrapers. Lico, *Arkitekturang Filipino,* 459–60.

52. On Filipino Art Deco, especially the Metropolitan Theater, see Lico and Dy, *Deco Filipino,* and Montinola, *Art Deco in the Philippines.*

53. In architecture, the term *tectonics* refers to the way a building's structure is expressed through its form. The term was introduced in architecture in the mid-nineteenth century, perhaps most notably by Gottfried Semper. See Semper, *Four Elements.*

54. On the bifurcation of the Philippine Islands' population into Christian and non-Christian peoples, see Kramer, *Blood of Government,* 391; and Aguilar, "Tracing Origins."

55. In an article published in the *Journal of International Relations,* for example, Maximo M. Kalaw outlined an "administrative program" toward the non-Christian people, administered by an all-Filipino legislature following the passage of the Jones Law in 1916. It closely mirrored the US colonial program for the Philippines at large. It included:

(a) A settlement policy whereby people of the semi-nomadic race are induced to leave their wild habitat and settle in organized communities; (b) The extension of the public school system and system of public health throughout the regions inhabited by the non-Christian people . . . (c) The extension of public works throughout the Mohammedan regions to facilitate their development and the extension of government control; (d) Construction of road and trails between one place and another among non-Christians to promote social and commercial intercourse and maintain amicable relations among them and with Christian people; (e) Pursuance of the development of natural economic resources, especially agriculture; (f) The encouragement of immigration into, and of the investment of private capital in, the fertile regions of Mindanao and Sulu. (Kalaw, "Recent Policy," 3)

56. In a message delivered to the First National Assembly on October 18, 1937, Manuel Quezon argued that the Philippines should abandon the transition period, noting that "there were tendencies in Congress to disregard the terms and conditions governing said trade relations even against the will of the Filipino people." Quezon, "Message of President."

57. On violent anti-Filipino sentiment and protests, including the Watsonville, California, race riots of January 1930, especially as related to immigration policy, see Baldoz, *Third Asiatic Invasion*, and Kramer, *Blood of Government*, 407–29.

58. Whatever the US's motivations for granting independence, Manuel Quezon, the newly elected president of the Philippine Commonwealth, began his term with big plans, doubling down on the modernization efforts introduced in the early US colonial period, but explicitly committed to correcting their social ill-effects. As Quezon put it, though the US colonial regime made "considerable progress in sanitation, in education, in the construction of roads and all kinds of communication . . . the main beneficiaries of this most remarkable progress were . . . the rich and the middle class." Pledging his commitment to a program of "social justice," Quezon promised dozens of physical improvements that centered the needs of the Philippines' laborers, including the construction of schools, workers' housing, and leprosariums; the development of hydroelectric power; the reforestation of denuded areas; and "the colonization and development of Mindanao" (reaffirming the internalized evolutionary hierarchy and "civilizing" program of the *Nacionalistas*). Very little of this was achieved during the Commonwealth period, which is best characterized as a period of ambitious planning, most notably for Quezon City, a "model community" conceived, in many ways, as the *Nacionalistas'* answer to Burnham's colonial plan. Its execution was delayed by Japanese occupation and by World War II. On the planning of Quezon City, see Pante, *Capital City at the Margins*.

59. Both the Department of Finance and the Department of Agriculture were reorganized several times over the course of US colonization and after. At the time of the completion of Toledo's buildings, they were actually a single department, the Department of Agriculture and Natural Resources, which supervised the Bureaus of Agriculture, Forestry, Lands, Science, and Weather, as well as matters concerning hunting, fisheries, and other sea products. See "History," Department of Agriculture, https://www.da.gov.ph/about-us/history/.

60. In an address to Congress in 1898 regarding whether the United States would take the Philippines as a colony, President McKinley famously wrote, "Incidental to our tenure in the Philippines is the commercial opportunity to which American statesmanship can

not be indifferent. It is just to use every legitimate means for the enlargement of American trade." McKinley, "Instructions to the Peace Commissioners," 907.

CHAPTER 9. STRENGTH: DEFENSIVE ARCHITECTURES AND MANILA'S DESTRUCTION

1. Marx and Smith, *Does Technology Drive History?*, ix.

2. These defense positions also included the islands of Corregidor (Fort Mills), El Caballo Island (Fort Hughes), Carabao Island (Fort Frank), and El Grande Island (Fort Wint), which sat several hundred miles north in the entrance to Subic Bay.

3. Officially Fort Mills and nicknamed "The Rock," Corregidor became the main post headquarters for the Harbor Defenses of Manila Bay. The island was fully equipped not only with its big sea defense batteries but also with several docks, shops, storehouses, an electric rail line, its own power plant, a large ice and cold storage plant, a radio intercept station, a small airfield, a hospital, officers' quarters, an officers' club, a nine-hole golf course, schools, and the 1500-feet-long, three-story reinforced concrete Mile Long Barracks—reputedly the longest barracks in the world—also provided a supposedly bombproof shelter for enlistees. Allen and McGovern, *Concrete Battleship*, 2–10.

4. The recommendation to replace brick masonry with reinforced concrete was published in 1866 by the Endicott Board, named after then Secretary of War William Crowninshield Endicott. Endicott, *Board on Fortifications*, 9, 27.

5. Strong, "Lean Years." Strong's narrative flair was also put to use as an adventure writer for *Boys' Life*, the official Boy Scouts' magazine, for which he wrote under the pseudonym Kennedy Lyons. In those stories Strong piled fantasy and adventure onto his limited knowledge of the archipelago, publishing for example in the November 1932 issue, the cover story "The White Sultan of Mindanao."

6. In 1931, as Britain headed into an economic crisis, Baldwin (a Conservative) entered into a coalition with Labour Prime Minister Ramsay MacDonald, which led to MacDonald's expulsion from his own party. Baldwin, as lord president of the council, became the de facto prime minister, deputizing for MacDonald until Baldwin officially became prime minister in 1935.

7. Stanley Baldwin, "Fear for the Future," Speech before the House of Commons of the United Kingdom on November 10, 1932, https://missilethreat.csis.org/wp-content/uploads/2020/09/A-Fear-for-the-Future.pdf.

8. On the history of aerial bombing see Kennett, *History of Strategic Bombing*. On military destruction in the colonies see Lindqvist, *History of Bombing*.

9. *Bilibid* is Tagalog for prison, though it was usually meant to refer specifically to Manila's central jail, known as Bilibid.

10. Strong, "Lean Years."

11. The Brussels Conference of 1874 stipulated that "open towns" which were "not defended" must not be attacked or bombarded. Article 25 of the Hague Regulations of 1907 abandoned the phrase *open town* but forbade "the attack or bombardment by any means whatever, of towns, villages, habitations, or buildings, which are not defended." The phrase *by any means whatever* was inserted expressly to cover bombing from the air.

Article 1 of the Hague Convention IX laid down a similar rule for naval warfare, with the important addition in Article 2 of a rule permitting the bombardment by naval forces of certain specified "military objectives." Jennings, "Open Towns."

12. Major General Robert Beightler, quoted in Scott, *Rampage*, 278.

13. In times of war, an "open city" is a locality that a belligerent has declared to be "open," that is, undefended, and, if the adversary accepts this status, it will not be bombarded. The purpose is to prevent unnecessary suffering to noninvolved civilians and to avoid unwarranted destruction. See, for example, Fleck, *Handbook of Humanitarian Law*, 457–63.

14. MacArthur, "General Douglas MacArthur's Proclamations," 1.

15. Haussmannian boulevards themselves, as many from Émile Zola to Lewis Mumford have argued, were also used to control urban populations in open revolt. Mumford, *Culture of Cities*, 96. Just three years after the Haymarket Affair in Chicago, and just four years before the opening of the Columbia Exposition there, *Inland Architect* published Burnham and Root's design for the First Regiment Armory. The armory was placed in close proximity to "Millionaire's Row." The armory complemented the city's new broad streets and avenues, which allowed for the quick deployment of military forces. "Design for the First Regiment."

16. *Japanese Defense of Cities*, 1.

17. Dower, *War Without Mercy*, 77.

18. Robert S. Beightler, quoted in Connaughton et al., *Battle for Manila*, 175. Major General Robert Beightler was not the only military official who weighed the value of buildings against human life. However, whereas Beightler would not entertain the thought of losing "a single American life to save a building," Dwight D. Eisenhower, when faced with the same question in the European theater, believed the choice "between destroying a famous building and sacrificing our own men . . . was not so clear-cut." Italy, Eisenhower reasoned, "has contributed a great deal to our cultural inheritance, a country rich in monuments which by their creation . . . and now in their old age illustrate the growth of the civilization which is ours." Thus, Eisenhower mapped battle plans that sacrificed "military convenience" in order to protect the landmarks of Western civilization. These European monuments—some destroyed, some preserved, in turn became the basis of a modern cult of architectural heritage—one that aligned neatly with a Western architectural history canon. Dwight D. Eisenhower, "Letter on Historical Monuments," December 29, 1943, National Archives and Records Administration (NARA) RG 165 CAD000.4 (3-25-43), quoted in Allais, *Designs of Destruction*.

19. Report of the 37th Division, quoted in Smith, *Triumph in the Philippines*, 264.

20. Smith, *Triumph in the Philippines*, 276.

21. *Japanese Defense of Cities*, 23.

22. *Japanese Defense of Cities*, 23.

23. Smith, *Triumph in the Philippines*, 291.

24. Scott, *Rampage*, 23.

25. Smith, *Triumph in the Philippines*, 294.

26. Manchester, *American Caesar*, 413.

27. With its first issue appearing in December 1923, the primary object of the *Philippine Republic* magazine was "to tell the American people facts about the Filipinos and

Philippine Independence that they ought to know, but do not know." Gabaldon and Guevara, "An Important Message," 20.

28. The "teeming millions" that Quezon is referring to are former colonized populations. Quezon, *Good Fight*, 11.

29. MacArthur, "Introduction," in Quezon, *Good Fight*, viii.

30. Quezon, *Good Fight*, xiii.

31. MacArthur, *Reminiscences*, 261.

32. Delinks, "Navy Construction in the Philippines."

33. Feeney, "The United States and the Philippines."

34. On the US's "pointillist empire," see Immerwahr, *How to Hide an Empire*, 214–17.

CHAPTER 10. RECONSTRUCTION: FROM COLONIAL PROJECT TO "FOREIGN AID"

1. Smith, *Triumph in the Philippines*, 304.

2. David Ekbladh points out how missions of technocratic reform more commonly referred to as development in the postwar period was earlier referred to as reconstruction, a term that while primarily linked to the post–Civil War era was often used during the Progressive Era to describe attempts to reconcile society to the abrupt changes introduced by industrial modernity. Ekbladh, *Great American Mission*.

3. According to Article IV of the "Agreement Between the United States of America and the Republic of the Philippines Regarding the Payment of the Public and Private Claims," "Where work is performed by contract . . . contractors who are citizens of the United States of America shall have equal rights with contractors who are citizens of the Republic of the Philippines on all rehabilitation projects financed by the Commission." Philippine War Damage Commission, *Semiannual Report*, no. 8 (1950), 79–80.

4. Gozum, *Historical Survey*.

5. Most of the $400 million was set aside for private claims. The eligibility of private claims was adjudicated on the basis of "insurable interest . . . actual cash value of assets at the time of loss, or on the postwar replacement cost, whichever was lower." Philippine War Damage Commission, *Semiannual Report*, no. 9 (1951), 9–15.

6. Philippine War Damage Commission, *Semiannual Report*, no. 3 (1947), 62.

7. Doane, "Architecture in the Philippines," 2.

8. Philippine War Damage Commission, *Semiannual Report*, no. 9 (1951) 1.

9. "Unrest in Pacific," 5.

10. After this date, tariffs would be imposed in both countries at an annually increasing rate of 5percent of the existing duty. Full duties would not be in force until 1974. Shalom, "Philippine Acceptance."

11. Romualdez, *Question of Sovereignty*.

12. Philippine-American Anti-Parity Committee, Report entitled "Independence and Interference" on the ramifications of the Bell Trade Act, also known as the Philippine Trade Act, on the independence and sovereignty of the newly independent nation of the Philippines, Ca. 1947–54, pp. 1–3, University Libraries, University of Washington, Special Collections, PNW01290, https://digitalcollections.lib.washington.edu/digital

/collection/pioneerlife/id/10586/. Further "parity" was achieved in the Laurel-Langley Agreement of 1955, a trade act which gave American citizens and businesses the ability to own 100 percent of companies in any area of the economy, a condition that explains why US corporations still control most foreign investments in the Philippines.

13. Filipinos were given a (required) one-year window in which to file private property claims. During that period, a total of 1,250,000 claims were filed, with a declared value of $1.225 billion.

14. Philippine War Damage Commission, *Semiannual Report*, no. 8 (1950), 3.

15. Philippine War Damage Commission, *Semiannual Report*, no. 9 (1951), 9–15.

16. Porter, "The Philippines as an American Investment," 219.

17. Philippine War Damage Commission, *Semiannual Report*, no. 9 (1951), 7.

18. Serafino et al., *US Occupation Assistance*, 5.

19. Ellender, *Review of the United States*, 320–32.

20. George P. Miller, speaking on the Philippine Rehabilitation Act, July 19, 1957, 85th Congress, 1st sess., Congressional Record 103, Part 9, p. 12240.

21. John F. Kennedy, quoted in "House Approves Bill," 3.

22. Indeed, the Philippines War Damage Commission and the Marshall Plan can be seen as early iterations of what Naomi Klein calls "disaster capitalism," in which a variety of political actors exploit the chaos that follows in the wake of natural disaster, war, and other crises to push unpopular policies. In the case of the Philippines, the need for rehabilitation aid compelled the Philippine government to accept even the most unpopular conditions contained in the Bell Trade Act. Klein, *Shock Doctrine*, esp. 273, 313–18.

AFTERWORD

1. Robinson, "The American Press," 195.

2. White, *Tropics of Discourse*, 81.

3. McCoy, "Philippines: Independence."

4. "Music for Primary Songs," 25.

5. For a detailed account of the Philippine-American War in Batangas, where, as Glenn Anthony May argues, it played out differently than in other parts of the Philippines, see May, *Battle for Batangas*.

6. Wallace, "Extract from Report," 99–100.

7. In the chapter "As We Encounter It at the Breakfast Table," Forbes describes the American breakfast table as a globe-trotting adventure into history, where our lips touch china, which is named so by "no mere coincidence"; our hands touch silverware, possibly smelted from mines in the "Andes in Bolivia, or from the blood-stained mines of Mexico . . . [or] perhaps Captain Kidd's treasure." The cocoa may have come from "Ecuador, Trinidad, Africa, Venezuela, Granada, Hayti, Cuba, Ceylon, Para, Bahia, Suriname, Martinique," and to it is added some sugar and vanilla, from dozens of more places. He turns often to the Philippines, where the cocoa industry struggles to take hold, but where sugar fields are vast. He concludes by exclaiming, "What a mine of hidden or lost romance lies about us!" Forbes, *Romance of Business*, 26–51.

8. All of the objects given to the author were duplicates of documents gifted to the Houghton Library, Harvard University.

9. Forbes, *Romance of Business*, 79 (emphasis added).

10. I once stumbled on a poignant example of this in the documentary film *Queen of Versailles*, in which one of the nannies, Virginia Nebab, relays that her father had dreamt of having a "concrete house," which she was never able to build for him. Instead, she built him a concrete tomb: "It is his own house," she says, "and I think it is good for him." Lauren Greenfield, director, *Queen of Versailles*, Evergreen Pictures, 2012.

Bibliography

"Act no. 173: An Act Restoring the Provinces of Batangas, Cebu, and Bohol to the Executive Control of the Military Governor." July 17, 1901. Accessed August 27, 2020. https://elibrary.judiciary.gov.ph/thebookshelf/showdocs/28/35639.

Adas, Michael. *Machines as the Measure of Men: Science, Technology, and Ideologies of Western Dominance,* Ithaca, NY: Cornell University Press, 2014

Agoncillo, Teodoro, and Oscar M. Alfonso. *History of the Filipino People.* Quezon City: Malaya, 1971.

Aguilar, Filomeno, Jr. "Tracing Origins: *Ilustrado* Nationalism and the Racial Science of Migration Waves." *Journal of Asian Studies* 64, no. 3 (2005): 605–37.

Ahern, George P. *Annual Report of the Director of Forestry of the Philippine Islands, 1906–1907.* Manila: Bureau of Printing, 1908.

Ahern, George P. *Opportunities for Lumber in the Philippine Forests.* Manila: Bureau of Printing, 1911.

Alatas, Syed Hussein. *The Myth of the Lazy Native: A Study of the Image of Malays, Filipinos, and Javanese from the 16th to the 20th Century and Its Function in the Ideology of Colonial Capitalism.* London: F. Cass, 1977.

Alharilla, Martín Rodrigo. *Un hombre, mil negocios: La controvertida historia de Antonio López, Marqués de Comillas.* Barcelona: Ariel, 2021.

Allais, Lucia. *Designs of Destruction.* Chicago: University of Chicago Press, 2018.

Allais, Lucia, and Forrest Meggers. "Concrete Is One Hundred Years Old." In *Evidence and Narrative,* edited by Aggregate Architectural History Collective, 75–89. Pittsburgh, PA: University of Pittsburgh Press, 2021.

Allen, Francis J., and Terrance McGovern. *The Concrete Battleship: Fort Drum, El Fraile Island, Manila Bay.* Missoula, MT: Pictorial Histories Publishing Co., 1999.

"All Nationalities Plead to Advance Philippine Interests." *Far Eastern Review*, August 1911, 89–90.

Anderson, Benedict. *Imagined Communities: Reflections on the Origin and Spread of Nationalism.* Rev. ed. New York: Verso, 2016.

Anderson, Benedict. *Under Three Flags: Anarchism and the Anticolonial Imagination.* New York: Verso, 2006.

Anderson, Warwick. *Colonial Pathologies: American Tropical Medicine, Race, and Hygiene in the Philippines.* Durham, NC: Duke University Press, 2006.

Anonymous [Berton Braley]. "Business Is Business." *Quarterly Bulletin, Bureau of Public Works* 6, no. 1 (1917): 20.

Aristotle. *Meteorologica.* Translated by H. D. P. Lee. Cambridge, MA: Harvard University Press, 1952.

Baldoz, Rick. *The Third Asiatic Invasion: Migration and Empire in Filipino America, 1898–1946.* New York: NYU Press, 2011.

Balfour, Andrew. "Problems of Acclimatisation." *Lancet* 202, no. 5211 (1923): 84–87.

Balfour, Andrew. "Problems of Acclimatisation." *Lancet* 202, no. 5214 (1923): 243–47.

Balfour, Andrew. "Sojourners in the Tropics." *Lancet* 201, no. 5209 (1923): 1329–34.

Banham, Reyner. *A Concrete Atlantis: U.S. Industrial Building and European Modern Architecture, 1900–1925.* Cambridge, MA: MIT Press, 1986.

Banham, Reyner. *The New Brutalism: Ethic or Aesthetic?* New York: Reinhold, 1966.

Barad, Karen Michelle. *Meeting the Universe Halfway: Quantum Physics and the Entanglement of Matter and Meaning.* Durham, NC: Duke University Press, 2007.

Barnes, Geraldine. "Curiosity, Wonder, and William Dampier's Painted Prince." *Journal for Early Modern Cultural Studies* 6, no. 1 (Spring-Summer 2006): 31–50.

Baumann, Frederick. *The Art of Preparing Foundations for All Kinds of Buildings, with Particular Illustration of the Method of Isolated Piers as Followed in Chicago.* Chicago: J. M. Wing, 1873.

Beardsley, James W. "The Progress of Public Works in the Philippine Islands." *Journal of Race Development* 1, no. 2 (1910): 169–86.

Benjamin, Walter. *The Arcades Project.* Translated by Howard Eiland and Kevin McLaughlin. Cambridge, MA: Belknap, 2002.

Benjamin, Walter. "On the Concept of History (Thesis VI)." In *Walter Benjamin: Selected Writings, Vol. 4: 1938–1940*, 389–401. Cambridge, MA: Harvard University Press, 2006.

Benjamin, Walter. "The Work of Art in the Age of Mechanical Reproduction." In *Illuminations,* edited by Hannah Arendt, 217–52. New York: Schocken, 1969.

Betts, Raymond. "Decolonization: A Brief History of the Word." In *Beyond Empire and Nation,* edited by Els Bogaerts and Remco Raben, 23–38. Leiden: Brill, 2012.

Black, Megan. *The Global Interior: Material Frontiers and American Power.* Cambridge, MA: Harvard University Press, 2018.

Blakeslee, George H. "Introduction." *Journal of Race Development* 1, no. 1 (1910): 1–4.

Boas, Franz. "Changes in the Bodily Form of Descendants of Immigrants." *American Anthropologist* 14, no. 3 (1912): 530–62.

Bowes, John P. "American Indian Removal beyond the Removal Act." *Native American and Indigenous Studies* 1, no. 1 (2014): 65–87.

Brands, H. W. *Bound to Empire: The United States and the Philippines.* New York: Oxford University Press, 1992.

Brody, David. *Visualizing American Empire: Orientalism and Imperialism in the Philippines.* Chicago: University of Chicago Press, 2010.

Bureau of Public Works (Philippines). *Road Book.* Manila: Bureau of Printing, 1909.

Bureau of the Census (US). *Census of the Philippine Islands: Taken Under the Direction of the Philippine Commission in 1903.* 4 vols. Washington, DC: United States Bureau of the Census, 1905.

Burnham, Daniel H., and William Pierce Anderson. "Report on Proposed Improvements at Manila." In *Sixth Annual Report of the Philippine Commission, 1905,* 627–35. Washington, DC: US Government Printing Office, 1906.

Burnham, Daniel H., and Edward H. Bennett. *Plan of Chicago.* Chicago: Chicago Commercial Club, 1909.

Cameron, H. F. "Manila-South Road System." *Quarterly Bulletin, Bureau of Public Works* 1, no. 4 (1913): 26–37.

Cameron, H. F. "Provincial Centers in the Philippine Islands." *Quarterly Bulletin, Bureau of Public Works* 2, no. 4 (1914): 3–4.

Carnegie, Andrew. "Distant Possessions: The Parting of the Ways." *North American Review,* August 1898, 239–48.

Carnegie, Andrew. "The Value of the World's Fair to the American People." *Engineering Magazine,* January 1894, 419.

Castillo, Greg. *Cold War on the Home Front: The Soft Power of Midcentury Design.* Minneapolis: University of Minnesota Press, 2010.

"Cement Tariff in the Philippines." *Cement Age* 1, no. 8 (1905): 338.

Césaire, Aimé. *Discourse on Colonialism.* New York: Monthly Review Press, 2000.

Chamberlin, Frederick. *The Philippine Problem, 1898–1913.* Boston: Little Brown, 1913.

Chang, Jiat-Hwee, and Imran bin Tajudeen, eds. *Southeast Asia's Modern Architecture: Questions of Translation, Epistemology and Power.* Singapore: National University of Singapore Press, 2019.

Chee-Kien, Lai. "Beyond Colonial and National Frameworks: Some Thoughts on the Writing of Southeast Asian Architecture." *Journal of Architectural Education* 63, no. 2 (2010): 74–75.

Chow, Rey. "The Politics and Pedagogy of Asian Literatures in American Universities." *Differences: A Journal of Feminist Cultural Studies* 2, no. 3 (1990): 29–51.

Clark, Victor S. "Labor Conditions in the Philippines." *Bulletin of the United States Bureau of Labor,* May 1905, 845.

Clifford, James. "The Others: Beyond the 'Salvage' Paradigm." *Third Text,* no. 6 (1989): 73–78.

Clutario, Genevieve. *Beauty Regimes: A History of Power and Modern Empire in the Philippines 1898–1941.* Durham, NC: Duke University Press, 2023.

Cochrane, Rexmond C. *Measures for Progress: A History of the National Bureau of Standards.* Washington, DC: US Department of Commerce, 1966.

Coleman, Ambrose. *The Friars in the Philippines.* Boston: Marlier, Callanan, 1899.

Collins, Peter. *Concrete: The Vision of a New Architecture.* New York: Horizon, 1959.

Conant, Charles A. "The Economic Basis of Imperialism." *North American Review,* 167, no. 502 (1898): 326–40.

Condit, Carl. *The Chicago School of Architecture: A History of Commercial and Public Building in the Chicago Area, 1875–1925.* Chicago: University of Chicago Press, 1964.

Connaughton, Richard M., John Pimlott, and Duncan Anderson. *The Battle for Manila*. Novato, CA: Presidio, 1995.

Constantino, Renato. *The Philippines: A Past Revisited*. With Letizia R. Constantino. Quezon City: Tala, 1975.

Coo, Stephanie. *Clothing the Colony*. Manila: Ateneo de Manila University Press, 2019.

Cox, Alvin J. *Eleventh Annual Report of the Bureau of Science*. Manila: Bureau of Printing, 1913.

Cox, Fitzhugh. "The Use of Concrete in India." *Professional Papers on Indian Engineering* 5, no. 22 (1876): 24–35.

Crawford, Christina E. *Spatial Revolution: Architecture and Planning in the Early Soviet Union*. Ithaca, NY: Cornell University Press, 2022.

Crawford, Margaret. *Building the Workingman's Paradise*. London: Verso, 1995.

Crinson, Mark. *Shock City: Image and Architecture in Industrial Manchester*. London: Paul Mellon Centre for Studies in British Art, 2022.

Cronon, William. *Changes in the Land: Indians, Colonists, and the Ecology of New England*. New York: Hill and Wang, 1983.

Cronon, William. *Nature's Metropolis: Chicago and the Great West*. New York: Norton, 1991.

"The Crust at Chicago." *New York Times*, October 18, 1891, 4.

Cullinane, Michael. "Bringing in the Brigands." *Philippine Studies* 57, no. 1 (2009): 49–76.

Darwin, Charles. *On the Origin of the Species*. London: John Murray, 1859.

Davis, Charles. *Building Character: The Racial Politics of Modern Architectural Style*. Pittsburgh, PA: University of Pittsburgh Press, 2019.

Davis, James F. *Who Is Black? One Nation's Definition*. University Park: Pennsylvania State University Press, 2001.

Davis, Will. "Palm Politics: Warfare, Folklore, and Architecture." PhD diss., University of California, Los Angeles, 2021.

Davis, Will. "Seeds That Float." *Architectural Theory Review* 25, nos. 1–2 (2021): 154–64.

Day, Beth. *The Manila Hotel: The Heart and Memory of a City*. Manila: National Media Production Center, 1980.

DeCanio, Samuel. *Democracy and the Origins of the American Regulatory State*. New Haven, CT: Yale University Press, 2015.

Delina, Laurence L. "Indigenous Environmental Defenders and the Legacy of Macli-ing Dulag: Anti-Dam Dissent, Assassinations, and Protests in the Making of the Philippine Energyscape." *Energy Research & Social Science,* 65 (2020): 1–13. https://doi.org/10.1016/j.erss.2020.101463.

Delinks, J. A. "Navy Construction in the Philippines." *Military Engineer* 54, no. 358 (1962): 107–9.

del Mundo, Fernando. *The Promised Land: Hacienda Luisita*. Manila: Philippine Daily Inquirer, 2012.

de los Reyes, Isabelo. "Nueva Ciudad y Boulevares Para Manila." *El Renacimiento*, January 24, 1903, 2.

Demolins, Edmond. *Anglo-Saxon Superiority, to What It Is Due*. New York: R. F. Fenno, 1899.

"Design for the First Regiment Armory, Chicago: Burnham & Root." *Inland Architect and News Record*, June 1889, 90.

di Palma, Vittoria. "Architecture, Environment, and Emotion: Quatremère de Quincy and the Concept of Character." *AAFiles*, no. 47 (2002): 45–56.

Doane, Ralph Harrington. "Architecture in the Philippines." *Quarterly Bulletin, Bureau of Public Works* 7, no. 2 (1918): 2–8.

Doane, Ralph Harrington. "The Story of American Architecture in the Philippines: Part I." *Architectural Review* 8, no. 2 (1919): 25–32.

Doane, Ralph Harrington. "The Story of American Architecture in the Philippines: Part II." *Architectural Review* 8, no. 5 (1919): 115–22.

Dolan, Ronald E., ed. *Philippines: A Country Study*. Washington, DC: GPO for the Library of Congress, 1991.

Dower, John. *War Without Mercy: Race and Power in the Pacific War*. New York: Pantheon, 1986.

Drexler, Arthur. *The Architecture of the École des Beaux-Arts*. New York: Museum of Modern Art, 1977.

Du Bois, W. E. B. "The Forethought." In *The Souls of Black Folk*. New York: Norton, 2022.

Ealham, Chris. *Anarchism and the City: Revolution and Counter-Revolution in Barcelona 1898–1937*. Edinburgh: AK Press, 2010.

Edison Portland Cement Co. *The Romance of Cement*. Boston: Edison Portland Cement Co., 1926.

Ekbladh, David. *The Great American Mission: Development and the Construction of an American World Order*. Ithaca, NY: Cornell University Press, 2011.

Elinoff, Eli, and Kali Rubaii. *The Social Properties of Concrete*. London: Punctum, 2024.

Ellender, Allan J. *A Review of United States Foreign Policy Operations*. Washington, DC: US Government Printing Office, 1958.

Endicott, William Crowninshield. *Report of the Board on Fortifications or Other Defenses Appointed by the President of the United States*. Washington, DC: US Government Printing Office, 1866.

Engels, Friedrich. "The Housing Question." In *Karl Marx and Friedrich Engels, Selected Work in Three Volumes*, vol. 2, 293–375. Moscow: Progress Publishers, 1969.

Engerman, David C., ed. *Staging Growth: Modernization, Development, and the Global Cold War*. Amherst: University of Massachusetts Press, 2003.

Estes, Lewis Alden. *Earthquake Proof Construction: A Discussion of the Effects of Earthquakes on Building Construction with Special Reference to Structure of Reinforced Concrete*. Detroit: Trussed Concrete Steel Co., 1911.

Facts and Figures About the Philippines. Manila: Bureau of Printing, 1920.

Fanon, Frantz. *Black Skin, White Masks*. New York: Grove, 1967.

Fanon, Frantz. *The Wretched of the Earth*. New York: Grove, 1965.

Faustino, Leopoldo A. "Nonmetallic Minerals." In *The Mineral Resources of the Philippine Islands for the Years 1917–1918*, edited by the Chief of the Division of Geology and Mines, Bureau of Science, 38–46. Manila: Bureau of Printing, 1918.

Feeney, William R. "The United States and the Philippines: The Bases Dilemma." *Asian Affairs: An American Review* 10, no. 4 (1984): 63–85.

Ferro, Sergio. "Concrete as Weapon." *Harvard Design Magazine* (special insert), Fall/Winter 2018, unpaginated.

Fetter, Frank A. "Review: *Anglo Saxon Superiority: To What It Is Due*." *Annals of the American Academy of Political and Social Science* 14 (1899): 117–20.

Fitch, George Hamlin. *The Critic in the Orient*. San Francisco: Paul Elder & Co., 1913.

Fleck, D., ed. *The Handbook of Humanitarian Law in Armed Conflicts*. Oxford: Oxford University Press, 1995.

Fletcher, Banister. *The Influence of Material on Architecture*. London: T. Batsford, 1897.

Forbes, William Cameron. *Inauguration Address as Governor General of the Philippine Islands*. Manila: Bureau of Printing, 1909.

Forbes, William Cameron. *The Philippine Islands*. Rev. ed. Cambridge, MA: Harvard University Press, 1945.

Forbes, William Cameron. *Reply to Jones: Replies to False Charges Contained in the Speeches Made by William A. Jones, of Virginia, in the House of Representatives, January 28 and February 13, 1913*. Manila: N.p., 1913.

Forbes, William Cameron. *The Romance of Business*. Boston: Houghton Mifflin, 1921.

Forbes, William Cameron. "What Had Best Be Done for the Material Advancement of the Philippines." In *Proceedings of the Twenty-Sixth Annual Meeting of the Lake Mohonk Conference of Friends of the Indian and Other Dependent Peoples*, reported by Lillian D. Powers, 117–23. New York: Lake Mohonk Conference of Friends and the Indian and Other Dependent Peoples, 1908.

Forbes, William Cameron, and Leonard Wood. *Report of the Special Mission on the Investigation to the Philippine Islands to the Secretary of War*. Washington, DC: US Government Publishing Office, 1921.

Forty, Adrian. *Concrete and Culture: A Material History*. London: Reaktion, 2012.

Foucault, Michel. *Security, Territory, Population*. New York: Palgrave MacMillan, 2007.

Foucault, Michel. "What Is an Author?" In *Language, Counter-Memory, Practice*. Translated by D. F. Bouchard and S. Simon. Ithaca, NY: Cornell University Press, 1977.

Fox, Carroll. *Annual Report of the Bureau of Health for the Philippine Islands, for the Fiscal Year Ended June 30, 1911*. Manila: Bureau of Health, 1911.

Frapier, Christel, and Simon Vaillant. "The Organization of the Hennebique Firm in the Countries of the Mediterranean Basin: Establishment and Communications Strategy." In *Building Beyond the Mediterranean: Studying the Archives of European Businesses (1860–1970)*, edited by Claudine Piaton, Ezio Godoli, and David Peyceré, 34–43. Arles: OpenEdition, 2021.

Freer, P. C. "The Bureau of Government Laboratories for the Philippine Islands, and Scientific Positions Under It." *Science*, October 10, 1902, 579–80.

Fuhriman, Walter U. "Federal Aid to Irrigation Development." *Journal of Farm Economics* 31, no. 4, pt. 2 (1949): 965–75.

Gabaldon, Isauro, and Pedro Guevara. "An Important Message From the Philippine Commissioners." *Philippine Republic*, December 1923, 20.

Garb, Margaret. "Race, Housing, and Burnham's Plan: Why Is There No Housing in the 1909 *Plan of Chicago*?" *Journal of Planning History* 10, no. 2 (2011): 99–113.

Getachew, Adom. *Worldmaking After Empire: The Rise and Fall of Self-Determination*. Princeton, NJ: Princeton University Press, 2019.

Getachew, Adom, and Jennifer Pitts, eds. *W. E. B. Du Bois: International Thought*. Cambridge: Cambridge University Press, 2022.

Giedion, Sigfried. *Bauen in Frankreich, Bauen in Eisen, Bauen in Eisenbeton*. Leipzig: Klinkhardt & Biermann, 1928.

Giedion, Sigfried. *Building in France, Building in Iron, Building in Ferroconcrete*. Translated by Duncan Berry. Santa Monica, CA: Getty Center for the History of Art and the Humanities, 1995.

Giedion, Sigfried. "The Need for a New Monumentality." In *New Architecture and City Planning*, edited by Paul Zucker. New York: Philosophical Library, 1944.

Gillis, Malcolm. "The Role of State Enterprises in Economic Development." *Social Research* 47 (1980): 248–89.

Gordon, C. E. "An Experiment in Macadam Asphalt Construction." *Quarterly Bulletin, Bureau of Public Works* 1, no. 4 (1913): 19–21.

Gozum, Lolito Gil. "A Historical Survey of the Postwar Operation of the Cebu Portland Cement Company." Master's thesis, University of San Carlos, Cebu, Philippines.

Guerdrum, George H. "A Novel House and Street Sewerage System for Portions of Manila P.I." *Engineering News* 64, no. 14 (1910): 356.

Guevarra, Dante G. *History of the Philippine Labor Movement*. Santa Mesa: Institute of Labor and Industrial Relations, Polytechnic University of the Philippines, 1991.

Guterl, Matthew. *The Color of Race in America, 1900–1940*. Cambridge, MA: Harvard University Press, 2004.

Gyger, Helen. *Improvised Cities: Architecture, Urbanization, and Innovation in Peru*. Pittsburgh, PA: University of Pittsburgh Press, 2019.

Hall, G. Stanley. "The Point of View Towards Primitive Races." *Journal of Race Development* 1, no. 1 (1910): 5–11.

Hall, G. Stanley. "The White Man's Burden vs. the Indigenous Development of Lower Races." *Journal of Education* 58 (1903): 83.

Halliday, Fred. "Three Concepts of Internationalism." *International Affairs* 64, no. 2 (1988): 187–98.

Han, Yikuan, and Zhaoyi Wang. "Transplantation and Adaptation: Research on Reinforced Concrete Structures in Modern Nanjing (1909–1949)." *Buildings* 13, no. 6 (2023): 1468–71. https://doi.org/10.3390/buildings13061468.

Harrison, Francis Burton. *The Cornerstone of Philippine Independence: A Narrative of Seven Years*. New York: The Century Co., 1922.

Hawkins, Mike B. "An Episodic History of Manila's Waterfront." Phd diss., University of North Carolina at Chapel Hill, 2022.

Heiser, Victor G. *Annual Report of the Bureau of Health for the Philippine Islands, July 1, 1908, to June 30, 1909*. Manila: Bureau of Printing, 1909.

Heiser, Victor G. *Annual Report of the Bureau of Health for the Philippine Islands, from July 1, 1909, to June 30, 1910*. Manila: Bureau of Printing, 1910.

Heiser, Victor G. *Annual Report of the Bureau of Health for the Philippine Islands, for the Fiscal Year Ended June 30, 1912*. Manila: Bureau of Printing, 1913.

Heizer, Robert. "The Background of Thomsen's Three-age System." *Technology and Culture* 3, no. 3 (1962): 259–66.

Henderson, Susan R. *Building Culture: Ernst May and the New Frankfurt am Main Initiative, 1926–1931*. Lausanne: Peter Lang, 2013.

Hines, Thomas. "American Modernism in the Philippines: The Forgotten Architecture of William E. Parsons." *Journal of the Society of Architectural Historians* 32, no. 4 (1973): 316–26.

Hines, Thomas. *Burnham of Chicago: Architect and Planner*. New York: Oxford University Press, 1974.

Hines, Thomas. "The Imperial Façade: Daniel H. Burnham and American Architectural Planning." *Pacific Historical Review* 41, no. 1 (1972): 33–53.

Ho, Enseng. "Empire Through Diasporic Eyes: A View from the Other Boat." *Comparative Studies in Society and History* 46, no. 2 (2004): 210–46.

"House Approves Bill on Philippine War Damage." *New York Times*, August 2, 1962, 3.

Huntington, Ellsworth. "A Neglected Factor in Race Development." *Journal of Race Development* 6, no. 2 (1915): 167–84.

Huntington, Ellsworth. *World Power and Evolution*. New Haven, CT: Yale University Press, 1919.

Hvattum, Mari. *Gottfried Semper and the Problem of Historicism*. Cambridge: Cambridge University Press, 2004.

Ileto, Reynaldo. "Cholera and the Origins of the American Sanitary Order in the Philippines." In *Discrepant Histories: Translocal Essays on Filipino Culture*, edited by Vicente Rafael. Philadelphia: Temple University Press, 1995.

Immerwahr, Daniel. *How to Hide an Empire*. New York: Farrar, Strauss, and Giroux, 2019.

"Importancia de las casillas de camineros en la planificación de la Isla." *Periódico El Adoquín*, March 21, 2023. https://eladoquintimes.com/2023/03/21/importancia-de-las-casillas-de-camineros-en-la-planificacion-de-carreteras-en-la-isla/.

Ingalls, Owen L. "Report upon the Sewerage System for the City of Manila." *Report on the Philippine Commission to the Secretary of War, 1905*. Washington, DC: US Government Printing Office, 1906.

Ingold, Tim. *Making: Anthropology, Archaeaeology, Art and Architecture*. London: Routledge, 2013.

Jackson, Donald E. "L'Enfant's Washington: An Architect's View." *Records of the Columbia Historical Society* 50 (1980): 398–420.

Jackson, Justin F. "'A Military Necessity Which Must Be Pressed': The U.S. Army and Forced Road Labor in the Early American Colonial Philippines." In *On Coerced Labor*, edited by Marcel M. Van der Linden and Magaly Rodríguez García. Leiden: Brill Academic, 2016.

Jackson, Justin F. "Roads to American Empire: U.S. Military Public Works and Capitalist Transitions, 1898–1934." *Journal of Historical Sociology* 33, no. 1 (2020): 115–33.

Japanese Defense of Cities as Exemplified by the Battle for Manila: A Report by XIV Corps. Headquarters Sixth Army: A.C. of S., G-2, 1945.

Jennings, Eric. *Imperial Heights: Dalat and the Making and Undoing of French Indochina*. Berkeley: University of California Press, 2011.

Jennings, R. Y. "Open Towns." *British Year Book of International Law* 22 (1945): 258–64.

Joaquin, Nick. *Almanac for Manileños*. Manila: Mr. & Ms., 1979.

Joaquin, Nick. *Manila, My Manila*. Makati City: Bookmark, 1999.

"The Jones Law of 1916." *Official Gazette of the Republic of the Philippines*, August 29, 1916. https://mirror.officialgazette.gov.ph/constitutions/the-jones-law-of-1916/.

Jones, Owen. *Details and Ornaments from the Alhambra*. London: Jones, 1845.

Jones, William A. *Misgovernment in the Philippines and Cost to the United States of American Occupation*. Washington, DC: US Government Printing Office, 1913.

"Juan Arellano." *Philippine Magazine*, February 1926, 461.

Junghändel, Max. *Die Baukunst Spaniens*. Dresden: J. Bleyl Gilbers, 1891.

Kalaw, Maximo M. "Recent Policy Towards the Non-Christian People of the Philippines." *Journal of International Relations* 10, no. 1 (1919): 1–12.

Kalaw, Maximo M. *Self-Government in the Philippines*. New York: Century, 1919.

Kawamura, Noriko. "Wilsonian Idealism and Japanese Claims at the Paris Peace Conference." *Pacific Historical Review* 66, no. 4 (1997): 503–26.

Kawehipuaakahaopulani Hobart, Hi'ilei Julia. *Cooling the Tropics: Ice, Indigeneity, and Hawaiian Refreshment*. Durham, NC: Duke University Press, 2023.

Kennett, Lee. *A History of Strategic Bombing*. New York: Scribners, 1982.

Kerkvliet, Melinda Tria. *Manila Workers' Unions, 1900–1950*. Quezon City: New Day Publishers, 1992.

Kincaid, Jamaica. *A Small Place: Some Perspectives on the Ordinary*. New York: Farrar, Strauss, and Giroux, 1988.

King, Albert E. W. "Physical Properties of Philippine Concrete and Concrete Aggregates." *Philippine Journal of Science* 18, no. 2 (1921): 105–220.

Kipling, Rudyard. *American Notes*. Boston: Brown and Co., 1899.

Kipling, Rudyard. "A Real Live City." In *The City of Dreadful Night*. New York: Alex, Grosset, 1899.

Klassen, Winand W. *Architecture in the Philippines: Filipino Building in a Cross Cultural Context*. Cebu City: University of San Carlos Press, 1986.

Klein, Naomi. *The Shock Doctrine: The Rise of Disaster Capitalism*. New York: Metropolitan Books, 2008.

Koch, J. C. "Methods and Practice in the Design of Reinforced Concrete with Special Reference to Tropical Conditions in the Orient." *Far-Eastern Review; Engineer, Commerce, Finance* 3, no. 8 (1907): 239.

Kramer, Paul A. *The Blood of Government: Race, Empire, the United States, and the Philippines*. Chapel Hill: University of North Carolina Press, 2006.

Kramer, Paul A. "Power and Connection: Imperial Histories of the United States in the World." *American Historical Review* 116, no. 5 (2011): 1348–91.

Kubo, Michael, Chris Grimley, and Michael Pasnik. *Heroic: Concrete Architecture and the New Boston*. New York: Monacelli Press, 2015.

Kusno, Abidin. *Jakarta: City of a Thousand Dimensions*. Singapore: National University of Singapore Press, 2023.

Lake, Marilyn. *Drawing the Global Colour Line: White Men's Countries and the International Challenge of Racial Equity*. Cambridge: Cambridge University Pres, 2008.

Lambert, Guy. "Bridges as Ambassadors: Hennebique's Expansion in North Africa." In *Building Beyond the Mediterranean: Studying the Archives of European Businesses (1860–1970)*, edited by Claudine Piaton, Ezio Godoli, and David Peyceré. Arles: OpenEdition, 2021.

Larson, John Lauritz. *Bonds of Enterprise: John Murray Forbes and Western Development in America's Railway Age*. Iowa City: University of Iowa Press, 1984.

Latour, Bruno. *Reassembling the Social: An Introduction to Actor-Network Theory*, Oxford: Oxford University Press, 2005.

Lefebvre, Henri. "Right to the City." In *Writings on Cities*. Translated by Eleonore Kofman and edited by Elizabeth Lebas. Cambridge: Wiley-Blackwell, 1996.

LeRoy, James Alfred. *The Americans in the Philippines: A History of the Conquest and First Years of Occupation, with an Introductory Account of the Spanish Rule, Vol. 2*. Boston: Houghton Mifflin, 1914.

Lesley, Robert Whitman. *History of the Portland Cement Industry in the United States*. Philadelphia: American Cement Co., 1900.

Lewis, W. H. "Bilibid: The Most Remarkable Penal Institution in the World." *Manila Times: Second Annual Edition*, edited by Eleanor Franklin Eagan. N.p.: Times Publishing, 1911.

Lico, Gerard. *Arkitekturang Filipino: A History of Architecture and Urbanism in the Philippines*. Quezon City: University of the Philippines Press, 2008.

Lico, Gerard. "'Manila Beautiful': Urban Hygiene and Colonial Architecture in the Age of American Imperialism (1898–1942)." In *Southeast Asia's Modern Architecture: Questions of Translation, Epistemology and Power*, edited by Jiat-Hwee Chang and Imran bin Tajudeen. Singapore: National University of Singapore Press, 2019.

Lico, Gerard, and Ivan Man Dy. *Deco Filipino: Art Deco Heritage in the Philippines*. Makati: Artpostasia, 2020.

Lindqvist, Sven. *The History of Bombing*. New York: New Press, 2001.

Link, Arthus S, ed. *The Papers of Woodrow Wilson*. Vol. 2. Princeton, NJ: Princeton University Press, 1977.

Ludovice, Nicolo Paolo. "The Ice Plant Cometh: The Insular Cold Storage and Ice Plant, Frozen Meat, and the Imperial Biodeterioration of Imperial Manila, 1900–1935." *Global Food History* 7, no. 2 (2021): 115–39.

Mabry, James C. "Regulation, Industry Structure, and Competitiveness in the U.S. Portland Cement Industry." *Business and Economic History* 27, no. 2 (1998): 402–12.

MacArthur, Douglas. "General Douglas MacArthur's Proclamations." *Congressional Record, Proceedings and Debates of the 79th Congress*. Washington, DC: US Government Publishing Office, 1944.

MacArthur, Douglas. *Reminiscences*. Annapolis, MD: Bluejacket, 2012.

Malacrino, Carmelo. *Constructing the Ancient World: Architectural Techniques of the Greeks and Romans*. Los Angeles: J. Paul Getty, 2010.

Manchester, William. *American Caesar*. New York: Back Bay, 2008.

Manela, Erez. *The Wilsonian Moment*. Oxford: Oxford University Press, 2007.

"Manila Waterworks and Sewer Construction." *Far Eastern Review* 4, no. 10 (1908): 308–11.

Martin, Reinhold. "Local Stone (A Fragment)." *Architectural Design* 77, no. 6 (2007): 56–59.

Martinez, Diana Jean. "Crystals in the Colony." *Architectural Theory Review* 26, no. 3 (2022): 384–404.

Martinez, Diana Jean. "Nation Building in the Philippines and the Racial Ordering of International Architecture." *Grey Room* 95 (2024): 42–73.

Marx, Karl. *Capital: A Critical Analysis of Capitalist Production.* Translated by Ben Fowkes. New York: Penguin, 1992.

Marx, Leo. *The Machine in the Garden: Technology and the Pastoral Ideal in America.* New York: Oxford University Press, 1964.

Marx, Leo, and Merritt Roe Smith. *Does Technology Drive History? The Dilemma of Technological Determinism.* Cambridge, MA: MIT Press, 1994.

May, Glenn Anthony. *The Battle for Batangas: A Philippine Province at War.* New Haven, CT: Yale University Press, 1991.

May, Glenn Anthony. *Social Engineering in the Philippines: The Aims, Execution, and Impact of American Colonial Policy, 1900–1913.* New York: Praeger, 1980.

Mazower, Mark. *No Enchanted Palace: The End of Empire and the Ideological Origins of the United Nations.* Princeton, NJ: Princeton University Press, 2010.

Mazrui, Ali. "From Darwin to Current Theories of Modernization." *World Politics* 21, no. 1, (1968): 69–83.

McCoy, Alfred. "The Philippines: Independence Without Decolonization." In *Asia: The Winning of Independence*, edited by R. Jeffrey. London: MacMillan, 1981.

McGregor, J. "Administrative Construction of the University Hall, University of the Philippines, Manila, P.I." *Quarterly Bulletin, Bureau of Public Works* 2, no. 1 (1913): 28–31.

McKenna, Rebecca Tinio. *American Imperial Pastoral: The Architecture of US Colonialism in the Philippines.* Chicago: University of Chicago Press, 2017.

McKenna, Thomas M. *Muslim Rulers and Rebels.* Berkeley: University of California Press, 1998.

McKinley, William. "Instructions to the Peace Commissioners." Papers Relating to the Foreign Relations of the United States, with the Annual Message of the President Transmitted to Congress, December 5, 1898, Document 776. Office of the Historian, Foreign Service Institute, United States Department of State. https://history.state.gov/historicaldocuments/frus1898/d776.

McNutt, Paul V. "Irrigation in the Philippines." *Reclamation Era* 33, no. 3 (1947): 49–53.

Merwood-Salisbury, Joanna. *Chicago 1890: The Skyscraper and the Modern City.* Chicago: University of Chicago Press, 2009.

Miller, E. Willard. "Industrial Resources of Indochina." *Far Eastern Quarterly* 6, no. 4 (1947): 396–408.

Miller, George Amos. *Interesting Manila.* Manila: E. C. McCullough, 1906.

Mitchell, Timothy. *Colonizing Egypt.* Berkeley: University of California Press, 1991.

Mitchell, Timothy. *Rule of Experts.* Berkeley: University of California Press, 2002.

Mitchell, Timothy. "The World as Exhibition." *Comparative Studies in Society and History* 31, no. 2 (1989): 217–36.

Monroe, Harriet, and Henry VanBrunt. *John Wellborn Root: A Study of His Life and Work.* Park Forest, IL: Prairie School Press, 1966.

Montinola, Lourdes R., ed. *Art Deco in the Philippines*. Manila: Art Post Asia, 2010.

Morley, Ian. *American Colonisation and the City Beautiful: Filipinos and Planning in the Philippines, 1915–35*. New York: Routledge, 2020.

Morley, Ian. *Cities and Nationhood*. Honolulu: University of Hawai'i Press, 2018.

Morley, Ian. *Remodelling to Prepare for Independence: The Philippine Commonwealth, Decolonisation, Cities and Public Works, c. 1935–46*. New York: Routledge, 2024.

Moses, Edith. *Unofficial Letters of an Official's Wife*. New York: D. Appleton, 1908.

Muir-Wood, Robert. *The Cure for Catastrophe: How We Can Stop Manufacturing Natural Disasters*. New York: Basic Books, 2016.

Mukherjee, Mithi. "Justice, War, and the Imperium: India and Britain in Sir Edmund Burke's Prosecutorial Speeches in the Impeachment Trial of Warren Hastings." *Law and History Review* 23, no. 3 (2005): 589–630.

Mumford, Lewis. *The City in History: Its Origins, Its Transformations, and Its Prospects*. New York: Harcourt, 1961.

Mumford, Lewis. *The Culture of Cities*. New York: Harcourt Brace Jovanovic, 1938.

Mumford, Lewis. *Sticks and Stones*. New York: Boni and Liveright, 1924.

Mundigo, Axel I., and Dora P. Crouch. "The City Planning Ordinances of the Laws of the Indies Revisited, Part I: Their Philosophy and Implications." *Town Planning Review* 48, no. 3 (1977): 247–68.

"Music for Primary Songs." *Philippine Public Schools: A Monthly Magazine for Teachers*, January 1929, 25.

Niemeyer, Victor E. "The American Historical Collection of Filipiniana." *Philippine Studies* 9, no. 3 (1961): 414–22.

"Noted Architect Once Posed as 'Wild Man' at Jamestown." *New York Times*, January 30, 1927, 13.

Notz, William. "The World's Coal Situation During the War." *Journal of Political Economy* 26, no. 7 (1918): 673–704.

Nye, David E. *American Technological Sublime*. Cambridge, MA: MIT Press, 1994.

Nye, Joseph R., Jr. *Soft Power: The Means to Success in World Politics*, New York: Public Affairs, 2004.

Odum, Howard W. "Standards of Measurement for Race Development." *The Journal of Race Development* 5, no. 4 (1915): 364–83.

Oleson, J. P., ed. *Building for Eternity: The History and Technology of Roman Concrete Engineering*. Oxford: Oxbow, 2014.

Onorato, Michael P. "Leonard Wood as Governor General: A Calendar of Selected Correspondence." *Philippine Studies* 12, no. 1 (1964): 124–48.

Onorato, Michael P. "The Philippine Independence Mission of 1922." *Philippine Studies* 16, no. 3 (1968): 558–62.

Orenstein, Dara. *Out of Stock: The Warehouse in the History of Capitalism*. Chicago: University of Chicago Press, 2019.

Orquiza, René Alexander D. *Taste of Control*. New Brunswick, NJ: Rutgers University Press, 2020.

Osborne, Michael A. "Acclimatizing the World: A History of the Paradigmatic Colonial Science." *Osiris* 15, no. 1 (2000): 135–51.

Osman, Michael. "The Managerial Aesthetics of Concrete." *Perspecta* 45, *AGENCY* (2012): 67–76.

Pante, Michael D. *A Capital City at the Margins*. Manila: Ateneo de Manila University Press, 2019.

Pante, Michael D. "The Politics of Flood Control and the Making of Metro Manila." *Philippine Studies* 64, no. 3 (2016): 555–92.

Parsons, William. "Report of the Consulting Architect." In *Report of the Philippine Commission to the Secretary of War, 1909*. Washington, DC: Government Printing Office, 1910.

Paulet, Anne. "To Change the World: The Use of American Indian Education in the Philippines." *History of Education Quarterly* 47, no. 2 (2007): 173–202.

Peck, Ralph B. *History of Building Foundations in Chicago: A Report of an Investigation*. Report. *University of Illinois Bulletin* 45, no. 29 (1948).

Philippine Bureau of Science. *The Mineral Resources of the Philippine Islands*. Manila: Bureau of Printing, 1913.

Philippine Bureau of Science. *The Mineral Resources of the Philippine Islands*. Manila: Bureau of Printing, 1920.

Philippine Bureau of Science. *The Philippine Islands: Cement Raw Materials of the Philippines*. Manila: Bureau of Printing, 1915.

Philippine Commission. "Act No. 854: An Act Providing for the Education of Filipino Students in the United States and Appropriating for Such Purpose the Sum of Seventy-Two Thousand Dollars, in Money of the United States." In *Public Laws and Resolutions Passed by the Philippine Commission*. Vol. 12. Manila: Bureau of Printing, 1904.

Philippine Commission, "Act No. 1511: An Act Providing for the Construction, Repair, and Maintenance of Public Highways, Bridges, Wharves, and Trails in Those Provinces Organized under the Provincial Government Act Which Shall Vote to Adopt the Provisions of this Act in the Manner Hereafter Provided, and Providing a Penalty for Malicious Injuries to Highways, Bridges, Wharves, and Trails." In *Public Laws Passed by the Philippine Commission*. Vol. 5. Manila: Bureau of Printing, 1907.

Philippine Habitations. Manila: Bureau of Printing, 1912.

Philippine War Damage Commission (US). *Semiannual Report of the United States Philippine War Damage Commission*. Washington, DC: US Government Printing Office, 1947–51.

"Port Works in the Philippines: A Mammoth Pile Driver." *Far Eastern Review* 17, no. 9 (1921): 587–90.

Porter, Catherine. "The Philippines as an American Investment." *Far Eastern Survey* 9, no. 16 (1940): 219–25.

Pratt, Wallace E. "Geology and Field Relations of Portland Cement Materials at Naga, Cebu." *Philippine Journal of Science* 9, no. 2 (1914): 151–62.

Prentice, Andrew N. *Renaissance Architecture and Ornament in Spain*. London: B. T. Batsford, 1893.

The Presidential Committee on Harvard and the Legacy of Slavery. *The Legacy of Slavery at Harvard: Report and Recommendations of the Presidential Committee*. Cambridge, MA: Harvard University Press, 2022.

"Project Notes from District Engineers: Pangasinan." *Quarterly Bulletin, Bureau of Public Works* 6, no. 4 (1918): 17–18.

Putzel, James A. *A Captive Land: The Politics of Agrarian Reform in the Philippines.* Manila: Ateneo de Manila University Press, 1992.

Quezon, Manuel L. *The Good Fight.* New York: D. Appleton-Century, 1946.

Quezon, Manuel L. "Message of President Quezon on Improvement of Philippine Conditions, Philippine Independence, and Relations with American High Commissioner, October, 1937." *Official Gazette of the Republic of the Philippines.* https://www.officialgazette.gov.ph/1937/10/18/message-of-president-quezon-on-improvement-of-philippine-conditions-philippine-independence-and-relations-with-american-high-commissioner-october-18-1937/.

Quezon, Manuel L., and Camilo Osias. *Governor General Wood and the Filipino Cause.* Manila: Manila Book, 1924.

Rafael, Vicente. "The Cultures of Area Studies in the United States." *Social Text*, no. 41 (1994): 91–111.

Rafael, Vicente. *White Love and Other Events in Filipino History.* Durham, NC: Duke University Press, 2000.

Rankin, William. *After the Map.* Chicago: University of Chicago Press, 2016.

Rebori, A. N. "The Work of William E. Parsons in the Philippine Islands, Part I." *Architectural Record* 41 (April 1917): 305–24.

Rebori, A. N. "The Work of William E. Parsons in the Philippine Islands, Part II." *Architectural Record* 41 (May 1917): 423–34.

Reeser Lawrence, Amanda. *The Architecture of Influence: The Myth of Originality in the 20th Century.* Charlottesville: University of Virginia Press, 2023.

Reibling, W. C. "A Bonus System for the Purchase of Portland Cement." *Philippine Journal of Science* 8, no. 3 (1913): 107–25.

Reibling, W. C., and L. A. Salinger. "Portland Cement Testing." *Philippine Journal of Science*, 3, no. 3 (1908): 137–85.

Reibling, W. C., and F. D. Reyes, "The Efficiency of Portland Cement Raw Materials from Naga, Cebu." *Philippines Journal of Science* 9, no. 2 (1914): 127–50.

"Report of the Philippine Commission." In *Annual Reports of the War Department.* Washington DC: Government Printing Office, 1904.

Reps, John W. *Monumental Washington: The Planning and Development of the Capital Center.* Princeton, NJ: Princeton University Press, 1967.

Ripley, William Z. "Acclimatization." *Popular Science Monthly*, March 1896, 662–75.

Roads in the Philippine Islands: Present Conditions and Proposed Betterment. Manila: Bureau of Public Works, 1909.

Robb, Walter. "Philippine Cement: The Cebu Portland Cement Company." *American Chamber of Commerce Journal* 5, no. 8 (1925): 23, 30.

Robinson, Cedric J. "The American Press and the Repairing of the Philippines." In *Cedric J. Robinson: On Racial Capitalism, Black Internationalism, and Cultures of Resistance*, edited by H. L. T. Quan. London: Pluto Press, 2019.

Robinson, Cedric J. *Black Marxism: The Making of the Black Radical Tradition.* Chapel Hill: University of North Carolina Press, 2022.

Romualdez, Eduardo. *A Question of Sovereignty: The Military Bases in the Philippines*. Manila: E. Z. Romualdez, 1980.

Romulo, Carlos P. *Mother America, a Living Story of Democracy*. Garden City, NJ: Doubleday, 1943.

Roosevelt, Theodore. "First Annual Message to Congress." Transcript, December 3, 1901. https://www.presidency.ucsb.edu/documents/first-annual-message-16.

Roosevelt, Theodore. *The Winning of the West*. 4 vols. New York: Putnam, 1900.

Root, John Wellborn. "Code for Guidance." In *The Meanings of Architecture: Buildings and Writings*. Edited by Donald Hoffman. New York: Horizon, 1967.

Root, John Wellborn. "A Great Architectural Problem." In *The Meanings of Architecture: Buildings and Writings*, edited by Donald Hoffman. New York: Horizon, 1967.

Ruskin, John. *The Nature of the Gothic*. London: George Allen, 1900.

Ruskin, John. *The Opening of the Crystal Palace*. London: Smith, Elder, 1854.

Ruskin, John. *The Stones of Venice*. Boston: Aldine, 1890.

Salman, Michael. *The Embarrassment of Slavery: Controversies Over Bondage and Nationalism in the American Colonial Philippines*. Berkeley: University of California Press, 2001.

School Buildings: Plans, Specifications, and Bills of Material for Standard Revised School Buildings of the Bureau of Education. Manila: Bureau of Printing, 1912.

Schueller, Malini Johar. *Campaigns of Knowledge: U.S. Pedagogies of Colonialism and Occupation in the Philippines and Japan*. Philadelphia: Temple University Press, 2023.

[Schuyler, Montgomery]. "Architecture Made Easy: Prospectus of the Classic Design and Detail Co." *Architectural Record* 7, no. 2 (1897): 214–18.

Schwarz, Karl. "Filipino Education and Spanish Colonialism: Toward an Autonomous Perspective." *Comparative Education Review* 15, no. 2 (1971): 202–18.

Scott, James M. *Rampage: MacArthur, Yamashita, and the Battle of Manila*. New York: Norton, 2018.

Scott, William Henry. "Minority Reaction to American Imperialism." *Philippine Quarterly of Culture and Society* 10, no. 1/2 (1982): 1–11.

Semper, Gottfried. *Der Stil in den technischen und tektonishen Künsten*. 2 vols. Munich: F. Bruckmann, 1861, 1863.

Semper, Gottfried. *The Four Elements of Architecture and Other Writings*. Cambridge: Cambridge University Press, 1989.

Serafino, Nina, Curt Tarnoff, and Dick Nanto. *U.S. Occupation Assistance: Iraq, Germany, and Japan Compared*. Washington, DC: Congressional Research Service, 2006.

Shalom, Stephen R. "Philippine Acceptance of the Bell Trade Act of 1946: A Study of Manipulatory Democracy." *Pacific Historical Review* 49, no. 3 (1980): 488–517.

Shankland, Edward Clapp. "The Construction of the World's Fair Buildings, Bridges, Piers and Docks." *American Architect and Building News*, September 23, 1893, 183–85.

Shibusawa, Naoko. "'U.S. Empire' and Racial Capitalist Modernity." *Diplomatic History* 45, no. 4 (2021): 855–84.

Shoemaker, Nancy. "A Typology of Colonialism." *Perspectives on History*, October 1, 2015. https://www.historians.org/research-and-publications/perspectives-on-history/october-2015/a-typology-of-colonialism.

Shuster, W. Morgan. "Our Philippine Policies and Their Results." *Journal of Race Development* 1, no. 1 (1910): 58–74.

Silkenat, David. "Workers in the White City: Working Class Culture at the World's Columbian Exposition of 1893." *Journal of the Illinois State Historical Society* 104, no. 4 (2011): 266–300.

Simmel, Georg. "The Metropolis and Mental Life." In *The Sociology of George Simmel*, edited by K. H. Wolff. New York: Free Press, 1950.

Simonnet, Cyrile. *Le Béton: historie d'un matériau*. Paris: Editions Parenthèses, 2005.

Simpson, William. M. R. *Hylomorphism*. Cambridge: Cambridge University Press, 2023.

Sklar, Martin J. *The Corporate Reconstruction of American Capitalism: The Market, the Law and Politics*. Cambridge: Cambridge University Press, 1988.

Sklar, Martin J. *The United States as Developing Country*. Cambridge: Cambridge University Press, 2010.

Slobodian, Quinn. *Crack-Up Capitalism: Market Radicals and the Dream of a World Without Democracy*. New York: MacMillan, 2023.

Smil, Vaclav. *How the World Really Works*. New York: Penguin Random House, 2022.

Smil, Vaclav. *Numbers Don't Lie*. New York: Penguin Random House, 2020.

Smith, Phillip Chadwick Foster. *Crystal Blocks of Yankee Coldness: The Development of the Massachusetts Ice Trade from Frederick Tudor to Wenham Lake, 1806–1866*. Salem, MA: Wenham Historical Association and Museum, 1961.

Smith, Robert Ross. *Triumph in the Philippines*. Washington, DC: Center for Military History, 1993.

Spector, Robert M. "William Cameron Forbes in the Philippines: A Study in Proconsular Power." *Journal of Southeast Asian History* 7, no. 2 (1966): 74–92.

Stanley, Peter W. *A Nation in the Making: The Philippines in the United States, 1899–1921*. Cambridge, MA: Harvard University Press, 1974.

Steinbock-Pratt, Sarah. *Educating the Empire: American Teachers and Contested Colonization in the Philippines*. Cambridge: Cambridge University Press, 2019.

Stierli, Martino, and Vladmir Kulić. *Toward a Concrete Utopia: Architecture in Yugoslavia, 1948–1980*. New York: MoMA, 2018.

Stierli, Martino, and Anoma Pieris. *The Project of Independence: Architecture and Decolonization in South Asia*. New York: MoMA, 2022.

"Stirred by Burnham, Democracy Champion." *Chicago Record-Herald*, October 15, 1910, 4.

Stocking, George W., Jr. *Race, Culture, and Evolution: Essays in the History of Anthropology*. Chicago: University of Chicago Press, 1982.

Strong, Paschal A. "The Lean Years." *Military Engineer* 41, no. 281 (1949): 179–81.

Strong, Paschal A. (Kennedy Lyons). "The White Sultan of Mindanao." *Boy's Life*, November 1932, 8–9, 37.

Sullivan, Louis. *The Autobiography of an Idea*. New York: Dover, 1956.

Summerson, John. "What Is the History of Construction?" *Construction History* 1 (1985): 1–2.

Tafuri, Manfredo. *Architecture and Utopia: Design and Capitalist Development*. Cambridge, MA: MIT Press, 1976.

Tallmadge, Thomas. *Architecture in Old Chicago*. Chicago: University of Chicago Press, 1941.

Tappin, Stuart. "The Early Use of Reinforced Concrete in India." *Proceedings of the First International Congress on Construction History* 18 (2002): 79–98.

Thompson, Carmi S. "Designed by Filipino Brains, Built by Filipino Hands." *Philippine Republic*, January–February 1927, 5.

Trachtenberg, Alan. *The Incorporation of America: Culture and Society in the Gilded Age*. New York: Hill and Wang, 1982.

Turak, Theodore. *William Le Baron Jenney: A Pioneer of Modern Architecture*. Ann Arbor, MI: UMI Research Press, 1986.

Turner, Frederick Jackson. "The Middle West." In *The Frontier in American History*. New York: Reinhard and Winston, 1962.

Turner, Frederick Jackson. "The Significance of the Frontier in American History." In *The Frontier in American History*. New York: Holt, Rinehart and Winston, 1962.

Turner, Frederick Jackson. "The Significance of the Section in American History." *Wisconsin Magazine of History*, March 1925, 255–80.

Twain, Mark. "Comments on the Moro Massacre." In *Mark Twain's Weapons of Satire: Anti-Imperialist Writings on the Philippine-American War*, edited by Jim Zwick. New York: Syracuse University Press, 1992.

United States Geological Survey. *The San Francisco Earthquake and Fire of April 18, 1906*. Washington, DC: US Government Publishing Office, 1907.

United States Philippine Commission. *Annual Report of the Philippine Commission to the Secretary of War, 1902, Part 1*. Washington, DC: Government Printing Office, 1903.

"Unrest in Pacific Held Dire Threat." *New York Times*, October 12, 1946, 5.

Vann, Michael G. *The Great Hanoi Rat Hunt: Empire, Disease, and Modernity in French Colonial Vietnam*. New York: Oxford University Press, 2019.

Vann, Michael G. "Of Rats, Rice, and Race: The Great Hanoi Rat Massacre, an Episode in French Colonial History." *French Colonial History* 4 (2003): 191–203.

Ventura, Theresa. "From Small Farms to Progressive Plantations: The Trajectory of Land Reform in the Philippines, 1900–1916." *Agricultural History* 90, no. 4 (2016): 459–83.

Viollet-le-Duc, Eugène-Emmanuel. *The Habitations of Man in All Ages*. Translated by Benjamin Bucknall. Boston: J. R. Osgood, 1876.

Vitalis, Robert. *White World Order, Black Power Politics: The Birth of American International Relations*. Ithaca, NY: Cornell University Press, 2015.

Vitruvius. *The Ten Books on Architecture*. Translated by Morris Hicky Morgan. Cambridge, MA: Harvard University Press, 1914.

Wallace, Charles S. "Extract from Report of Lieutenant Charles S. Wallace, Signal Corps, United States Volunteers." In *The Annual Report of the Chief Signal Officer made to the Secretary of War for the Year 1899–1900*. Washington DC: Government Printing Office, 1900.

Weber, Benjamin. *American Purgatory*. New York: New Press, 2023.

Wells, Ida B. *The Reason Why the Colored American Is Not in the World's Columbian Exposition: The Afro-American's Contribution to Columbian Literature*. Urbana: University of Illinois Press, 1999.

West, Augustus P., and Alvin J. Cox. "Burning Tests of Philippine Portland Cement Raw Materials." *Philippine Journal of Science* 9, pt. A, no. 2 (1914): 79–102.

White, Donald Wallace. *The American Century: The Rise and Decline of the United States as a World Power*. New Haven, CT: Yale University Press, 1996.

White, Hayden. *The Tropics of Discourse: Essays in Cultural Criticism*. Baltimore: Johns Hopkins University Press, 1978.

Williams, William Appleman. *The Tragedy of American Diplomacy*. New York: Norton, 1988.

Wilson, Woodrow. "Democracy and Efficiency." *The Atlantic*, March 1901, 289–99.

Wilson, Woodrow. "Eighth Annual Message to the US Congress." December 7, 1920. The American Presidency Project, University of California, Santa Barbara. https://www .presidency.ucsb.edu/documents/8th-annual-message.

Wilson, Woodrow. "First Annual Message to the US Congress." December 2, 1913. The American Presidency Project, University of California, Santa Barbara. https://www .presidency.ucsb.edu/documents/first-annual-message-18.

Wilson, Woodrow. *A History of the American People: Illustrated with Portraits, Maps, Plans, Facsimiles, Rare Prints, Contemporary Views, etc.* New York: Harper & Bros., 1902.

Wilson, Woodrow. "The Ideals of America." *The Atlantic*, December 1902, 721–54.

Witt, Joshua Chitwood. *Portland Cement Technology*. New York: Chemical Pub., 1966.

Witt, Joshua Chitwood. "Why Concrete Is the Master Building Material in the Philippines." *Engineering World*, September 1921, 159–62.

Wood, Christopher. *Forgery, Replica, Fiction: Temporalities of German Renaissance Art*. Chicago: University of Chicago Press, 2008.

Wooley, Monroe. "New Hotel Building in Manila: A Seven-Story Structure of Reinforced Concrete Resting on Piling of Native Hardwood—Impressive Architectural Features." *Building Age*, January 1913, 17–18.

Worcester, Dean C. *The History of Asiatic Cholera in the Philippines*. Manila: Bureau of Printing, 1904.

Worcester, Dean C. *The Philippines Past and Present*. 2 vols. New York: MacMillan, 1914.

Wright, Frank Lloyd. "Daniel Hudson Burnham, An Appreciation." *Architectural Record*, August 1912, 175–84.

Wright, Frank Lloyd. "The Meaning of Materials—Concrete." *Architectural Record*, August 1928, 99–104.

Wright, Gwendolyn. *The Politics of Design in French Colonial Urbanism*. Chicago: University of Chicago Press, 1991.

Wurfel, David. "Trade Union Development and Labor Relations Policy in the Philippines." *ILR Review* 12, no. 4 (1951): 582–608.

Yanne, Andrew, and Gillis Heller. *Signs of a Colonial Era*. Hong Kong: Hong Kong University Press, 2009.

Zheng, Hongbin, and James W. P. Campbell. "History of Reinforced Concrete in Modern Shanghai 1890–1914." *Construction History* 36, no. 2 (2021): 81–122.

Ziolkowski, Jan M. *The Juggler of Notre Dame and the Medievalizing of Modernity*. Vol. 3, *The American Middle Ages*. Cambridge: Open Book, 2018.

Index

Page numbers followed by *f* refer to figures.

Europe, 58, 155; Arellano and, 236n9; colonies of, 8, 149; de los Reyes and, 120; housing reform in, 70; immigrants from, 35; Kahn system in, 33; modernists in, 79; public buildings in, 217n2; Western, 202

expansion, 16; Barcelona's, 230n33; of durability, 8; of fort modernization program, 174; of French and British Empires, 18; Hennebique's, 214n15; imperial, 6, 27, 150; of reinforced concrete construction, 24; US, 4, 10–11, 62, 112, 150

exploitation, 12, 150, 197; colonial, 33; of natural resources, 198

Fanon, Frantz, 157–58, 223n15, 237n21
Fenhagen, George Corner, 95, 98–101, 226n6
festoons, 95, 140, 144, 195
Filipinization, 28, 136, 153–54, 226n6, 235n4; reversal of, 232n24
Filipino architects, 95, 136, 157, 159, 168, 226n6
First Philippine Republic, 9, 67, 227n35
Fischer-Credo, Otto, 162f, 164–65, 167, 194, 238n39
Fitch, George Hamlin, 1–2
floating raft foundation, 25, 54, 59
Forbes, William Cameron, 12, 25–26, 40–42, 59–60, 62–63, 105–7, 109–12, 210–11; Burnham and, 83–86, 90; leisure and, 227n28; Philippine independence and, 122, 214n15, 230n30, 232n24; Pier 7 and, 116; ports and, 114, 222n30; prison labor and, 227n32, 230n18; *The Romance of Business*, 42, 117–20, 210, 230n31, 244n7; Smith and, 230n19. *See also* Emerson, Ralph Waldo
Foreign Affairs, 34, 218n16, 237n25
Forty, Adrian, 23, 47, 217n63, 231n4, 239n49
Foucault, Michel, 79, 214n9

Germany, 126, 145, 167, 202; architectural organicism in, 234n27; cement and, 121, 125, 231n4; Frankfurt, 225n34
Giedion, Sigfried, 7, 22, 81
Gomez, Dimonador, 46, 98, 219n48
governance, 3, 41; colonial, 26, 40, 92, 134; federal, 62; postcolonial, 123; self-governance, 171

government buildings, 2, 6, 41, 93, 196, 233n3; reconstruction of, 200f; reduction of, 188
Great Lakes, 50; region, 53, 117
Guerdrum, George, 70–72

Hacienda Luisita, 105, 229n5
Haiti, 34, 214n12
Hall, Granville Stanley, 34–35, 44–45
Hanoi, 67, 223n15
Hansom, Joseph, 23
Harding, Warren G., 154, 230n30, 232n24
Harrison, Francis Burton, 127–28, 135f, 141, 148–49, 168–70; administration of, 143; anti-miscegenation stance of, 166, 238n33; Philippine independence and, 122, 136
Heiser, Victor, 71–74
hemp, 41, 45, 109
Hennebique (company), 4, 214n15; "stirrup" system, 32, 88, 231n6
historicism, 22, 88, 143, 234n27
housing, 25, 69–70, 75–76, 78, 81, 191; council, 193; workers', 224–25n34, 240n58
Huntington, Ellsworth, 36, 218n16

Igorots, 155–56, 165, 236n14
Ileto, Reynaldo, 67, 223n3
Iloilo, 93, 94f, 99, 140, 146, 208
Ilustrados, 156, 163
immigrants, 35, 63, 237n26
imperialism, 143, 226n23; prison, 229n17; US, 150
India, 4–5, 197, 231n2, 231n4, 233n11
Indochina, 5; French, 4, 121, 123, 216n59, 231n2
Indonesia, 5, 191, 216n59
industrialization, 22, 40, 81, 132, 229n6
Industrial Revolution, 22, 224n34
industry, 14, 40, 172; building, 23, 33, 47, 83, 96; captains of, 12, 127; heavy, 118; insurance, 42; lumber, 7; marine insurance, 51; Philippine construction, 191; Portland cement, 33, 62, 123, 128, 217n1, 231n7; sugar, 229n6; US, 222n34
infrastructure, 15, 22, 34, 59, 188, 207, 235n31; concrete, 5, 13, 28; hygienic, 77; in landscape art, 113; military, 204; modern, 75; transportation, 10; of the White City, 56. *See also* sanitary barrios
Ingalls, Owen L., 69, 223n7

Robinson, Cedric, 12–13, 44, 206

Romulo, Carlos P., 156, 236n14

Roosevelt, Theodore, 26, 42, 44, 62, 103–4, 112, 174; Dewey Monument and, 206*f*; Great White Fleet, 223n6; Wood and, 151

Root, John Wellborn, 19, 25, 52–55, 58–59, 221n11, 242n15

rot, 3, 7, 50

Rough Riders, 43, 151. *See also* Roosevelt, Theodore; Wood, Leonard

Roxas, Manuel, 191, 195–96

Ruskin, John, 22, 99, 169, 225n2, 239n47

Sabang Bridge, 113, 114*f*

sand, 7, 60, 123–25, 213n5

sanitary barrios, 2, 25–26, 70–78, 224n26, 224n33, 225n35

sanitation, 25–26, 65, 71, 75, 77, 240n58; native, 69

Schuyler, Montgomery, 22, 141, 234n20

science, 20, 34, 39, 70, 143; bogus, 13, 34; social, 42, 44, 219n40

self-determination, 8–9, 152, 164, 168

Semper, Gottfried, 22, 39, 220n49, 234n27, 239n53

settlement, 32, 49, 51; of agricultural land, 111; of the American frontier, 7; even, 54; informal, 78; mixed pattern of, 68; policy, 239n55; theories of, 236n11; of the West, 58, 105

sewer systems, 6, 69; of Hanoi, 67, 223n15; Manila's, 25, 58, 67, 69, 73–74, 223n8

Shankland, E. C., 55

Shibusawa, Naoko, 12, 215n21

Singapore, 86, 191, 231n2

slavery, 12–13, 215n38, 226n23

Smith, Robert Ross, 188, 194

Sorsogon, 98–99, 100*f*

sovereignty, 164, 190; colonial, 6–7, 36, 132, 134, 139, 201, 203; indigenous, 218n16; national, 8, 27–28, 122, 127, 134, 139, 154, 167, 170–71, 197, 207, 237n22; Philippine, 29, 36, 153, 161, 171, 199, 226n6, 243n12; US, 134; postcolonial, 146

Soviet Union, 225n34; former, 4

Spain, 8, 82, 141, 155, 227n35; First Republic, 230n33

Spanish-American War, 3, 8, 46, 113, 120, 155, 173

standardization, 79, 133; of architecture, 99

steel, 19–20, 52–53, 116, 140, 142, 228n43; beams, 174; benders, 8; machines, 114; market, 97; rails, 54; reinforcement, 7, 17, 60, 122, 127, 217n2, 231n6; ships, 173–74; tanks, 185; workers, 88

Strong, Paschal N., 176–78, 241n5

Subic Naval Base, 191–92

sugar, 12, 41, 89, 10, 126, 229n4, 244n7; industry, 229n6

Sullivan, Louis, 19–20, 22, 216n51, 234n25, 234n27

Summerson, John, 23

surplus population, 74, 224n32

Tabacalera, 105–6, 216n45, 229n4

Tabaco, 80*f*, 109, 230n18

Taft, William Howard, 27, 40, 44, 46, 91, 219n48, 222n25, 223n6; Pensionado Act, 95

Talim, 60, 124*f*, 235n31

Tampinco, Vidal, 140, 234n19

Tarlac, 106, 107*f*; Canal, 216n45

technology, 20, 59–60; American, 4, 118, 188; artificial ice as, 222n24; concrete as, 50; empire-killing, 11; fireproofing, 52; foundation, 60–61; machine, 113; modern, 104, 144; US military, 174, 177–78. *See also* reinforced concrete

tectonics, 239n53; indigenous, 171

termites, 3, 7, 42, 82

Thompson, Carmi S., 153, 157, 237n16

timber, 7; boom towns, 32, 53

tobacco, 41, 126, 229n4; company, 216n45; farms, 89; workers, 46

Toledo, Antonio, 95, 97*f*, 144*f*, 145*f*, 172, 186, 237n22, 240n59

Treaty of Chicago (1833), 50, 220n5

Treaty of Paris (1898), 8–9, 227n35; US ratification, 9

TrusCon, 32–33, 231n6. *See also* Kahn (trussed bar) system

Turner, Frederick Jackson, 10–11, 220n6

Tydings-McDuffie Act, 171–72, 190, 195

typhoons, 3, 7, 42, 67, 220n49

Unión Obrera Democrática (UOD), 46, 219n48

www.ingramcontent.com/pod-product-compliance
Lightning Source LLC
Chambersburg PA
CBHW032345280326
41935CB00008B/461